CITY OF LIES

CITY OF LIES

Love, Sex, Death and the
Search for Truth in Tehran

RAMITA NAVAI

PUBLICAFFAIRS
New York

PublicAffairs books are available at special discounts for bulk purchases in
the U.S. by corporations, institutions, and other organizations. For more
information, please contact the Special Markets Department
at the Perseus Books Group, 2300 Chestnut Street, Suite 200,
Philadelphia, PA 19103, call (800) 810-4145, ext. 5000, or e-mail
special.markets@perseusbooks.com.

Typeset by GroupFMG within BookCloud

Library of Congress Control Number: 2014942565

ISBN 978-1-61039-519-9 (HC)
ISBN 978-1-61039-520-5 (EB)

First Edition

10 9 8 7 6 5 4 3 2 1

For all Tehranis, wherever you may be.

For my husband Gabriel,
honorary Tehrani and the love of my life.

Most of all, for my parents: my mother Laya,
for inspiring me, and my father Kourosh,
who is all that is good and great about Tehran.

CONTENTS

Better the lie that keeps the peace than the truth that disrupts

دروغی مصلحت آمیز به که راستی فتنه انگیز

Sa'adi Shirazi, The Rose Garden of Saadi

PREFACE

Let's get one thing straight: in order to live in Tehran you have to lie. Morals don't come into it: lying in Tehran is about survival. This need to dissimulate is surprisingly egalitarian – there are no class boundaries and there is no religious discrimination when it comes to the world of deceit. Some of the most pious, righteous Tehranis are the most gifted and cunning in the art of deception. We Tehranis are masters at manipulating the truth. Tiny children are instructed to deny that daddy has any booze at home; teenagers passionately vow their virginity; shopkeepers allow customers to surreptitiously eat, drink and smoke in their back rooms during the fasting months and young men self-flagellate at the religious festival of Ashura, purporting that each lash is for Imam Hossein, when really it is a macho show to entice pretty girls, who in turn claim they are there only for God. All these lies breed new lies, mushrooming in every crack in society.

The truth has become a secret, a rare and dangerous commodity, highly prized and to be handled with great care. When the truth is shared in Tehran, it is an act of extreme trust or absolute desperation. Lying for survival in Iranian culture goes back a long way; in the early years of the Islamic conquest, Shias were encouraged to lie about their faith to avoid persecution, a practice known as *taqiya*. The Koran also states that, in some cases, lying for the greater good is permitted. While this pathology of subterfuge has leaked out of the city and flowed into the towns and villages across the country, Tehran remains at its source.

But here is the rub: Iranians are obsessed with being true to themselves; it is part of our culture. The Persian poet Hafez begs us to seek the truth to discover the meaning of life:

This love you now have of the Truth
Will never forsake you
Your joys and sufferings on this arduous path
Are lifting your worn veil like a rising stage curtain
And will surely reveal your Magnificent Self

The characters in Iranian soap operas are nearly always on a quest to find their real selves and many a fatwa deals with the dichotomy between the burden of religious obligations and honest human desires. So most Tehranis are in constant conflict, for how do you stay true to yourself in a system in which you are forced to lie to ensure survival?

Let me be clear about one last thing. I am not saying that we Iranians are congenital liars. The lies are, above all, a consequence of surviving in an oppressive regime, of being ruled by a government that believes it should be able to interfere in even the most intimate affairs of its citizens.

While living (and lying) in Tehran I heard the stories of the Tehranis you are about to meet. Not all of them are ordinary Tehranis; some exist at the very margins of Iranian society. But I hope that even the most extreme stories in this book will help an outsider understand everyday life in this city of over twelve million people. In my experience, the defining trait of Tehranis is their kindness, for no matter how hard life gets, no matter how tight the regime turns the screw, there is an irrepressible warmth; I have felt it from diehard regime supporters to ardent dissidents and everyone in between.

I have changed all names and some details, time frames and locations to protect people, but everything here has happened or is still happening. These are all true stories from the city of lies.

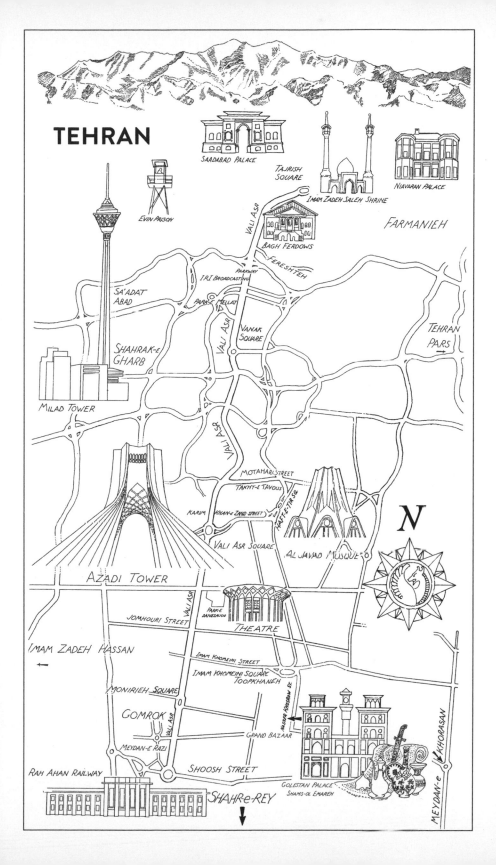

PROLOGUE

Vali Asr Street

From above, Tehran has an ethereal glow. An orange mist hangs over the city, refracting sunrays: a thick, noxious haze that stubbornly clings to every corner, burning the nose and stinging the eyes. Every street is clogged with cars coughing out the black clouds that gently rise and sit, unmoving, overhead. The fumes even creep up the caramel Alborz mountains in the north. Here, clusters of high-rise buildings look down across the city, like imams standing over a prostrating congregation. A mass of humanity fills the valley below them. Every inch is covered, with no discernible style, logic or reason. Old neighbourhoods are crudely carved open by spaghetti junctions, and ugly postmodern buildings rear up over manor houses.

In the middle of the city, cutting straight through the chaos and slicing Tehran in half, is one long, wide road lined on either side by thousands of tall sycamore trees. Vali Asr Street runs from the north of Tehran to the south, pumping life through it and spitting it out into the deepest corners of the city. Vali Asr is the single road that sums up Tehran for all Tehranis. For decades Iranians have come here to celebrate, to protest, to march, to commemorate, to mourn. One of my clearest childhood memories from Tehran is journeying along the street by car; I can still remember the feeling of being cocooned by the trees, tenderly bowing towards each other, protecting us below with their green canopy.

Alongside the trees' aged, overgrown roots, twisting and protruding from the cracked concrete, deep gutters known as *joobs* carry icy water that gushes out of the mountains in the north. The farther south the water flows, the murkier and darker it becomes. Just past the middle of Vali Asr is downtown, a bubbling, densely packed concentration of the city, where thousands of motorbikes and cars and people roar along and across it. Squeezed between the apartment blocks, the dying remains of a few grand old houses can still be found, clinging on to life. Farther south, the buildings become smaller and more decrepit: houses of raw cement and crumbling brick with broken windows and corrugated iron shacks set up on rooftops. Rusting gas flues and air conditioning units hang from walls, like metal guts pushed outside. Here the colour is sucked from the streets, into the shadows of conservatism and poverty. Black shrouds of women's chadors weave silently among the dark suits and headscarves: the shades of mourning that all bear the Islamic stamp of approval, broken only by lurid murals of war heroes, religious martyrs and political propaganda. At the very southern end, Vali Asr opens its mouth onto Rah Ahan Square, Tehran's main railway station, where travellers arrive from all over the country: the Lors, the Kurds, the Azeris, the Turkmens, the Tajiks, the Arabs, the Baluchis, the Bakhtiyaris, the Qashqa'is and Afghans.

Vali Asr Street and the hundreds of roads that run off it is a microcosm of the city. Just over eleven miles from top to bottom, it connects the rich and the poor, the religious and the secular, tradition and modernity. Yet the lives of the people at either end seem centuries apart.

The road was built by Reza Shah, although when work first began on it in 1921, he was not yet King. After a military coup that ousted Ahmad Shah, the last Qajar monarch, the road really began to take shape. Orchards and exquisite landscaped gardens belonging to aristocrats, statesmen and royal Qajar princes were destroyed to make way for it, with Reza Shah saving the best plots of land for himself and his family. It took another eight years for the road to be completed as it was stretched further north, through the countryside, connecting the Shah's palaces; the winter residences in the warmer south of the city and the summer residences nestled in the cooler mountains in the north. The road was part of Reza Shah's programme of massive expansion, as he attempted to drag Iran into the modern world. It was to be the envy of the Middle East; magnificent and awe-inducing, with the refinement and beauty of French tree-lined boulevards and the majesty of a great, big Roman road. Reza Shah personally oversaw the planting of about 18,000 sycamore trees. He named the road after himself: Pahlavi.

When the Islamic Revolution toppled Reza Shah's son, Mohammad Reza Shah, in 1979, anti-Shah nationalists renamed the road Mossadegh Street, in honour of the former Iranian Prime Minister, Dr Mohammad Mossadegh, an eccentric, European-educated lawyer who was ousted in a CIA-backed coup when he attempted to nationalize the country's oil, propelling him to hero status. The name lasted almost as long as his incumbency – just over a year. The godfather of the revolution, Ayatollah Ruhollah Khomeini, was never going to allow the country's most famous road to remain named after a man who stood for Persian nationalism rather than Islam, and whose popularity he envied. Khomeini commanded the road be called Vali Asr, after the revered Imam Mahdi, also known as Imam Zaman, the last

3

of the twelve Shia imams and the man who many Shias believe will be the Last Saviour of the world. The messiah's reappearance will herald a new era of peace and Islamic perfection, but until then the Last Saviour will be in hiding. A fitting name for a road that symbolizes a city whose real life force is so suppressed under Islamic rule.

It happens in the middle of the night. No one knows exactly what time, nor how many men are involved. But the next morning, everybody is talking about it. The evidence is dotted along stretches of Vali Asr Street: dozens of tree stumps protrude from the concrete. Municipal workers with chainsaws have cut down over forty of the road's sycamore trees. Tehranis complain. They write letters, call the mayor's office, take photos. They tweet and start a Facebook page. The story makes headlines. A well-known human rights group claims many more trees have been cut. A cultural heritage group calls the slaying of the 'innocent' trees a 'devastating' act. Radio Farhang, a national radio station, is inundated with calls on its live discussion show. 'Every tree is a memory for me. If the trees are cut, my memories will die. It's as though they're cutting my very soul,' says one tearful woman, with typical Iranian passion and drama. Tehranis are angry.

A war veteran with no legs takes up his usual spot on the pavement near Park-e Mellat on the north of Vali Asr. He places his dirty crutches next to him and spreads out his goods on the ground: batteries of different sizes and colours. A giant rat scampers across the gutter behind him. A music student, with his violin slung over his shoulders, has heard about the cutting of the trees and has come to see for himself.

'At least I went to war, what did that poor tree do to deserve the same fate as me?' jokes the veteran. The young man smiles and walks north to Bagh Ferdows, a public garden in front of an elegant Qajar palace. This is where he comes to think and watch the world on Vali Asr. He sits on a bench and opens his laptop; on it he plays a live performance of Mozart's Requiem. An old man in a three-piece suit joins him, sitting at the other end of the bench so he can hear the sublime music above the sounds of the city.

Where Vali Asr careers towards downtown, near Jomhouri Street, a bearded man in green trainers and a red shirt is busking on his accordion, playing mournful Persian classics for commuters stuck in their cars. When someone hands him a note, he fishes out a strip of paper from his bumbag directing people to his Internet page, a blog about the evils of the world: the devil, materialism and our obsession with sex.

Near the southernmost tip of Vali Asr, the road has come to a standstill. But this is not rush-hour traffic. Thousands are gathered in the cold, on the pavement and on the street outside a mosque; there is no room inside. It is a funeral. Men carry seven-foot-high displays of white gladioli tied with black ribbon. Inside the mosque, a *ghaari*, religious reader, is reciting from the Koran. Afterwards he leads the eulogy about the dead woman: 'She was from a generation who knew the true meaning of honour. She turned to God and never looked back,' he says. 'She was an honest woman.'

ONE

DARIUSH

Mehrabad Airport, Tehran, March 2001

'You've been away a while.' The young officer did not look up as he flicked through the passport. 'And now you've decided to come back.' Still flicking. 'After all these years.' He picked the plastic corner of the first page.

Dariush could not remember being this scared since he was a little boy. He slid his tongue along the hard plastic side of the cyanide pill lodged between his gum and cheek. They had told him the regime had a list of all their names, a blacklist of dissidents wanted by the state. They had said that prison would mean torture and a slow death.

The officer was staring at him. 'Why did you leave?'

'My parents left because of the war, I wish I'd stayed but they took me.' He had answered too quickly.

'Why are you back?' The man scanned his passport. It had cost 20,000 US dollars from a Shia militant in Baghdad who had supplied passports for some big names. It was a work of art; you could not buy a better fake.

'I've come to see some relatives. I – I miss my country,' his voice was trembling. The officer leant over his desk and pressed his hand on Dariush's chest.

'Your heart's beating like a little sparrow,' he said. Then he burst out laughing and tossed Dariush's passport across the counter.

6

'You new ones, you're always so scared. Don't believe what you read mate, we won't eat you. You'll see life is better for people like you here. You'll never leave.'

It was as easy as that, returning to the country that had haunted his every day since he had fled the revolution with his mother over twenty years ago. It seemed almost too easy. He should be cautious, as they might still be onto him. Dariush knew Iranians were masters of double-bluffing.

As the Group had forewarned him, his bags had to be X-rayed before he was allowed out. The tightened security wasn't just regime paranoia or fear of separatist movements. It was also fear of people like him, it was fear of the MEK, the Mojahedin-e-Khalq, the Warriors of the People.

It had been just over a year since Dariush had officially joined the MEK. His mother, a primary school teacher, had reacted angrily when he had first started to talk about them. The MEK had played a crucial role in the 1979 Islamic Revolution that brought down the Shah and Dariush's mother blamed them as much as the Islamists for having ruined her life. She had hoped he was going through a phase; the MEK were Iran's first modern Islamic Revolutionaries and she remembered how, as a student, some of her own friends had been impressed by their talk of socialist values and equality. But she began to start to notice more serious changes in Dariush; he began praying, and even though she practised her faith, her son's new-found religiosity unsettled her. He had started lecturing everyone around him about the *sazman*, the organization – the Group – showing photographs of MEK prisoners of conscience. She argued back, reeling off anecdotes about family friends who had become involved and been brainwashed and separated from their loved ones. His mother had been proud of his American education and of their new life in a small town near Washington, DC. She could not abide watching him pouring all his savings and earnings into the Group's bank account. Dariush did not accept a word of what she said. He started spending less and less time visiting home until he stopped calling her. She begged him to leave the MEK. Instead, he cut her out of his life.

Dariush stepped out into the early-morning spring sky, breathing in the dusty smell of Tehran. It was the smell of his childhood: mothballs, dried herbs, earth and petrol. He was home.

Walking to the taxi queue he savoured every small step, his head jolting around like a pigeon scanning for food. The familiarity was almost overbearing; everywhere he looked it was as if he were surrounded by relatives. He had never felt such a strong sense of belonging, not even with the Group.

'Listen, we haven't got all day, get in the car or out the queue.' A man in a bib and a clipboard was staring at him.

'Sorry, deep in thought. Vali Asr Street, Parkway, please.'

Dariush had been surprised when the instructions came to meet in north Tehran, but the Group had learnt from bitter experience that there are few places in the city where they could blend in. People are less interested in your business on the streets of north Tehran; too involved in their own conversations and recoiling at anything that may prick the bubble in which they live. In the early days, first meetings between an operative and his handler used to happen in secluded downtown parks, but now those were full of drug addicts, dealers and cops. Even when there appears to be no one around, in every alley and corner in downtown Tehran there are hidden eyes and ears. Once, a meeting of comrades near the bazaar had gone disastrously wrong. Whispers of a hushed conversation spread through the area. Two group members saw the police coming and ran for their lives. They lived in hiding for three months before they were smuggled out on donkeys over freezing mountains by outlaw Kurds, having persuaded them that they were student protesters, for the Kurds would never have taken them if they had known they were MEK members. They still remember how the MEK helped the Iraqi President Saddam Hussein battle Kurdish uprisings. Under the Shah, most political prisoners and those executed on political grounds were members of the MEK and that had helped swell their support. Just two years after the revolution, the MEK had half a million active followers. Feeling threatened by its burgeoning power, the real men behind the Islamic Revolution – the clerics and the fundamentalists – did what they would repeatedly do when faced with a threat from within: they turned against their own. Calling MEK members *monafeqin*, hypocrites colluding with imperialist Western powers to wage an unholy war, the revolutionaries hanged or shot thousands as part of a systematic cleansing. Survivors escaped to Iraq, where Saddam gave them protection and installed them in Camp Ashraf, a stretch of land north of Baghdad where he armed and trained them. The MEK had even joined the Iraqi army to fight against Iranian soldiers during the Iran–Iraq war, killing many of their own countrymen. That is when attitudes towards them shifted.

'God, you haven't been here for a while, where d'you get that accent from? Sorry sir, I don't mean to be rude, but that accent's thicker than George Bush's – it's got to be America?'

The driver stretched his neck as he laughed and gave him the once-over in his rear-view mirror. Dariush winced.

'Yes, America, near Washington. But we never wanted to leave Iran, we had no choice.' He was apologizing.

'Twenty years! You've earned that accent, not like these rich kids who go on holiday for a week and come back pretending they've forgotten their Farsi. Ah, the Great Satan, what I'd give to go and live with that devil. My girlfriend spent three days queuing up at the US consulate in Istanbul and they practically laughed in her face. We're all terrorists you know.' He turned up the tinny Euro-techno that was softly thudding away. When Dariush had fled, Gloria Gaynor's 'I Will Survive' had been a taxi favourite.

Even though the windows were all shut, cold streams of wind blew through the cracks and gaps of the white Peykan, Iran's improvised version of the 1960s Hillman Hunter, as it thundered along, full-throttle.

There is only one driving speed in Tehran: the fastest your machine will go. The battered old Peykans can still manage a lurching eighty miles an hour with a new engine, nearly as good as any Peugeot, the middle-class car of choice. The Group had joked it was more likely Dariush would die on Tehran's roads than at the hands of the regime, and they were probably right. Mangled cars, bloodied passengers and even dead ones lying on the tarmac are familiar sights in Tehran. Of course the traffic was also a major concern for the Group; they had decided on using a motorbike as the getaway vehicle, as a car would get stuck. But at this time of day the freeway was eerily clear. Dariush watched Tehran unfold from his window, his eyes tracking the rise and fall of houses, apartment blocks, offices, hospitals and schools.

He had not remembered Tehran being so ugly. His memories were of old stately homes, winding alleys, elegant French-built apartments; villas and orchards and gardens; a clean city with no traffic. But now all he could see was an unsightly mash of grey concrete slabs, gaudy blocks of flecked marble, towering mock-Grecian pillars and primary-coloured plastic piping for good measure. They had pissed all over it. Dariush clenched his teeth shut as the hate convulsed him. The anger was always a relief. There were moments when he could feel the rage dissipating from his body, it was a physical sensation; his muscles would loosen and his chest would rise. He would panic in anticipation of losing his motivation, of giving up the struggle. But not now. They had taken over his city, and he was ready.

The taxi turned into Vali Asr Street, the road that reminds all Tehranis of home. At first glance Vali Asr looked more or less the same. There were still the greengrocers, the boutiques, the cafés and restaurants, the glitzy shop fronts and the hawkers. Only the bars were gone, the whisky joints his parents loved, the smoky billiard halls open all night, the discos with their queues outside. It pained him to admit that Tehran was better off without all these things – the pernicious, corrupting influence of the West that had taken root in his country and cracked the foundations of his land. It pained him because this was the time his parents had been happiest, dancing and drinking up and down Pahlavi Street. But it also hurt Dariush to think his parents had indulged in a culture that was so louche. He had tried to exonerate them in his mind; they had simply embraced the aspirations of any young middle-class Tehrani in the 1970s. But he had turned his back on all that. The Group had shown him the way and he knew God was watching.

The roads were not so empty now, the city slowly crawling out of its slumber. An old, bent man pushing a wheelbarrow stacked with oranges edged past the car. Despite a full head of hair, he looked 100 years old, and sounded even older, his frail croaks muffled by the engines and snatched by the spring breeze.

'Poor old thing. OI, GRANDDAD, HOW MUCH?' The driver beckoned him over.

'Three hundred tomans for a kilo of oranges my son, they're fresh today, picked from the sweet soil of Mosha,' whispered the old man, lifting his small eyes, shimmering with cataracts, from under his hunched back. Even his clothes looked ancient: a threadbare, stained shirt with incongruously starched collar and cuffs hung from his little emaciated body, the worn folds of his peasant trousers billowing towards the ground.

'Granddad, you've got more hair than me and him put together – keep the change.'

'It's the only thing I've got more of than anyone else,' the old man's smiling gums glistened, 'may God give you a long life.' The taxi rattled forward and the driver shook his head at the image of the old farmer in his rear-view mirror. 'Even if he sells all the fruit from his village, that guy still won't have enough to feed a family. This ain't living, it ain't even surviving. This city's fucked.'

The Peykan emerged from the tunnel of trees into Parkway, a huge concrete intersection stuffed with people and cars zigzagging in every direction underneath a flyover. The driver stopped at an island in the middle, clipping the side of an office worker's briefcase. The man didn't even bother turning his head as he waded out into the roar. Dariush got out of the taxi and into the middle of the morning mayhem. He realized there would be no lull and he would have to cross the road Iranian style, throwing himself into the oncoming traffic. It took him over five minutes to cross the ten yards to the other side; each time he inched forward a car or a motorbike screamed towards him. Finally an old woman in a chador told him to follow her, and as her hefty body waddled through the onslaught of cars she told him he must have been away a long time. He sighed.

Dariush walked north to a café on the corner of Vali Asr and

Fereshteh Street. It had been open for hours, serving *kalepacheh* breakfasts, an entire sheep's head: tongue, eyes, cheeks and all. It looked more like a laboratory than a café, with shiny white tiles on every wall and surface. The waiters even wore spotless lab coats as they dished out the dissected cuts of soft, slippery meat, the unforgiving glare of the high-voltage strip lights piercing through every slither of fat and muscle on the cheap white china plates. Dariush breathed in the sweet, warm stink of disintegrating flesh, bones and cartilage. His mother had tried to make *kalehpacheh* in America a few times. They had eaten it glumly, in silence, for *kalehpacheh* is a man's dish and it reminded them of his father, who could make it better than anyone. His father, a devout monarchist, had been a civil servant in the Shah's government. When the militia had been roaming the streets and rounding up anyone they could find, he had been taken in for questioning and was never seen again.

Dariush spotted an empty table at the back, near the kitchen counter. He weaved his way through the room and, as he sat down, a small glass of tea was banged on the table by a passing waiter. Behind him, steel pots puffed out streams of steam, the gentle murmur of boiling broth a steady hum underneath clashing plates and voices. He had kept an eye out in the taxi to see if he was being followed. From where he was sitting he had a clear view across the restaurant to outside. Nobody. He was early. He relaxed a little, allowing himself to survey the room.

The diners were a curious mix. Bearded lone workmen and office clerks eating quickly, heads bowed. Old regulars in pressed shirts trading banter across the tables, their breakfast rituals unchanged for decades. Bright-eyed ramblers in windcheaters and woolly socks fuelling themselves after treks in the Alborz mountains, walking sticks and rucksacks propped up against the tables. They ate the slowest, enjoying every morsel after their dawn summit visits, having beaten the merciless sun and the trails clogged up with the amateurs.

In the middle was a sight that both excited and disgusted him. A group in their teens and early twenties were slumped in their chairs and across the tables, heads resting on each other, feet sprawled out, sunglasses on their heads. They giggled and flirted and in whispers gossiped about their night. The girls were breathtakingly beautiful, even with smudged mascara and backcombed hair falling out of tiny headscarves, stray strands stuck on their sweaty foreheads. Beautiful, despite their improbable upturned noses carved and chiselled by the surgeon's knife. They pouted their juicy lips, pushing out slurred words, throwing heads back and breasts forward as they laughed, showing off slender brown arms. They filled the room with their laughter, their dilated, spaced-out ecstasy-pilled eyes and the sweet smell of vodka moonshine that clung to their party clothes peeking through their *manteaus*, the Islamic regulation overcoats that women are obliged to wear in order to conceal curves. They slurped down the revellers' morning-after favourite, big bowls of brain soup, a perfect hangover cure to soak up the drugs and booze that were still coursing through their bodies.

Dariush was staring so intently at the girls that he did not notice his comrade enter the restaurant.

'Salaam brother. Welcome home.' Dariush had been easy to spot; apart from the agreed set of keys and a packet of red Marlboro cigarettes on the table, he was gawping.

Dariush looked embarrassed. He had taken his eye off the ball.

'Don't worry, it's always a shock to see these young kids behaving like animals while their country goes to shit. And you're the one who's going to be saving us all, right?' He smirked and then lowered his voice to a whisper. 'I know your mission. Jahangir briefed me. Call me Kian. You know the drill.'

They ate their food in silence, and without waiting for the bill Kian left a stack of notes on the table and walked out. Dariush followed him north up Vali Asr where the road bends to the east towards Tajrish Square. They passed the gardens of the old palace of Bagh Ferdows, the fresh breeze licking their ankles. Vali Asr was bursting with the signs of spring: dazzling green buds sprouting out of the trees, the sticky smell of the sweet sap that coated the year's new leaves; mounds of unripe almonds, jade-coloured plums, apricots and figs from the south, and bunches of tarragon and mint spilt out of boxes in front of shops.

They turned left and into the backstreets of the old neighbour-hood of Shemiran, and entered a square grey block of flats; the air was filled with the smell of frying onions. Up to the sixth floor. From the balcony, hundreds of high-rise rooftops looked like toy houses in the shadow of the mountains, a coating of winter's snow still stubbornly clinging to their peaks.

'The flat's clean, no bugs, I checked it last night.' A shroud of dust covered the room. Kian took a plastic cover off an old leather sofa. From his jacket pocket he unfolded a map, discoloured by summer sun. He smoothed out the creases as he laid it out on the table.

'They told me to give you this. It's marked up so don't leave it lying around. Learn where you have to go, then burn it.'

Dariush studied the map, tracing his hand along Tehran's perimeter, marvelling at its unfamiliar new shape; fat fingers of concrete and brick poking up into the mountains, out towards the desert and into the plains and the countryside. In the centre, two black circles marked the home and workplace of his target: Tehran's former police chief.

'Here are a few SIM cards. Don't use any of them for more than two weeks. Don't order cabs, just hail them in the streets. That's it from me. Good luck.'

Dariush's head jerked, 'You're leaving? Is that it? What about a gun? The getaway driver?'

'Don't tell me they haven't arranged that for you? They've got to sort their shit out.'

Dariush slammed his hand on the table, scattering a cloud of dust. 'This is a joke! We're working our guts out over there, I'm putting my life on the line for the cause, and it seems you don't even give a fuck!'

Kian lit a cigarette and took a deep drag before resting his head in the palms of his hands. He did not bother looking up. 'Brother, I appreciate what you're doing. I really do. Things are just different here. It's not what they've been feeding you. You know how much pressure we're under? The old boys are monitored twenty-four-seven. You're lucky they didn't give you some young gun with no experience who would have landed you in prison.' He scribbled down a number on a scrap of paper. 'Say Pedram says the shop's been opened again. That's all you have to say. I'll sort out the driver.' He turned round when he got to the door. 'Just so you know, don't be surprised when you hear people don't much like us here. And by the way, this isn't the first time the *sazman* has fucked up.' He walked out shaking his head.

If someone had told Dariush two years ago that he would become involved with the MEK, he would have laughed at them. Dariush had never been interested in politics; at least, no more than any other exiled Iranian who grew up with revolution talk. His childhood in Virginia had been uneventful. Arezou had changed everything.

He had met Arezou at university, where he was studying computer engineering. From their first conversation, they were both struck by the inevitability of what was going to happen. In many ways they were similar: serious and bruised by life. Arezou told Dariush that both her parents had been killed during the revolution for being political activists. She was guarded and evasive when it came to ordinary questions about her family. Other students found her cold; Dariush was intrigued. They approached their inchoate love cautiously. When she finally submitted, Dariush was utterly captivated. He had found his soulmate.

They had just made love when Arezou first told him that she was a member of the Group, the MEK. Dariush had sat up in shock. He had heard the MEK were a bunch of crazies, just as bad as the mullahs, and that they were loathed by all.

Dariush argued with Arezou against them, but she became indignant and defensive, ranting at him. Even though he disagreed with what she said – that the MEK were freedom fighters, that everyone in Iran was rooting for them and that they were the only credible dissident group – he could not help but be impressed by her knowledge, by her grasp of history and her ability to reel out facts. Arezou began to talk of the *sazman* more often. It would always end in an argument. She tried to persuade him to go to meetings; he always refused.

One evening, in the middle of cooking supper, she told him it was over. He had burst out crying. She told him that unless he respected the cause, and accepted it was a part of her life, she could not be with him. She spoke with absolute dispassion. 'This is who I am. If you love me, you have to accept all of me.' Dariush had no choice but to say yes; he promised to try.

It had taken another few months for Arezou to reveal the whole truth to Dariush. That her parents were not dead, but

were living in Camp Ashraf in Iraq. They had been forced to
separate from each other by the leader of the MEK, Massoud
Rajavi. He had ordered a mass divorce, part of an 'ideological
revolution' that Massoud and his wife Maryam had launched
for members to prove their loyalty. Hundreds were forced to
cut ties from all they loved, and that included legally divorcing
their spouses. Massoud had even demanded members in Camp
Ashraf hand over their wedding rings. Arezou was only a few
years old at the time and had been living in the camp with her
parents. She was immediately sent away to a 'group house' in
Washington where a distant relative worked. Arezou's parents had
long cut off contact with anyone who did not agree with the
sazman. Arezou had been brought up in a big suburban home
run by her father's second cousin. The second cousin took care
of three other children, all victims of the mass divorce.

Instead of being angry that Arezou had lied to him, Dariush
was grateful that she had entrusted him with her secrets. The
revelation brought them closer together. It also helped him
appreciate what the Group had done for her.

Dariush had turned against his religion in his teens, blaming
it for the revolution that had ruined their lives; all he saw in
it was a list of restrictions, of what one was not allowed to do.
But Arezou painted a different picture: one of real social justice
and where women had equal rights. She told him how there
were women fighters in Camp Ashraf who drove tanks and fired
weapons. Dariush was fascinated.

The gun-runner spotted Dariush immediately. 'You don't half
stick out. You look like a spy. Follow me.'

Dariush had followed Kian's instructions and had arranged
to meet the gun-runner outside a fruit juice shop on Haft-e

Tir Square, midtown Tehran. It was a symbolic meeting place; Dariush wondered whether the gun-runner was a member. Haft-e Tir was the 28th of June, the day in 1981 when the Chief Justice Ayatollah Beheshti and seventy-five high-ranking officials of the regime were blown up by an MEK-planted bomb in the square. For Dariush, Tehran's streets were dotted with victories, where Group members had bombed, rocket- and mortar-attacked government and military buildings. In 1998 there was the assassination of the director of Evin prison, who had been involved in the mass killings of MEK members during the late 1980s. In 1999 the MEK executed the Supreme Leader's military adviser outside his house, as he left for work.

On the way to meeting the gun-runner, Dariush had noticed that the map Kian had given him was out of date; new alleys had sprung up and many of the street names had changed. There were times when the Group seemed so sophisticated, and times when they looked like a bunch of cowboys.

The gun-runner raced through the backstreets and disappeared into a concrete block of flats. Dariush followed him to the third floor and into a messy living room with black eighties furniture and brown velvet curtains.

'I can get you an AK-47, but that's about it at the moment.'

'Well I'll take it then. Are you with the *sazman?*'

'No fucking way!' The gun-runner was laughing. 'Listen, I've dealt with quite a few of your lot. You all come here thinking we're all waiting to be saved by you. The truth is that we can't stand you. Nothing personal. But I bet you 1,000 US dollars that in one month, you won't find one Tehrani here who supports you. Better the devil you know, mate. The sister will sort you out,' he said, nodding towards a voluptuous redhead in a pink velour tracksuit. And the gun-runner was gone.

The woman lit a cigarette and stared at Dariush. Everything about him was attractive: he was tall and broad with thick hair, but his boyish features gave him a clean-cut, unassuming appearance. The woman disappeared into the corridor, talking into her mobile. She returned holding a shiny new AK-47 and a bag full of bullets. Dariush tried to make small talk as he handed over the cash, but she ignored him.

'If you make it out alive, tell your people to leave Iran alone,' she said, slamming the door shut.

To outsiders, the Mojahedin-e Khalq is an enigma. Their largest base is in Paris, where they work under the banner of their political wing, the National Resistance Council of Iran. Even some members struggle clearly to define the Group's principles and politics: a mixture of Marxism, Islam and nationalism. It has been led by Maryam Rajavi ever since her husband, Massoud, mysteriously disappeared out of public view in 2003. Maryam and Massoud are worshipped by their supporters and revered as gurus. Maryam, green-eyed, middle-aged with a make-up-less face and perfectly plucked eyebrows – a prerequisite for any respectable Iranian female regardless of attempts at modesty – wears a headscarf pulled down past her hairline. She looks more like a suburban, conservative housewife than a leader of Iran's biggest dissident group. In her soothing, nasal voice she successfully lobbies European and American politicians for support in fighting the Iranian regime, and speaks movingly of a free Iran.

The MEK spends millions on getting Western governments on side, often paying handsomely for endorsements and speeches by politicians. It is gearing up for a revolution. Or for when the USA or Israel may attack. Or for the moment when they can seize power from the clerics and destroy the regime.

The first MEK meeting Dariush attended was in a church hall. There were about fifty others there: middle-aged, friendly housewives, professionals, students and a few Americans. Only a handful were card-carrying members, the others called themselves 'supporters'. The women wore red headscarves pulled down low over their foreheads. They called each other *khaahar*, sister, and *baradar*, brother.

The Americans gushed about these brave 'freedom fighters'. They gave updates on the latest senators who had agreed to campaign for the MEK (for a healthy fee). The revered leader of this local branch, *Baradar* Fereydoon, spoke of human rights abuses in Iran – people being imprisoned and tortured. Pictures of bodies hanging from cranes, lashed backs and prisoners with lifeless eyes flashed up on an overhead projector. Nearly all the victims were members of the Group. Dariush was outraged.

Afterwards, they sat around tables eating *zereshk polo ba morgh*, barberry rice and chicken, chatting about their children and their jobs. It was more like the gathering of a town council than a rebel group. Dariush was astonished by the ordinariness of it all. Arezou was warm and open, unlike how she was in public. She was the happiest he had seen her.

The meetings became a regular part of Dariush's life. He found himself increasingly maddened by the atrocities meted out by the Islamic Republic towards members. *Baradar* Fereydoon singled out Dariush for special attention, spending time with him. He began confiding in him, explaining that the reason he walked with a limp was from an injury during a secret operation that had killed his comrade, now a war martyr. He entrusted Dariush with nuggets of top-level information and spoke of the Group's spies on the inside, MEK members who had infiltrated the government and who were even working on nuclear sites. Soon

Dariush was spending hours a day listening to taped messages from the leaders. It was impossible not to believe what they said. He fundraised for the Group and learnt about its main base in Camp Ashraf, where he hoped to be sent. The situation in his mother country was an emergency, and he had to act. Dariush began parroting *Baradar* Fereydoon's lines: 'Our people love us, they are waiting to be saved from hell.'

BANG. It sounded like a bomb. Dariush instinctively dived under his bed. BANG BANG BANG. BOOM. Now he could hear whizzing. He had heard the sounds of all sorts of artillery during training but these were not noises he recognized. Then there was screaming, and what sounded like laughing. As he crept towards the window, he saw an explosion of white sparkles glittering in the sky like a flower. He had forgotten it was *chaharshanbeh souri*, the fire festival.

The Group had sent him during *norooz*, New Year, which in Iran coincides with the first day of spring. The Group had said it was good cover, as it was when exiles returned to visit family. Dariush would just have to bide his time for a while. He read books that Kian had brought round for him, including one of his favourites, *Marxism and Other Western Fallacies: An Islamic Critique* by Ali Shariati.

He took a walk. Hundreds of kids were in the streets, jumping over bonfires they had made in the middle of the road, chanting an ancient Zoroastrian mantra to burn away bad luck and ill health. Packs of boys and girls were playing chase, sparklers in their hands. On Vali Asr firecrackers hurtled up and down the road. The cars were at a standstill, music blasting, people hanging out of the windows. The government had tried to ban *chaharshanbeh souri*; it was a pagan remnant of Zoroastrianism and the regime had declared it un-Islamic. But *norooz* and all that came with it was as culturally important to Iranians as the Islamic festivals; try as the government might, this was one battle they could not win. He stared at the people in wonder, surprised they could be enjoying themselves under the circumstances. He could not understand why there were so many discrepancies between what the Group had been telling them and what was happening in the country. But it was still possible to read the situation through the Group's prism: these kids were brave, for they were demonstrating audacious disobedience. He watched a group of teenagers down a side street start dancing and clapping; a few were on car bonnets singing and hip-swinging; one of the girls even whipped off her headscarf and waved it in the air as the crowd around her shrieked in appreciation. Dariush realized he was witnessing a mass act of rebellion.

When Dariush was especially chosen for the mission, Arezou said she had never felt so proud. Senior members had recognized his dedication and seen that he was prepared to die in the fight against the Islamic Republic. It did not matter that he had only been a member for a short while, it did not work like that. There were some who had been with the Group for years, had given their money (which they were all expected to do), had offered their services, yet they never progressed up the ranks, never got near the inner sanctum. You had to be prepared to give *all* of yourself to the Group. It was about discipline, sacrifice and loyalty. The Group had sent Dariush from America to Paris, where he met even higher-ranking MEK members. Everybody was impressed by him. He had thrown himself into ideological training, submitting detailed reports on his feelings for the Rajavis and learning their speeches off by heart. That is when it was decided Dariush should be sent to Camp Ashraf in Iraq to prepare for a mission.

Life at Camp Ashraf was strict. His training was intense: handling guns, using hand grenades, making bombs, stalking victims, using bugs and surveillance equipment, shooting targets. The sexes were segregated. Lustful thoughts were reported. Dariush attended obligatory group 'confessional' sessions to cleanse the mind; they made Dariush feel closer to his brothers and sisters. There were many like him, who had cut ties with their families. They spoke continually about the wide support they had in the motherland. Nobody seemed to know how many active members were living in Iran, but they assured Dariush there was a big, active network and that once there he would have a dedicated team helping him.

It was the day of the assassination. Dariush had started the morning doing breathing exercises to calm his nerves. It was all planned. He had been following the ex-police chief for weeks. The first morning after the public holidays, he had left the house at dawn, wearing tatty, ragged clothes and a pair of scuffed shoes. He arrived at the ex-police chief's road just after five in the morning and squatted on the side. Nobody noticed him.

Every day the ex-police chief would drive himself to a small office – unlike when he was the police chief and was driven in a bullet-proof car complete with a security convoy. Dariush thought the hit would be easy. He would strike as his target drove back home from work, in peak traffic.

Kian had found a getaway driver, a young mechanic who was a new member, itching for word of his loyalty to reach the

Rajavis. As they left the apartment, the getaway driver put his hand on Dariush's shoulder, 'I'm ready to die for the cause.' Dariush squeezed his hand, 'So am I.'

On time, the ex-police chief stepped out of the building and into his car. They followed him. His car began to slow as it reached a pile of traffic ahead. Dariush tapped the driver on the back – their signal. He drove up behind the police chief's car, up very close; Dariush could see the hairs on the police chief's neck through the window. He shot. He saw glass shatter. He looked back, the AK-47 still in his hand. There was a splatter of blood. The chief was slumped forward. *Was he still moving?* Then Dariush was in the air. On the ground, with a thud. He could not breathe. Men were pushing down on him, pressing his head into the tar-soaked gravel of the road. His body throbbed. His vision was blurred. How long did it take for him to understand what had happened? A minute, two minutes, ten minutes? He could not say.

He pieced it together: something had hit the motorbike and he had been catapulted in the air. Three police officers had jumped onto him. He had wet himself. He could not see his driver. When the cops made him stand on his feet, guns trained at his head, he knew it was over. The Group had told him: *if they catch you, they will torture you mercilessly, perhaps for years. They will rape you.* He remembered the photos. That is why he had the cyanide capsule in his mouth. It was still lodged there, despite the fall. He bit into the vial. A burst of liquid oozed out. Nine seconds. That is how long they told him it would take. Now it was at least fifteen seconds for sure, or does time slow when you die? Dariush squeezed his eyes tight to concentrate on death. But he was still very much alive. At least thirty seconds. Maybe the Group had been out by a few seconds; they seemed to be out about a lot of things.

'I said get into the back of the van!'

He opened his eyes. Still alive. Surely it was over a minute now. He took a tentative step forward.

'He's on drugs. Seriously, he's a total freak.'

He did not die on the way to the police station. Not only were their maps old and out of date; so was their cyanide. It must have degraded. Expired. Unlike him, who faced years of torture and rape.

At the police station, they took his handcuffs off and locked him in a small room. Somehow the police had not even frisked him. At least he had gone back to the gun-runner and ordered a hand grenade. It was tucked into his trousers. The minute the officer shut the door on him, he pulled the pin out. Only it went off before he had time to raise it to his head. He saw his own hand fly across the room. And then he fainted.

The judge looked weary. There was a time when he would send hundreds of these idiots to the firing squads or the noose; when the weight of his authority was encapsulated in four short, neat syllables: *hokm-e edam*, death penalty. He looked at Dariush standing in front of him. He was shaking with fear. He had a bandaged stump instead of a right hand. His lawyers said he had been brainwashed. He had repented. He had not killed anyone; the bullet had simply grazed the side of the ex-police chief's neck. The judge fiddled with his biro as he delivered the verdict.

Fatemi Street, midtown Tehran, several years later

The halogen strip light buzzes overhead, bathing everyone in a vicious blue light that picks out the hollows of cheeks and darkens circles under eyes. Three families are sitting on plastic chairs in silence, in a shabby office block. Nobody has touched the small cups of tea laid out on the plastic table. Their eyes are fixed on the door. Dariush walks in, wearing jeans and a crisp white shirt. Three men, heads slightly bowed, eyes scanning the room, follow him. The sobbing begins. The three men are soon encircled. Mothers clutch their sons to their chests; one man sinks to his knees; a sister strokes her brother's hair; a father simply buries his head in his hands, wrists wet with tears. One of the three men has been away for over twenty years. Over and over again he whispers one word: *sorry.*

Dariush watches from the corner of the room, cradling a crude plastic hand that has been attached to his stump. He has witnessed many such reunions, but he still cries every time. The three men he led into the room are former members of the MEK; now they are deserters, like Dariush. The men begin to recount their time with the Group. As the stories of brainwashing and regret tumble, Dariush silently nods. He remembers the beatings and the public confessionals at Camp Ashraf; his comrade was forced to confess to masturbating, which was banned. He remembers the isolation, of not being allowed out of a small compound, and the strict segregation of the sexes – one of the returnees Dariush had helped had not been allowed to be with his wife for fifteen years, even though they were both at Camp Ashraf together. He remembers families of members turning up at the camp, begging to see their loved ones. He remembers being part of the MEK cult.

After his botched assassination attempt, Dariush was sent to a military hospital, where doctors and nurses tended to him with care until he was healthy enough for prison. He had been given a life sentence. It was reduced to eight years. He spent just under four years in Evin prison. He was in the political wing and Dariush's cellmates were dissidents and students. It was in prison that Dariush was de-programmed, and it was in prison where he learnt the truth about his country, and learnt the lies that the MEK had fed him. He claims that in prison he was never tortured.

Nobody knows why the government did not kill Dariush, why he got such a light sentence. The most likely explanation is that he cut a deal: his freedom for his knowledge of the inner workings of the MEK. The Iranian love for a conspiracy theory went into overdrive; some said that Dariush was a regime spy all along. Whatever the truth, it was a cunning move by the government; when the Islamic Republic announced an amnesty on all deserters, dozens returned to the motherland. After Saddam Hussein's fall, the MEK was no longer welcome in Iraq and conditions in Camp Ashraf deteriorated. Dariush was paraded as a member who had been pardoned by the Islamic Republic of Iran and used as bait to lure others away, a perfect ploy to weaken the Group. As soon as Dariush was released from prison, he helped set up a government-backed charity rescuing MEK recruits and reuniting them with their families.

Once the families leave the office, Dariush locks up and heads home. He is meeting his mother at Yekta on Vali Asr, a café where she used to have milkshakes and burgers in her youth. The place has hardly changed: the same yellow sign and seventies interior. She flew to Tehran after his release, and he persuaded her to stay.

Arezou denounced him as a traitor, as did the rest of the Group. He tried to contact her, to convince her to leave them, but she never spoke to him again.

TWO

SOMAYEH

Meydan-e Khorasan, south Tehran

The day that Somayeh witnessed a miracle was the hottest day of the year. The shade under the sycamore trees on Vali Asr gave no sanctuary. The sun scorched the dark green leaves, burning the road below. The trees' roots ached with thirst, the *joobs* running above them dusty and dry.

Somayeh wiped bubbles of sweat from her top lip that kept popping up despite the best efforts of the ancient, juddering air-conditioning unit. Her damp fingers fiddled with the combination lock on the briefcase. With six rows of numbers, this was an impossible mission, but she was stubborn. She cried to God and to her favourite imam for help.

'Oh God, Oh Imam Zaman, I beg you to help me open this case, and I swear to you that I will sacrifice a lamb for the poor every year until I die,' she said her *nazr* prayer out loud, bruising her fingertips against the metal digits. Somayeh's *nazr* prayer was in keeping with tradition; she knew that for her wish to be granted she must vow to help those less well off than herself. She always channelled her prayers through Imam Zaman, even though so many believe that the patient and peaceful Abol Fazl, half-brother of Imam Hossein (the Prophet's grandson), responds to requests the quickest.

And then something extraordinary happened. At that precise moment the numbers snapped into alignment – a gentle click as the lock and God and Imam Zaman all acquiesced. The briefcase popped its mouth ajar.

It was a miracle. Of that, there was no doubt.

It had all started on an equally hot summer's day a few years earlier. Somayeh was seventeen and in the neighbourhood of her birth, Meydan-e Khorasan, east of the bazaar in south Tehran and as old as the city itself. The day had begun like any other, at six in the morning with her daily prayers. She breakfasted with her beloved father, Haj Agha, sipping her tea as he read the conservative daily *Kayhan* newspaper that he bought on his way back from the baker's. The *sangak* bread was still warm and pitted with crispy indents where the hot stones that lined the furnaces had cooked it; on it they slathered home-made cherry jam, sweet and sour and red as fresh blood. She then wrapped her black chador round her and walked to school with her younger brother, Mohammad-Reza.

They wound their way through the snaking alleys to the main road. The city was already at full throttle, roaring into the morning. There was never a gradual awakening in this part of town, just a sudden bang of activity that burst onto the streets. A line of shopkeepers were hosing down their patches of pavement. The day's newspapers were piled in stacks on the ground next to the tobacconist's stand; the Supreme Leader's face stared up from some of them, headlines speaking of martyrs, Zionists, blackmail and America: IRAN'S HEAVY FIST SMASHES THE FACE OF IMPERALISM and IRAN'S MILITARY EXCERCISE STRIKES FEAR IN ITS ENEMIES' HEARTS.

Meydan-e Khorasan is a small island, and Somayeh had seen

its shores slowly eroded by waves of modernity and youth. Shiny marble slabs and glossy stone cladding have risen up from the ruins of old houses, oiled by backhanders to foremen and civil servants to avoid expensive earthquake building codes. Yet religious, working-class values remain at the core of Meydan-e Khorasan; its residents battle to keep social strictures in place. For families like Somayeh's, religion means living by the words of the Koran and the Supreme Leader's fatwas to earn a place in paradise. In the knot of streets surrounding Somayeh's home, most of the women still wear chadors, as they have done for hundreds of years. Somayeh's family have been rooted in Meydan-e Khorasan for generations: it was the only world that Somayeh had ever known.

At school, the lessons were predictably uninspiring and Somayeh concentrated on her daydreams of life as an actress, an absurd fantasy considering that she was in agreement with her parents that acting was a dubious profession suited to those with loose morals. At break time the girls discussed the latest gossip. They were hooked on the Islamic-approved soap operas, where the evildoers were clean-shaven Iranians with old Persian names like Cyrus and Dariush and the heroes had Muslim names and beards. About half the pupils had satellite television at home and obsessively watched Latin American telenovelas on Farsi1, the Dubai-based channel part-owned by Rupert Murdoch. Satellite dishes are all over Iran, from Tehran to rooftops of remote villages, hanging off the homes of those from all classes, secular and religious alike. Even a member of government announced there were 4.5 million satellite television receivers in Iran. Somayeh's father declared foreign television an unnecessary and un-Islamic extravagance, and no amount of pleading could change his mind.

At two o'clock, just before the end of school, the girls were summoned by the headmistress they called Dog-Duck, an angry woman with the face of a bulldog and the waddling gait of a duck.

'Tahereh Azimi has been expelled for having improper relations with a boy,' barked Dog-Duck. There was a collective gasp. Everyone knew about the incident, Tahereh had not been to school since it happened, but nobody had been expelled before. It took over five minutes for Dog-Duck to calm the girls. She shuffled her big bottom across the room and launched into a lecture about modesty and God, lying to your parents and the corrupting influence of satellite television. It did not matter that Tahereh Azimi's hymen was still intact, that she rarely lied or that her family had never owned a satellite dish. The fact that she had been caught leaving a boy's house while his parents were out was enough to brand her a whore, which is what her teachers, classmates and it seemed most of the neighbourhood intimated. It did not help that Tahereh Azimi was beautiful, a fact that no *hejab* and lack of make-up would ever hide.

Dog-Duck soon ran out of steam, her crusade interrupted by stabs of hunger brought on by the succulent smell of grilled *shishlik* that was wafting through the windows. The girls grouped urgently outside the school gates.

'She's a *jendeh* through and through,' said Mansoureh, spitting out the word *jendeh* – whore – with surprising force. 'You can see it in her eyes and the way she walks. And she has a collection of *red* headscarves in her room, I've seen them. I find the whole thing really quite base.' Mansoureh's words triggered vigorous nodding.

'She's perverse. Remember her notebook, the one filled with porn,' said Narges, referring to Tahereh's pencil sketches of nudes.

Even though all the girls in Somayeh's year were virgins, a handful had experienced illicit encounters, mostly with their cousins, who were the only males they were allowed to be in contact with. Mansoureh and her cousin had fondled each other a year ago, and afterwards she was convulsed with shame. She took the palliative measure of viciously condemning any turpitude she encountered; she was in a perpetual state of disgust.

'I always thought it was weird the way she made such a point of telling us all she didn't like make-up, it was like she was trying to prove something, *hide something*,' batted Nika, whose real name was Setayesh, which she had deemed ugly and old-fashioned. Nearly half the girls in Somayeh's class had adopted names they thought sounded more chic than their own.

Jealousy quickly turned to outrage, a more palatable and acceptable response. Tahereh Azimi had broken the rules; but more than that, she had done something that they all longed to do.

'And I never saw her with a chador. Well, this serves her parents right, because if they don't even care if she wears a chador or not, how can they expect their daughter not to turn into a *jendeh*?' said Vista (real name Zohreh) whose *bazaari* father had promised her a nose job for her eighteenth birthday. Vista's father sold copper pipes, and even though he did not work in the bazaar itself, he was still referred to as a *bazaari*, which usually meant a merchant with strong traditional values. *Bazaaris* vote according to their personal interests and are never seen as any higher than middle-class, no matter how much money they make.

Tahereh's sartorial habits were carefully dissected. The girls concluded her clothes were suspiciously tame for a girl who sneaked into a boy's house behind everyone's back.

'Just because you wear a red headscarf or you don't wear a chador the whole time doesn't mean you're a bad girl,' Somayeh said, too prudish to use the word whore. 'She just has different values.'

'Yes, *Western* values,' said Mansoureh using one of their favourite euphemisms for 'slutty'. 'Her parents should move to *bala shahr*, north Tehran, where she can act all *Western*.' The girls laughed. It was a cruel joke, for Tahereh's parents were poor and everyone knew they had struggled to keep afloat. Moving to a chichi neighbourhood in north Tehran was about as likely as them buying a second home in Paris.

Somayeh was as troubled by Tahereh's behaviour as her friends; she was devout and religious; morals mattered to her. 'Let's face it, she dressed modestly, and I don't think there was any ulterior motive to that. But we're missing the point here, I think we all agree that having sex before marriage is just sinful. *Very, very sinful.*' The group cooed their approval.

Somayeh had a flair for appearing tolerant without sabotaging her own moral reputation. This made her popular with everyone, not just her own kind. Strong principles, a demure appearance and religious fervour meant that the *Hezbollahi* girls counted her as one of their own, and they were always the hardest to crack. *Hezbollahis* are the most zealous defenders of the regime, using religion and politics to ensure its survival. Somayeh never looked down on the poorer girls. Even the *Western*-looking girls who tried to emulate the uptown girls – and there were only a few of them in this school – did not feel judged by her. But Somayeh did judge them. She avoided being seen with them because she was embarrassed of the image they portrayed. Embarrassed that others might think she was cut from the same (inappropriate) cloth. Somayeh believed the way you clothed yourself was a litmus test for morality. The brighter and tighter the dress and the thicker the make-up, the higher up the *jendeh* scale you scored.

Somayeh and her friends strongly believed that the *hejab* should be enforced. They agreed with the law, which states that if your make-up and clothes are contrary to public decency and you intend to attract attention, you can be arrested and taken straight to court. The sexy excuses for *hejab* being paraded on the streets confirmed their suspicions that a dress code free-for-all would result in a speedy degeneration of morals and would be the undoing of the city. 'If the *hejab* wasn't compulsory, these women would be walking around half naked, men wouldn't be able to help themselves and we'd all be in trouble,' as Vista put it.

The girls were not to blame for their misogynous views. They had been fed the regime's line on *hejab*, which was usually touted around the city via huge billboard advertisements, since birth. The government had two basic tactics: to warn of the physical dangers of bad *hejab* (which was judged to be 'asking for it'), and to disseminate a culture of shame. A recent campaign showed a picture of two boiled sweets, one that had been opened and one that was still in its wrapper. The sweet that had been opened was surrounded by three flies looking ready to pounce. Underneath were the words: VEIL IS SECURITY. Some were not so subtle: 'We ourselves invite harassment' was the strapline on another advert. Some posters purported to use science. Underneath a picture of a couple of girls looking decidedly *Western* (lashings of make-up; blonde hair falling out of brightly coloured headscarves that were pushed back as far as they would go; short, tight *manteaus*) were the words: 'Psychologists say those who dress inappropriately and use lots of make-up have character issues.'

Most of north Tehran looked like a whorehouse to Somayeh, but she accepted that it was impossible for all these women to have loose morals. She accepted that they were not as devoted to God as she was. But the Tehran around her was changing so fast, it was hard to tell who was a *real* prostitute and who was not. There was bad *hejab* everywhere. Somayeh also knew that a chador could hide many sins. Her brother had once pointed out a spot near Shoosh Street, at the southern tip of Vali Asr, where *chadori* women were real-life *jendehs*. Poor souls selling their hidden bodies for the price of a *kabab*. Somayeh cried when she first saw their sullen faces and dead eyes.

Somayeh loved her chador, for it was part of her *sonat*, her culture. It symbolized far more than a respect for tradition. The simple black cloth stood for modesty and piety; for supplication to God and a spiritual, ordered world where rules were in place to protect. It was all these things and more. It was her oversized comfy cardigan, hiding her when she had her period and she was feeling bloated. It was her protector, concealing hints of curves from men's lustful stares. Her favourite look was black chador, skinny jeans and Converse trainers, the juxtaposing of old and new – a dual-purpose ensemble that kept her simultaneously connected to God and fashion. But most of all she wore her chador because of her father, Haj Agha. For him, it was the only acceptable form of *hejab*. 'A girl in a chador is like a rosebud, the beauty hidden inside, making it all the more beautiful and closer to God,' he would say.

Modesty was a serious business in Haj Agha's household. The only men who had ever seen Somayeh's hair or even her bare arms were her father and her brother Mohammad-Reza. In Somayeh's Tehran, it was inappropriate for even her dearest uncles to set eyes on her slim body. Sometimes, instead of a chador she wore a headscarf and *manteau*, mostly for practical reasons, when she went hiking in the mountains with her friends and on family picnics. Her *manteau* was always loose, below the knee and coloured dark. Underneath she wore the benign uniform of the high-street chain: Zara, Mango, Topshop and Benetton.

Some of the girls decided to go back to Mansoureh's house after school as her family had a big living room. There were few public places to hang out in this part of town. The nearby parks were mostly full of drug addicts and there were no cool coffee shops. The traditional tea houses were men-only dens, full of hookah-pipe smoke and banter.

Somayeh left the other girls; she had to help her mother prepare for a party. Tonight was a big night, they were celebrating Haj Agha's latest pilgrimage trip and all the neighbours were invited. As she turned the corner into her street she saw them. Tahereh Azimi and her elderly parents were standing by a small van laden with their possessions, fleeing in shame, back to the village they came from.

Tahereh Azimi had never fitted in. Her parents seemed normal: poor and working-class. They prayed and her mother only ever wore a chador in public. Tahereh's mother was nearly fifty when she had given birth to her, after thirty barren years. Tahereh's father, Sadegh, had endured decades of pressure from his family to leave his sterile wife for younger, more fecund ground. Sadegh had refused. He was a good man who could not stand to cause pain. Tahereh was their miracle baby, even if Hazrat Abol Fazl had responded to their *nazr* prayers with perverse delay.

They were sturdy country people, but the city had sucked the vitality out of them. Tahereh's parents had moved to Tehran in their youth when their village had crumbled to mounds of rubble after an earthquake had rumbled its way up from the earth's crusty layers. Half their house had smashed in on the ground in less than six seconds. Whole lives were reduced to particles of brick and dust. A few scores were killed, including Tahereh's extended family. Their bodies were buried in the cemetery under the orange trees. A village that had once been so vital, on a fertile plain, encircled by mountains that gushed water and fed orchards near where wild horses roamed, became a sad, forgotten place.

The transition to the city had been less painful than they had expected. Although Tehran's brash, ugly urbanity, its motorways, concrete high-rises and festering underbelly suggest an impersonal metropolis, it can still feel like a village. In Tehran, urban privileges like privacy and anonymity are still Western concepts. Hidden in its seams is the stitching that holds the city together: the bloodlines, the clans, the kindness, the prying and the meddling.

Tahereh's family soon stumbled on distant relatives and friends. But their new community did not last long. Many around them were felled by heart disease, cancer and medical incompetence. As their lives contracted, they became more solitary, leaning in towards each other, with Tahereh at their centre. The net began closing in on them too. Tahereh's mother suffered a stroke. They had no medical insurance and Sadegh juggled three jobs. Tahereh began working as a seamstress in the tiny back room of a dressmaker's shop in a shopping mall on Vali Asr, a job that was kept a secret. There would have been whispers if the neighbours found out that Tahereh was a working girl at sixteen, even if her time was spent with a Singer sewing machine sitting opposite an Afghan tailor in his seventies. Vali Asr opened a new world for Tahereh, where teenagers hung out in coffee shops and fast-food joints. Super Star and Super Star Fried Chicken were always brimming with teenage boys and girls flirting with each other, exchanging numbers and setting up dates.

Tahereh spent all her free time walking up and down Vali Asr, marvelling at its beauty, which seemed to intensify the farther north she ventured. She started walking up as far as Bagh Ferdows near the furthest reaches of Vali Asr. She would sit on a bench and watch the city; people here seemed to come from a different race. It was on one of these trips that she bumped into Hassan, the son of a neighbour. He had come to look at football kits in the sports shops on downtown Vali Asr, near Monirieh Square. Away from family and neighbourhood spies, they spoke differently to each other, at once understanding the other's need to discover a world outside the Meydan. The chance meeting became a treasured weekly tryst. Tahereh started reading *Zanan*, a daring women's magazine that covered everything from literature to sex and argued for gender equality. Tahereh visited exhibitions and plays. She was a gifted artist; but her teachers were not interested in drawing and painting. Only her parents understood the remarkable talent of their girl, but they had neither the money nor the education or foresight to encourage her.

Tahereh's parents were religious and traditional, but they came from a liberal village where men and women celebrated weddings together, where chadors were white and where it did not matter if your *hejab* slipped off your head. Sadegh thought the revolution had been a big mistake and he still lamented the fall of the Shah. He believed that the *hejab* should not be compulsory; it was a matter of personal choice and one's relationship with God was private. He never drank, but was not against alcohol. He thought modernity was not at odds with Islam. Sadegh also believed that people should be virgins until marriage, but he thought that relations between men and women were nobody's business but their own. Sadegh soon realized his views did not belong in Meydan-e Khorasan, so he kept them to himself, truths only shared with his wife and child.

When Sadegh found out about Hassan, he believed Tahereh when she said her honour was intact, but he was devastated that her reputation had been shredded to worthless pieces.

When Hassan's mother returned home she was so enraged that she called the police, telling them there was a prostitute in her house. The police took Tahereh to the station and summoned her father. He told the officers his daughter was pure and begged them to release her. They mocked his village accent, and spoke down to him as though he were a simple peasant.

'Your daughter behaves like a whore and you defend her! Where's your honour? Is that what they do in the villages? They'd have stoned her from where you come from!' They all laughed, not knowing that life in his northern village had not changed much since the revolution – in some ways it was more liberal than the laws enforced by the police in Tehran. As for Hassan, he got a few hearty slaps on the back from his friends. Only his best friend knew the truth: that he and Tahereh had fallen in love, that they spent their time visiting art galleries and listening to Pink Floyd. They had only ever dared to kiss.

Tahereh did not notice Somayeh loitering at the corner of the road, waiting for her and her parents to leave. It would not have surprised her; since the episode everyone had cut her off.

The smell of saffron and buttery steamed rice filled the flat and vats of rich stews bubbled on the stove. Somayeh's mother, Fatemeh, had been cooking for the last two days. Any morsel of food that passed through her soft, plump hands was transformed into succulent dishes. Fatemeh's mother had told her that if you kept your husband well fed, he would never leave you to taste forbidden fruit. Fatemeh had learnt her skills from a young age. She was famed for her cooking and their parties were always packed. Fatemeh stirred and fried and washed while Somayeh set out bowls of fruit, cucumbers, walnuts and pistachios. She cleaned the dust off the plastic maroon flowers that were displayed around the room. Even with windows closed, the dust somehow worked its way into apartments and houses across the city, sheeting everything in a fine grey powder.

Mohammad-Reza sat at the kitchen table playing the *Quest of Persia* video game on the family PC. Haj Agha was watching television. A turbaned mullah was wagging his fingers, doing what mullahs do so well: lecturing. Iran's mullahs are not only authorities on Islamic theology, but are also experts at finding moral decay in the most unlikely of places. Today it was to be found in a new 3G mobile Internet service: 'It endangers public chastity…it will destroy family life!' moaned the mullah, disgusted by the idea of video-calling. Four grand ayatollahs, no less, had issued a fatwa condemning the new service. The Internet operator had ignored them.

Haj Agha always looked like he was in contemplation. His permanently furrowed brows and small, squinting eyes gave the aura of a serious, reserved man. He was shy with strangers and mostly kept his thoughts to himself. He had been remarkably handsome in his youth, but an unfulfilled marriage and dull, poorly paid government jobs had prematurely ground his looks down. Haj Agha had spent most of his life toiling to make ends meet. When he married Fatemeh, she moved in with him and his parents. The four of them lived between three rooms, even when the children came along. For years he barely seemed to sleep, working two jobs, just enough to keep everyone fed. Two events changed his fortunes: the deaths of his parents and the arrival of a new President in the summer of 2005, Mahmoud Ahmadinejad, whom he had voted for on the Supreme Leader's advice. With one of Ahmadinejad's new easily accessible, low-interest government loans, Haj Agha joined Tehran's construction boom. He knocked down the small brick house his parents had bequeathed him and he built four floors upwards. He sold one apartment and was now renting the two below him. Never again would he live in a ramshackle brick house struggling to make ends meet. He could now afford to send his children to university. Haj Agha's boosted income also meant that even though Fatemeh did not have time to spend on religious pursuits, she had the money to buy spiritual peace of mind. When Fatemeh's father died, she paid a mullah one million tomans – just over 300 US dollars – for a year's worth of daily *namaaz* prayers for him, in case he had missed any during his lifetime. Ahmadinejad had served them well.

Haj Agha's social status had risen exponentially in line with his growing income. His rank in the neighbourhood had also been nudged up several places thanks to his religious devotion. The party tonight was to celebrate his second trip to Mecca. In the last few years he had been immersed in demonstrating his love to God and the imams: two trips to Karbala in southern Iraq to visit the tomb of Hossein, the most important Shia martyr and the Prophet Mohammad's grandson. From there on to Najaf to pay his respects at Hossein's father's tomb, Imam Ali, the first Shia imam and, as Shias believe, the rightful successor to Mohammad. Not forgetting two visits to Syria to the resting place of Imam Ali's daughter, Zeinab, granddaughter of the prophet.

Piety struck Haj Agha late in life. Fatemeh blamed herself for his affliction: soon after their marriage she had asked him to take her to Imam Reza's shrine in Mashhad, Iran's holiest city, for their honeymoon. Imam Reza was the only Shia imam buried in Iran, rumoured to have been murdered with poisoned grapes. But Haj Agha refused to take Fatemeh. He could not afford the trip and thought pilgrimages unnecessary. He was a stubborn man and could not be persuaded. Fatemeh was devastated but also fearful of angering her new husband. Instead she had cried to her mother, who had told her father, who had a quiet word with Haj Agha. There was no way of refusing his new father-in-law. Fatemeh was overcome with joy, not because he had agreed to the trip, but because, in changing his mind, he had shown his love for her. She was never told he had been forced to take her.

Mashhad and the world's busiest Islamic shrine were not what Haj Agha had in mind for his honeymoon, although the city was packed with honeymooners. Afghan migrants, pilgrims, hawkers, tourists, beggars and noxious fumes swirled around them on the crowded streets. The colossal shrine was open for business twenty-four hours a day and twinkled at night like an Islamic Disneyland.

Haj Agha and Fatemeh walked into this beguiling world of gilded domes, glittering mirror mosaics and exquisite alcoves tiled luminous blue and green. Somewhere between a vast court-yard shadowed by minarets and a dazzling six-tiered chandelier dripping light from a vaulted ceiling, their emotions took over. Fatemeh felt a rush of love for God and all He had given her. She felt a rush of love for this quiet, reserved man she barely knew, whom she had met only once before her wedding and had not wanted to marry. Haj Agha was stricken with regret for his academic failures and his laziness. But most of all for agreeing to marry Fatemeh, and being bound to a life of sexual frustration. Fatemeh and Haj Agha edged towards the inner chamber where the imam's body is entombed.

Shia shrines are not usually peaceful havens of reflection and meditation. Each shrine marks the spot on the trail of Arab caliphs, sheiks and horse-backed fighters as they journeyed towards war and death; they are monuments to murder, betrayal and sacrifice. Tragedies to be mourned. Lucky, then, that Iranians make excellent mourners. We embrace sorrow like no one else, wailing on demand, tapping into the vats of love and loss that simmer in the cauldrons of our hearts. We were always doomed, lied to and betrayed from the very beginning. Shrines are usually a tumult of sobbing and chest-beating and Imam Reza's shrine is no exception. From the female entrance Fatemeh stepped into what looked like a battleground. Howling women barrelled against her as they charged their way towards the tomb. Stewards holding neon feather dusters tried to beat them back. Even the scrums that broke out at Fatemeh's local bank were not this vicious. She was annoyed that she was unable to conjure even a few tears. So she pushed her way into the throng until the crush of wailing bodies sent her into a trance. She did not even notice when the tears trickled out of her eyes.

Fatemeh was spat out the other end, exhilarated. She edged towards the Perspex partition that separated the sexes, to look for Haj Agha. That is when she saw him. Crouching near a corner in the distance. He was wailing uncontrollably, an unstoppable flood of tears gushing from his eyes. She was dumbfounded. He had outdone all the other mourners, some of whom kept a competitive eye on him, forcing them to up the ante just to be heard over the din Haj Agha was making. Haj Agha seemed unaware of his surroundings. He had been overwhelmed by sorrow for a life half lived and half lost. Fatemeh had no idea he was such a sensitive, religious soul.

The trip changed both their lives. Fatemeh had new-found respect for her husband. Haj Agha appeared less miserable. It was as though he had discovered the mystic power of his religion, the essence of Shia Islam that seemed to elude so many. Whatever it was, Haj Agha was hooked. It was several years before he would take his next trip, as any extra cash was quickly sucked up after the children were born. When the money did start to roll in,

Haj Agha began his pilgrimages, always going alone. His dedication became a compulsion and it irked Fatemeh. The mould of Fatemeh and Haj Agha's marriage had been cast: an uncommunicative husband and a wife who was desperate to please, forever disappointed and yet resigned to her life. Fatemeh consoled herself that at least her husband was addicted to mourning and not to opium, like so many of the men in the neighbourhood.

In Tehran, his spirituality was hard to fathom. He rarely spoke of God, rarely read the holy book or the hadiths, rarely attended mosque. The strongest devotion he showed was to the television set. But Fatemeh could not complain too harshly, for she was riding in the slipstream of Haj Agha's holy journeys, which saw them hurtling up the social ladder; paying your respects to the imams gave you status in this neighbourhood. Ever since Haj Agha had actually earned his moniker of *Haji* by completing the pilgrimage to Mecca, people treated Fatemeh differently too. She was now *Haj Khanoum*, Mrs Haj. His trips accumulated spiritual chips, the only currency in Iran that never devalued, and which in Meydan-e Khorasan commanded deference and respect. Soon Haj Agha had been on more pilgrimages than the local mullah, and it was not uncommon for neighbours to come round to seek his advice on all matters, from the ethereal to more earthly affairs, such as nagging wives and children who talked back. He would receive his guests crouched, leaning against cushions as Fatemeh served them platters of fruit and piping-hot tea. He would suck the tea through lumps of sugar wedged in his cheek as he ruminated. His answers were brief and practical, and he would almost always end with a line that nobody really understood: 'You can only be true to God if you are true to yourself.'

*

The sun dipped past the suburbs of west Tehran and the city lights blinked into the descending darkness. The moon was big and fat and tinged ginger. It had just started its ascent when Haj Agha's family, friends and neighbours began to arrive, laden with pastries and cakes.

The women hovered together near the kitchen – a flock of crows, clasping black chadors that radiated wafts of sweaty perfume and hot, smoky city air. The men braced themselves on chairs against the wall, sipping the sweet-sour iced mint and vinegar cordial, *sekanjabin*, that Fatemeh served the guests. After the customary and laboriously detailed questioning of relatives' health and well-being, the two groups launched themselves into the favourite subject of most Tehranis: politics.

Politics invades conversations in every corner of the city. Even the crack addicts in south Tehran can turn political pundit in moments of cognizance. It is impossible to take a taxi without the driver delivering his verdict on the latest scandals and power battles. Talk of politics allows people to feel they have a stake in their future, that they are not powerless spectators. Behind the confines of walls and hidden in cars, most ordinary Iranians are surprisingly free in venting frustrations. For those who are not monitored, few subjects are off-limits. Internal mud-slinging and accusations traded between politicians and panjandrums give ordinary citizens freedom to do the same. Some say that verbal freedom is greater now than under the Shah, when people had been too scared to badmouth the king even in private.

Many religious and working-class families flourished after the revolution, including those in Meydan-e Khorasan. The Islamic Revolution had been the making of men like Haj Agha. The poorer members of society enjoyed a sudden rush of financial benefits laid on by the regime. Factory workers were given a minimum wage. Working hours were eased. And with the onset of war, as rations kicked in, basic items like bread, cheese, sugar and cooking oil were subsidized. But it was not just a matter of economic welfare. It was also a matter of respect. The residents of Meydan-e Khorasan had felt they were being slowly pushed to the fringes of the new, modern Tehran that the Shah was building, caught in limbo between development and tradition. The Shah had been impatient for change, dragging Iran into the First World; they had been fearful of a world with which they did not identify. Even though, unlike his father, the Shah did not ban the *hejab* and the chador, wearing it marked you out as from the lower classes. But under the Islamic regime, the people of the Meydan now felt a part of society. In government offices, they were no longer strangers in their own land. The way they worshipped and the way they lived their lives not only had the state's seal of approval, their lifestyle was now paraded as an exemplar of living. They felt close to this state, whose religious language they understood. Most had never been very political, but this integration provoked passionate support for the regime. It worked both ways. Their godliness proved useful, especially when the absolute rule of a spiritual leader was enshrined in the law, after Khomeini introduced the concept of *velayat-e-faqih*, rule of the Islamic jurist, a concept that gave him ultimate and unchallenged political authority over his subjects. With a God-ordained regime on their side, many in the Meydan had no need to question its authority.

Somayeh's neighbours shared common values, such as the importance of a woman's virginity before marriage and of modest *hejab*. Even though they varied in degrees of religiosity, their attitudes towards their faith were similar. But when it came to politics, they were divided. It was not a polarization of views, nor a simple division between those who supported the regime and those who did not; there were countless variations. 'So you're not still going to vote for that monkey, *Ahmagh*-inejad?' was the ice-breaker from next-door neighbour Masoud, who had inserted the word *ahmagh* – stupid – in place of *Ahmad*.

'At least he's not letting *Amrika* bully us.'

'At least he's not a mullah,' added Masoud, scooping up a handful of pistachios. Masoud not only prayed every day; he had also been to Mecca. Yet he despised mullahs. He blamed them for everything, from the bad state of the economy to corruption. Being from a *sonati* – traditional – family or a duti-fully observant Muslim did not mean automatic support for the regime. Masoud believed in a separation between the state and religion. He did not support the absolute rule of the Supreme Leader. While the Islamic Revolution suited most of Masoud's neighbours, his life had remained unchanged. Fatemeh shouted from the kitchen that mullahs were blameless and it was the politicians who were bad.

'We're in this mess because of those sly foxes, the English,' said Abbas, the local greengrocer. *Engelestan* always got a bad rap, and the British were held accountable by Iranians of all political persuasions for a long list of crimes, including backing a coup in 1953 that ousted popular Prime Minister Mossadegh, and a widely held conspiracy theory that BBC radio helped bring about the downfall of the Shah.

'It's all of them, they're all rotten to the core and Ahmadinejad's the worst one of the lot. He knows nothing about economics and he's going to be the ruin of us,' said Ali, a *bazaari* trader of electrical goods whose wife and daughters wore the chador, yet who believed that *hejab* should not be enforced.

'Ahmadinejad's the best thing that's happened to the country in a long time. The price of oil keeps going up, he's straight-talking and he understands what normal people like us want,' said Haj Agha. A group of women shouted out their agreement from the kitchen.

The conversation ran a familiar course, from politics to the economy to the sharing of personal misfortunes. Somayeh, like her mother Fatemeh, was indifferent to politics; but they were both devoted to the Supreme Leader, Ali Khamenei. Whatever the Supreme Leader would say, they would follow. Sometimes when they watched him on television they would be so moved by his words they would break down crying. The Supreme Leader was a saint; a representative of God and as sacred as the imams. Through his divine body the word of Allah was channelled. He was not sullied by dirty politics, for his role on this earth was pure: simply to ensure the law and practice of Islam. The Supreme Leader had taken over the mantel from Khomeini, who had rescued the country from moral corruption and who had saved the country's poor. These two old men were Somayeh's heroes and she could not abide criticism of them.

The women soon drifted out of the political discussions, partly because of the physical separation of the sexes, and partly because they had their own news to share. After twenty years of marriage, Batool Khanoum had got a divorce, the first woman aged over fifty to do so in the neighbourhood. Nobody knew the reasons for the divorce, but it was a scandal. 'What's the point?' said Fatemeh. 'After all those years, I just don't understand it. How could she do that to her children? They have to live with the shame.'

Batool Khanoum had been encouraged to divorce her husband by her own children. They had all had enough of his crippling opium habit and his abusive behaviour. Women can only divorce husbands with their permission, unless they can prove that a man has failed to fulfil his marital duties (which includes impotency and insanity), so Batool's daughter had helped her by secretly filming her father hitting Batool Khanoum and smoking opium. When the judge saw the grainy footage on Batool's mobile phone, he granted her a divorce on the spot. Batool Khanoum had already experienced the fallout of a divorce in the Meydan, for a divorcee was considered to have loose morals. Unbeknown to the women now disdainfully discussing her divorce, several of their husbands had already tried their luck with her. Batool Khanoum had slapped each of them across the face. Apart from Ozra's husband, who was attractive and rich.

'Getting a divorce is failing yourself and God,' said Somayeh.

'Everyone's getting divorced these days and the whole of society's falling apart. It's the government's fault for making a divorce easier than opening a bank account!' said Hamideh, not knowing that her best friend Akram had been begging her husband for a divorce for over a decade, but he refused to give it to her. Even though Hamideh tried to keep her opium addiction quiet, she thought it far more socially acceptable than a divorce.

Opium has been part of the culture for centuries. It is a classless drug smoked the length and breadth of Vali Asr and beyond, a panacea for everything from aches to boredom to joblessness.

The heaps of food being laid on the table were enough to distract the hungry guests from politics and divorce. At that moment too the entryphone buzzed. It was Fatemeh's sister Zahra, whom she had not seen for five years. The falling-out had been about money, as falling-outs in the city so often are. Fatemeh had asked to borrow some and Zahra said they had none to lend. It was a brazen lie. Zahra had married into a family of wealthy carpet traders and her husband Mohammad had already started the upward climb to a glitzier lifestyle. Zahra had not invited Fatemeh to their new home, scared that in the profusion of silverware and the Italian leather furniture the truth would be revealed – which was that Zahra's family were now richer than everyone they had left behind in the Meydan. Mohammad and Haj Agha kept out of it. They had tried to intervene between the competing sisters' feuds in the past and both had emerged as injured parties, heads and tongues bitten off by jealous rage. Recently word had reached Fatemeh that Zahra was repentant, and more importantly that she was ill with acute diabetes. When Zahra heard Fatemeh's voice on the phone she had cried, and when Fatemeh had invited her older sister to Haj Agha's pilgrimage party she had cried some more. It helped matters that Haj Agha was now self-sufficient. It reassured Zahra that a rapprochement would not mean having to part with cash.

Zahra looked better with diabetes. Her fatter face had plumped out her wrinkles. Standing beside her was her husband Mohammad and their two sons, now grown up and one with a new wife in tow. The unmistakable smell of money emanated from all of them. Ambergris and musk. Velvet-smooth nappa leather. Chador of softest silk. Fingers and lobes laden with gold. Mohammad was hugging a gigantic casket of clashing-coloured flowers bound with pastel ribbons, a generous gift given the high price of flowers these days. The two sons wore sharp Western-looking suits, which meant that they fitted properly and were not made from polyester. The three men were clean-shaven. They were a modern, *sonati* family and when they entered the room, Haj Agha felt a stab of jealousy. They were what he wanted to be.

Mohammad had heard of his brother-in-law Haj Agha's new-found religious zeal and was struck with respect. Mohammad was so busy making money, he did not have time for spiritual pursuits. As he congratulated Haj Agha on his latest holy jaunt, the sisters embraced and immediately retreated into the kitchen.

Zahra's oldest son, Amir-Ali, had done everything possible to get out of coming to the party. But when he walked into the flat, he saw that he had a reason for staying: Somayeh. Amir-Ali was taken aback by her transformation from unattractive little girl to alluring teenager. She had hazel eyes and, below a handsome straight nose, red lips sculpted in a defined Cupid's bow. Her skin was flawless and her make-up subtle. Her *roo-farshee* house shoes were black sequinned ballet pumps, not the usual ugly plastic slip-on *dampaee* slippers that most girls in the neighbourhood wore at home. When she loosened her grip on her chador, an earlobe studded with three earrings peaked out from under wisps of highlighted hair. This surprised Amir-Ali; he had not expected his poor cousins from Meydan-e Khorasan to know about multiple piercings. These were details that mattered to him. Details that told him she would understand his world.

Amir-Ali wanted a woman with traditional values but who appreciated the need to look good. In Amir-Ali's experience, *chadori* girls were usually one of two types. They were unsophisticated with ugly, clumpy shoes or they had Botox-smooth foreheads and wore stripper heels, the rich ones picking up their vulgar, red-soled Louboutins in Dubai – wolves in black chadors. Too rebellious and deceiving to make good wives.

A few young men in the corner of the room were trying to steal glimpses of Somayeh. Amir-Ali's competitive streak pulsed into action. She was *his* cousin, and he would be damned if any of these lowly upstarts would get her.

The attraction between them was instant. Somayeh felt her face reddening when he walked through the door. Amir-Ali was tall and muscular with a confident laugh and a sharp jaw. She noticed that his nose had shrunk in size, the handsome aquiline ridge now shaved off by the surgeon's knife. She always ridiculed the boys in her neighbourhood who had nose jobs. You get the nose you pay for. Many of the residents in the Meydan could not afford the city's certified plastic surgeons and had to make do with local dentists with a sideline in crude cosmetic surgery. The results were not always pretty. But Amir-Ali's nose was so expertly shaped, it was a work of art. A mark of success and good taste.

'So Mohammad-Reza, Persepolis or Esteghlal?' Amir-Ali was asking the obligatory football question, but his mind was not on Mohammad-Reza or Tehran's top competing clubs; his eyes were locked onto Somayeh, carefully tracking her around the room. She could feel his stare burning through her chador. She grabbed it tight round her, partly for comfort and partly because she knew it would cling to her and reveal her sylph-like body. Amir-Ali saw she was nubile and slim. You never knew with *chadori* girls. A few too many times chadors had slipped off to unveil dumpy hips and bounteous, fleshy stomachs, bounty he had not been looking for.

'So Somayeh, are you still at school?'

She blushed. 'Yes.' She hurried away. It would be inappropriate for her to talk to him for too long. In the neighbourhood, when puberty hit, cousins were no longer treated as close family. From her first period, Somayeh was not allowed to play unsupervised with the cousins she had considered as brothers. They had become potential sexual partners. 'Boys and girls are like cotton wool and fire, you can't put them anywhere near each other because they'll explode in flames!' her grandmother would say whenever she protested.

Marriage between cousins was considered lucky and heaven-sent, a strengthening of families that brought unity. Prized above all was the marriage between children of brothers; there was even an expression for it, declaring it was written in the stars.

Zahra had noticed her son staring. Testosterone oozed out of him. When everyone sat around the *sofreh,* a tablecloth placed on the ground, with plates full of food (men at one end, women and children at the other), she grabbed him by the arm and snapped in his ear, 'For the love of God pull yourself together. Unless you're serious about her, don't even think about it. You can't mess around with family, especially after everything that's happened; even *you* know that.' Without looking at his mother he replied: 'I'm serious.'

When Amir-Ali got home, he told his parents of his plan. He wanted to marry his cousin Somayeh. He was surprised at how quickly they agreed. She was perfect: pretty, shy, modest and an excellent homemaker. Most of the Tehrani girls that Amir-Ali knew acted as though their private parts were lined with gold, even when they were not attractive. Zahra and Mohammad had for a long time been praying that Amir-Ali would meet a good girl from a *sonati* family. Their son was immature and spoilt. He needed the responsibility of a wife and child to snap him into manhood. They had tried to tempt him with the daughters of rich *bazaaris* and industrialists, but Amir-Ali's reputation had spread farther than they had hoped. He had been seen in gambling houses. He drank. He had girlfriends. Nobody would allow a man like that near a daughter. It made no difference that Amir-Ali had no appetite for these rich religious girls who, deep down, he suspected wanted to be Western. He needed a woman who knew his culture and his tradition. An honest woman.

Amir-Ali had lost his virginity at sixteen to the forty-five-year-old wife of a neighbour. Fear of discovery (on his part) and guilt (on her part) put an end to the dalliance and he moved on to girls his own age. Mostly it was fumbling and frottage. Sometimes they would have *la-paee*, 'between the legs' thigh sex. He would pump vigorously between a girl's clenched thighs. *La-paee* sex was the most popular form of sex among teenagers and girls in their early twenties from *sonati* and religious families; these were girls who did not have the same strength and devotion to God as Somayeh.

Every now and again Amir-Ali and his friends would get lucky, but it was nearly always anal sex so the girl's hymen would remain untouched and she would still be a virgin for her wedding night.

'This guy gets married to this gorgeous girl,' was the opening line of one of Amir-Ali's favourite jokes. 'She's absolutely stunning. And of course, she says the usual crap: No one's ever touched me! I've saved myself for you all these years! And on his wedding night, he realizes that she really is a virgin. He can't believe it. He's overjoyed. So he says to her father, you did an amazing job, such a beautiful daughter and you brought her up to be a virgin until marriage. I must thank you. But the father says: No, don't thank me, thank her mother. So he says the same to her mum, and she replies: No, don't thank me, thank her; she's the one who kept herself pure. So finally he goes to his beautiful wife and says, thank you darling, for respecting yourself and for keeping your virginity. And she turns round and says: No, don't thank me, thank my arse!' The guys always fell about laughing at that one. Amir-Ali and his friends quipped that Tehran must be the world capital of anal sex.

Amir-Ali's good looks and a family move to Shahrak-e Gharb, a middle-class neighbourhood in the north-west of the city, propelled him to a different world, which finally brought with it a fully functioning sex life. This change of fortune was mostly down to his neighbour Arash, a cool kid in ripped jeans and Prada sunglasses with liberal parents. Arash's life consisted of girls and parties. In this part of town, some girls would have sex after only one date. Which was all very well when they were sitting astride Amir-Ali, but he did not want to marry a slut. That was when he realized that, when it came to marriage, he needed his own kind. He had never felt comfortable with the liberal, secular kids. Somehow, they could always tell him apart, no matter how much he spent on designer clothes. They thought it was cool that his father was a real *bazaari* done good, but he soon tired of being a novelty. More than that, he did not like the way the boys allowed the women to be so independent; it had not only spoilt the girls, but these rich men were being emasculated: they seemed to have lost their place in the world; they were constantly depressed even though they had it all, everything a young man from the Meydan dreamt of. Amir-Ali felt much more comfortable with his childhood friends, and that even included the more religious ones who disapproved of his new life. At least they behaved like men and were respected by their wives. He hung out with those who had turned out more like him; they were flexible in their adherence to religion. They slept with prostitutes and the one time in their lives they had a little extra cash, they had blown it on lads' holidays to Turkey. At weekends, Thursday and Friday nights, they smoked pot and *sheesheh*, crystal meth. Amir-Ali's best friend Reza, a judo champion, had started to spend more time with his *sheesheh* pipe than at the gym. Even the middle-class kids of Shahrak-e Gharb smoked *sheesheh* at parties.

Life was changing for Amir-Ali; at twenty-six years old, most of his friends were married and they saw each other less. He realized it was time for a wife.

*

The call to Somayeh's parents was made early the next morning. Haj
Agha was flattered that Mohammad thought Somayeh good enough
for his family. Amir-Ali could have anyone, but they had chosen
Somayeh. Fatemeh had cried, 'She's still a girl, she's so young.' They
had agreed that while they should approve any *khastegars*, suitors,
Somayeh should be free to choose her own husband.

When she got back from school Fatemeh and Haj Agha were
listening to a cleric on television discussing virgins in paradise.

'They are always fresh, energetic and young, they never age.
And they're untouched! In the Koran, it says their eyes look
downwards; now we know this type of look to mean *khomaar*
[a sultry come-hither look] but they don't give this look to just
anyone, only their husbands!' The presenter was rapt. Discussing
the virgins of paradise with the cleric was probably one of the
highlights of his career.

'Darling, you have a new *khastegar*,' said Fatemeh as Somayeh
walked through the door. Since she had turned fifteen, her parents
had repelled a stream of *khastegars* on her behalf, but she knew
instantly the identity of this latest one. And she did not want
him batted off.

'Amir-Ali wants to come round for *khastegari*.' *Khastegari* is
the first step of a marriage proposal, when the suitor visits the
bride's house with his family. Somayeh wanted to scream. Instead
she cocked her head and shrugged her shoulders as if to say *I
couldn't care less.*

'We'll just tell them no. Darling, you know I think you're
too young.'

Haj Agha came to the rescue, 'But he's an excellent catch!
They're rich – it would be a good life. And they're family...'

'Well, if *baba* thinks it's a good idea, they may as well come and I can think about it.' The *khastegari* was arranged for the following evening.

Fatemeh had recognized the look in her daughter's eye and she was worried. She saw that Somayeh was flattered by the attentions of her urbane cousin. What she could not see was whether marriage with him would lead to happiness. She needed some guidance. There was only one person she trusted to give it: Mullah Ahmad. Moments like this called for Islamic divination and Mullah Ahmad was Fatemeh's go-to mullah for *estekhareh,* Koranic divination. All personal conundrums were resolved, usually via telephone and in under four minutes. She would simply ask her question, Mullah Ahmad would consult the Koran and then shoot back a decisive 'yes' or 'no' answer. Job done. Problem solved. He never got it wrong. There were cowboys out there, as there were in any business. Turbaned charlatans riding on the wings of people's misery and pain. These were the clerics who charged a fortune for their divination services. Some even offered magic spells at premium rates. Fatemeh had once visited a mullah in Qom, a holy city south-west of Tehran. The mullah was famed for the accuracy of his predictions. He was surrounded by a small crowd of cross-legged men, hands raised, waiting to ask their questions. Two assistants manned telephones, answering a non-stop stream of calls. The mullah worked the floor faster than a stock-market trader. Using a long, thin shard of camel bone (so as to not pollute the Koran with the touch of his unwashed hands), he would randomly whip open the Koran, speed-read the verse in front of him and shoot out a reply. All matters, from property to inheritance to love and adultery, were solved with the flick of a page. Fatemeh had been watching the mullah from behind a diaphanous green curtain that separated the sexes. An assistant pressed a receiver to the mullah's ear.

'Yes to the first, no to the second.' Click.

A man handed the mullah his mobile.

'Bad, danger involved.'

A young boy whispered in his ear.

'Terrible. Lots of hardship.'

The women shouted out their questions once the men were done. 'Should I borrow money from my sister?' Fatemeh had asked.

'Excellent. The outcome will be excellent.' Fatemeh never went back to that mullah again.

Mullah Ahmad was different. He was a cleric of repute. Fatemeh had deduced this partly from his clientele, which included a growing coterie of upper-class devotees whom Fatemeh considered better educated and less gullible than herself; and partly from the fact that he was descended from a long line of mullahs. Mullah Ahmad was a kind man, and only occasionally accepted payment for divination; he got paid handsomely enough as it was. He could rake in up to 500,000 tomans for a one-hour sermon, which was nearly what a teacher earned in a whole month, and he was hired for funerals, prayer services and festivals. But he never refused gifts. Fatemeh had thrust a large envelope stuffed with money into his hands after their first appointment and ever since then Mullah Ahmad had given Fatemeh his mobile hotline number; she could call it any time of the day or night and he would answer.

When he saw Fatemeh's number flash up, Mullah Ahmad picked up immediately. She rushed through the rigmarole of polite enquiries about his family and his health and then fired her question at him.

'Somayeh has a *khastegar* coming round tonight, it's my sister's son. Would this be a good union?' Pause. Mullah Ahmad was opening his book.

'Neither good nor bad, it depends on the purity of their hearts. If they want the union to go ahead, so it must, but only time will tell.'

This was not the answer she was looking for, but as it was not an outright negative, the tension in her body was released anyway. She parroted Mullah Ahmad's prophetic words to Haj Agha, who was equally relieved. Now it was up to the kids.

That night the yearning that throbbed between Somayeh's legs was stronger than it had ever been. She always fought the feeling, squeezing her eyes tight and willing it to leave her body alone. She no longer dried herself with a towel, scared that her own touch might ignite forbidden desire. At these moments she would pray to God and ask forgiveness. Apart from when she was a little girl, she had not given in to her desires. Her grandmother had quoted a verse in the Koran often enough to scare Somayeh with the potential consequences of succumbing to desire: 'And whoever seeks any other avenue of lust besides with these [wife and female slaves] they are the transgressors.'

Somayeh often consulted *Find a Fatwa* websites to help solve her more personal dilemmas. She had read a lengthy testimony from a doctor on the psychological damage caused by masturbation, not to mention the havoc it wreaked on the nervous system. There was also advice on how to resist the urge: exercising, reading about the prophets, fasting, avoiding anything that would stimulate lustful thoughts, avoiding people who were not religious, attending religious ceremonies, keeping busy and marriage. Beneath the advice were the ubiquitous words: *Allah Knows Best*. Somayeh followed all these instructions.

Someone had posted a question on the Supreme Leader's website: *I was talking to a woman (I was not related to) on the phone during Ramadan and although I did not masturbate, and even though I did not intentionally phone her for (sexual) pleasure, I felt myself ejaculating. Please tell me if my fasting has been invalidated? If it has been invalidated, should I atone for this?* The worried ejaculator had got a reply: *If you usually speak to a woman on the telephone without getting (sexual) pleasure from the conversation and without ejaculating, (in this case) if you ejaculated without masturbating, your fasting has not been invalidated, and you do not have to atone for this.*

Somayeh's relationship with God was the best relationship of her life. She was not going to jeopardize it by needless masturbating. She felt closer to God than to anybody else. He was her best friend. He was her protector. She had heard that some people were godless; this filled her with pity, as it signalled a lack of self-belief. She could not countenance a more meaningless existence. Somayeh also adored the imams. Her favourite was Imam Mahdi, whom she always referred to as Imam Zaman, the Imam of All Time. Mahdi was still alive, but he was simply lost. God had hidden him. With every molecule in her body she believed he would appear for judgement day, when he would save the world from evil. The Mahdi also happened to answer all her prayers, which was not only fortuitous but yet further proof of his powers.

Doubt and second thoughts had kept Amir-Ali awake much of the night. Maybe he had been wrong about Somayeh. Maybe she was not as pretty as he had remembered.

'If you decide you don't want her, start eating cucumbers,' Zahra offered helpfully, sensing the waning of her son's enthusiasm, 'I'll handle it with Fatemeh and say it was me, that I think she's too young.'

'What if they don't have cucumbers?'

'For God's sake everyone has cucumbers! When have you ever been to a house without cucumbers?' She was right, of course.

Somayeh and Fatemeh were plotting similar tactics. Over the years they had devised an intricate code of signals involving coughs, statements about the weather and eating certain fruit and nuts. For tonight, a bunch of grapes was the sign for love.

Somayeh put on her best outfit: a smart white shirt and elegant tight black trousers that would remain concealed by her chador, and snakeskin *roo-farshee* heels that would be on show. A poster of Imam Ali was tacked above her desk on her bedroom wall. The imam's dreamy green eyes, lined thick with black kohl, stared into the distance. A green scarf was tied round his head, the sun emanating around him like a halo. Fat droplets of blood dripped sensuously out of a gash on his forehead and trickled down his angular cheekbones towards a handsome square jaw framed by chocolate-brown, wavy hair. Below him, either side of her laptop, were two blue-glass Ikea tea-light holders that she had bought from the Ikea boutique in the uptown Jaam-e Jam shopping centre on Vali Asr. It was Somayeh's favourite shop, full of chic, rich Tehranis. The tea-light holders had been all she could afford. Stacked on her desk were books including *Harry Potter and the Philosopher's Stone*, *Nights of Loneliness*, a Mills-and-Boon-style love story by the prolific romance author Fahimeh Rahimi, and a copy of the Koran.

Somayeh rushed into the kitchen when Amir-Ali and his family arrived. Her first job was to serve the tea. If a girl could serve a tray of tea without spilling a drop then she would make a good bride. Not all families took the custom seriously, but they had fun with the ritual. Mohammad-Reza was making faces at Somayeh as she walked into the living room.

'You little devil, stop making me laugh, I'll spill it over you on purpose!'

'*Bah-bah*, what delicious tea,' smiled Zahra encouragingly.

Somayeh bent down to serve Amir-Ali and dared to meet his eyes. He was staring right at her as he picked up his glass. Somayeh's hands began to shake. She retreated back to the kitchen to catch her breath.

Fatemeh passed the fruit bowl round. Zahra's eyes were glued to the cucumbers. Amir-Ali picked out a peach.

'Maybe you two should chat things through on your own?' said Fatemeh, sensing the tension. Zahra agreed.

Somayeh and Amir-Ali sat on the floor in Mohammad-Reza's bedroom, three feet apart. An appropriate distance. His stare was animalistic. Somayeh cleared her throat.

'I have some questions for you.'

'Ask me anything you like, but you're so beautiful that you can't expect me to concentrate.' Somayeh giggled nervously. She had prepared a list of exactly eleven questions and she needed to stay focused. Her future would be determined by his answers. She held her chador close. Whenever she spoke, it slipped.

'Do you ever get angry?' A flash of pale hand.

'Never. My friends say I'm one of the calmest guys they know.' His friends often berated him for his explosive temper.

'How will you support us?'

'I've worked hard all my life. As you know, I'm working for *baba*'s company and I hope to take over one day.' Amir-Ali's parents regularly complained that he would not know what work was even if it hit him in the face.

'Do you pray?' He saw a blaze of white shirt, but could not make out her breasts. Right now he certainly was praying – praying that her breasts were not bee stings. Even plums would do.

'When I hear the *azan*, call to prayer, it doesn't matter where I am, I have to pray. It's like an automatic reaction. Even if I'm reading the newspaper.' Amir-Ali never read the newspaper. And after years of enforced learning, he still could not remember all the Arabic words to the prayers.

Somayeh smiled. Her arm dropped slightly. A glimpse of her neck – long. A sliver of a collarbone – sharp, disappearing into a soft nape.

'Will you let me get my university diploma?'

'With eyes like that, I'd let you get anything you want.'

Somayeh laughed. A perfect laugh. Not too loud, not too forthright. You could tell a lot from a girl's laugh. Amir-Ali's mother had warned him of women who laughed too heartily; the voraciousness of a woman's laugh was in direct proportion to her morals. The louder, the looser.

Somayeh's questions were businesslike and perfunctory, but her voice was gentle, her eyes sensual. Amir-Ali danced around the probing, tiptoeing across her questions, generously scattering lies and half-truths. Somayeh trod purposefully forward, every word carefully placed. They each analysed the other, interpreting every move and gesture.

For Amir-Ali, it was usually easier to read girls when it came to his own kind. He knew what was expected of them. The rest was working out what was from the heart and what was for show. There was never any guarantee, but experience told him that Somayeh was genuine. He could also tell that she was already wildly in love with him. Tehrani girls usually acted disinterested and that was part of the ploy, but Somayeh's lack of game-playing showed an innocence and naivety that was beguiling.

Somayeh was too young to have learnt the art of discerning the truth. To her, Amir-Ali was the most charismatic man she had ever met.

After an hour, they returned to a living room that was silent and heavy with expectation. Fatemeh handed the fruit bowl round and watched her daughter like a hawk. Somayeh looked at her mother as she picked out a bunch of grapes and popped one in her mouth. Fatemeh jumped up and whispered to Haj Agha to bring out the *shireeni* sweet pastries, the sign understood by all: a wedding.

The hulking machinery of marriage chugged into motion. At the *bale-boroon* ceremony, when engagements are officially announced, Amir-Ali gave Somayeh six gold bracelets, a colossal bouquet of flowers and a silk chador. The four parents thrashed out a deal for Somayeh's *mehrieh*, dowry, an Islamic pre-nuptial agreement that ensures the woman will be looked after in the event of a divorce. Somayeh could hear Fatemeh and Haj Agha bartering over her worth.

'She's a beautiful, educated girl and Amir-Ali will be getting her in her prime! He'll have the best years of her life!'

'I know she's priceless, Fatemeh *joon*, but we're not made of money.'

The negotiating was usually the men's job, but as usual the two sisters had taken over. Zahra soon relented, and the *mehrieh* was set at 192 gold coins, sixteen for each of the twelve Shia imams. It was a low amount for Tehran, but high for the Meydan and in keeping with tradition here, which regarded very high *mehriehs* as vulgar. Unusually for an Iranian mother, Zahra knew her son was getting the better deal. The rest of the terms of the marriage were set: Amir-Ali promised to allow Somayeh to attend university and Zahra and Mohammad would give the couple their old apartment in the Meydan as, given Somayeh's young age, she should remain close to her family and friends for the first few years of married life.

The two families careered towards the *aroosi* wedding party, with the marriage sucking up mounds of money, food and relatives in its path. In between the gatherings and the blood test (a prerequisite for all Iranians, not just cousins) and the extra cooking and cleaning, Fatemeh remembered her own *aroosi* as a sad, small affair. She had not wanted to marry Haj Agha. She could have resisted, but was afraid of disappointing her parents, who were thrilled at the pairing. He came from a good family of homeowners. It was a different era then: a woman accepted the fate chosen for her by others. She had been relieved when she saw him for the first time. He had been disappointed, and she had seen it in his eyes. He had been pressurized into marrying Fatemeh too, because her father was known to be a respectable man. She had expected little from a marriage, just financial stability and, if she was lucky, companionship. Instead she got a man who rarely acknowledged her. Despite Somayeh's tender age, Fatemeh consoled herself that at least Somayeh was marrying for love, and that Mullah Ahmad had seen its potential in the verses of the Koran.

Somayeh's wedding was everything she had dreamt it would be. She wore a strapless white beaded gown under a white hooded cape and she spent nearly a million tomans on a make-up artist who transformed her into one of the *Western*-looking girls in the government poster warnings on bad *hejab*. Once the ceremony was over, the men and women partied separately, each group dancing until the early hours. In her wedding photographs Somayeh looked like an alien: her eyes had been Photoshopped blue, her skin digitally retouched and she had been given a new nose, pinched and thin – the Tehranis' style of choice. Somayeh was delighted.

Somayeh's married life began the day after the end of school and a few weeks after the wedding party. Amir-Ali broke his promise almost immediately. He pleaded with Somayeh to abandon her plans for university. In a flush of love Somayeh agreed. She interpreted his wish for her to stay home as passion; that he could not bear to be parted from her and see her life grow in a different direction from his own. Amir-Ali had chosen a tradi-tional wife for good reason. He might as well have married an uptown girl if Somayeh was going to spend the next few years of their married life with her nose in books. Fatemeh and Haj Agha were angry at first, but Somayeh assured them it was her decision. She seemed so happy, the matter quickly passed.

The first year of marriage was exciting. Amir-Ali was tender in bed. She embraced lovemaking, seeing it as a spiritual act and a religious duty to satisfy her man. Only one of her friends had married. Most of the women in her neighbourhood waited until their early twenties, and then would move in with their husbands' families as they could not afford the extortionate rents. Somayeh did not have to endure her in-laws and the new apartment was big and modern. She had a forty-six-inch television, a breakfast bar and black leather sofas. Her friends were envious of her new-found independence. A few of the girls had started university (mostly because it increased their marriage prospects) and they had been disappointed how little it had changed their lives.

Most days Somayeh would cook Amir-Ali's evening meal when she woke up and then spend time with her mother and her friends. They would keep up to date with the latest news, which revolved around gossip about relationships and plummeting morals. Dog-Duck had been sacked as headmistress for being a lesbian, Batool Khanoum the divorcee was now servicing virgin boys and Tahereh Azimi was pronounced a real-life whore living and working in a brothel in the centre of town.

Marriage for Amir-Ali was not too different from life with his parents. He had his meals cooked, his clothes cleaned and a spotless house. Although he had the added bonus of regular sex and of being adored.

Then the inevitable happened. Amir-Ali got bored. He took immediate action, spending more time with his friends. They drank *aragh sagee*, 'dog sweat' booze, the slang name for home-brewed vodka made of raisins, and they smoked *sheesheh* with Reza, who had given up judo and now devoted himself to his pipe full-time. Amir-Ali discovered a new gambling den run by an old gangster near the south end of Vali Asr.

Somayeh had been shocked the first few nights he had turned up late, smelling of alcohol. At first she was too submissive to get angry. She sobbed in the bathroom with the shower on, hoping Amir-Ali would not hear her. The passing of time and the worsening of Amir-Ali's behaviour emboldened her, but Amir-Ali was impervious to Somayeh's pleading and crying. The number of his Facebook friends swelled. Girls with tumbling ash-blonde hair and plunging vest tops appeared. He swore on his mother's life they were friends from his old life. He became secretive, hiding his mobile phone. Somayeh incessantly asked Amir-Ali if there was another woman. He did what he always did when she dared to question him: he shouted at her. Her traditional outlook was suddenly not so appealing. It had lost its romance. Now she was just a pain.

'Don't I provide for you? What more do you want? Go back to your parents' house if you don't like it here.' Amir-Ali wanted a woman, not a little girl who cried because he enjoyed life.

The unravelling of their relationship was drawn out and hidden from view. It happened mostly within the confines of their apartment, but also in Somayeh's head. Doubts and paranoia set in. Somayeh did not tell a soul. She was too ashamed to go back to her parents' house. Her friends had placed her at the pinnacle of success, and she could not endure the humiliation of the fall.

When autumn sapped the green from the trees on Vali Asr, exposing the road below to the white November sky, their baby was born. Somayeh hoped the birth of her girl Mona would change Amir-Ali. It did not. Instead the disappearances started. The first time, he left for work and did not come back all weekend. After thirteen missed calls and twenty frantic messages, he had texted back: *I'm fine stop hassling me.* Once he texted her from the airport to tell her he was going to Dubai for a week. Otherwise, she would not hear from him for days, sometimes weeks.

Somayeh had managed to keep the first disappearance to herself. By the second, she confided in his parents, Zahra and Mohammad, unable to withstand his behaviour alone. They were not surprised. They knew everything. Amir-Ali had not turned up to work for the past six months. He had done this many times before; they had hoped Somayeh would tame him. Somayeh felt cheated. She had been lied to, as had her parents.

Zahra and Mohammad became co-conspirators in concealing the truth from Fatemeh and Haj Agha. They were complicit in her lies to them. 'We will have no *aberoo* left if he continues like this,' Zahra had sobbed. *Aberoo.* Honour; saving face. It was a cornerstone of their world, and Amir-Ali had robbed Zahra and Mohammad of their *aberoo* too many times.

For a while nothing changed; Amir-Ali refused to give Somayeh any answers, and she learnt to adapt to her new reality, focusing her attentions on little Mona. Soon a new cycle of disappearances began; this time they lasted longer. They were also marked by the arrival of a brown leather briefcase. Amir-Ali kept it hidden under his clothes in the back of a cupboard in Mona's room. Some nights, he would head straight for the cupboard and she could hear the numbers of a lock clicking into place. He began to change its hiding place. Somayeh would always find it. She became as obsessed with it as Amir-Ali; she was sure the answer to her misery was in the briefcase.

For three months her small hands worked the locks, sometimes for hours, trying to figure out the combination. Until now. The moment of the miracle. His briefcase gaping wide open in front of her, her *nazr* prayer answered in an instant. Her sweaty hands shook as she lifted the compartments apart. Underneath a mound of receipts and bank statements was what she had been looking for: the truth. It was spelt out in dozens of letters written in childish handwriting. It was in words she had never heard from Amir-Ali: *I adore you, You are my life, The thought of your pussy makes me so hard.* It was in a box of Durex condoms. It was staring back at her through black eyes, round breasts and a mass of blonde, highlighted hair imprinted on a photograph. There was an ecstatic moment of liberation before the searing pain took hold; it was the serene hit of vindication before the rage. Then she started to cry. The heat was now maddening. She started grabbing the contents of the briefcase and hurling them across the room. As she was about to pick up another handful, she saw half a dozen scratched DVDs in a Bambi sleeve. She scrambled to her laptop and pushed one in. A woman was on her knees being fucked from behind. After that clip, a close-up of genitals, the camera revealing a woman having sex with her headscarf on. Another clip was a black man with two white women. Somayeh was sick to her stomach. By now she was sobbing and praying at the same time. She had never seen porn before.

Somayeh fled to Fatemeh's house. Fatemeh had long known that her daughter's marriage was in turmoil, but Somayeh would not admit it. The last few years had taken their toll; stress and heartbreak had left Somayeh pale and emaciated. She told her mother everything, even about the DVDs.

Life in the Meydan has changed in the years since Somayeh got married. Iran has a new President, Hassan Rouhani, a (comparatively) moderate English-speaking cleric with a Ph.D. in Constitutional Law from Glasgow Caledonian University. Rouhani is a regular Tweeter and speaks of equality and rapprochement with the West. Although many Iranians were elated at his election, not everyone in the Meydan was happy at the results.

'Rouhani's *bee-dean!*' said one of Haj Agha's *Hezbollahi* neighbours, using the word for 'irreligious', 'he's just an agent of the English, like Khatami. These types of clerics are dirty! It'll all come out in the wash.'

They did not want to be friends with the Great Satan, *Amrika.* A few weeks after Rouhani's historic phone call with President Obama, anti-American posters sprang up across the city (before they were taken back down as yet another internal power battle between government factions was played out). Some of the posters depicted an outstretched Iranian hand about to shake the clawed hand of the devil. On each were the words, written in both Persian and English: THE US GOVENMENT STYLES [*sic*] HONESTY.

Rouhani had been left with the mess Ahmadinejad had left behind. Discontent had sunk its teeth into the Meydan. Sanctions against Iran had ground the economy to a halt, sending the currency into free fall, slashing it to a third of its value in less than two years. Under Ahmadinejad subsidies of petrol had been scrapped and the government had doled out cash handouts instead, but these had not kept up with the soaring inflation that hovered between thirty and forty per cent. Jobs were even more scarce and badly paid. The sinking economy bred resentment and mistrust.

For the first time, even criticism of the Supreme Leader was no longer out of bounds. It had started after protesters were killed, beaten and raped after the disputed elections in 2009.

There were other, smaller changes. Somayeh's friends were now addicted to Turkish soap operas like *Forbidden Love* and *The Sultan's Harem* with juicy story lines shown on GEM TV, an entertainment satellite channel based in Dubai. Halfway through the series all the characters suddenly had new voices as the actors in Iran secretly dubbing the show had been arrested. And everyone knew about a hit show that had taken the country by storm: *Googoosh Music Academy*, an Iranian X Factor on Manoto TV, a Persian-language station run from London that had bought the format of hit British programmes like *Come Dine With Me*, another Tehrani favourite. And nowadays, Fatemeh and her friends had far fewer pistachios at home since their price had almost tripled.

Fatemeh's attitude to divorce had also changed. While the residents of the Meydan thought the moral fabric of their world was made of stronger stuff than in the rest of the city, they soon learnt they were wrong. Batool Khanoum's divorce seemed to have opened the floodgates. Already four young couples in their area had separated. Over the last ten years, divorces have tripled in Iran, with one out of every five marriages ending – the number is even higher in Tehran.

From thinking it was a shameful act, even Fatemeh had considered divorce. She had been looking for her birth certificate to replace a lost identity card. They were usually kept in a shoebox under the bed, but they were not there. As she pushed the box back in its place, she felt it knock something. She squeezed her leg under the gap and slid it out. Another shoebox, one she had never seen. Inside were old photographs and a brown envelope. Inside that, a stash of passports. Fatemeh flicked through the pages. She sighed. Haj Agha's journey of spiritual enlightenment was stamped across the pages in colourful visas. One of them was a recurring bright-red crest. Could this be Iraq, or Syria? She squinted at the strange blue writing on it. She held the passport closer. It was not Arabic. Definitely not Arabic. Without her realizing, her heart had started to race. She scrambled for her reading glasses. The blurred picture snapped into sharp focus; a winged demon with cock's feet stared back at her. Beside him words in English, which she could not read. She frantically turned the pages, and on every single one the scarlet demon pounced up at her. A neighbour three streets down knew how to read English, but she had a feeling she should ask a stranger. She slumped her body next to the scattered papers and passports beside her as she considered what she should do. Somayeh walked into the room to find her mother splayed on the floor like a bear on its back.

'I'm fine, I'm fine, just had a dizzy turn, nothing serious,' Fatemeh panted. Now she was clambering up to get her chador. She ran out of the door and headed straight towards the bazaar, to a *daroltarjomeh* translation office. She thrust Haj Agha's passport into the hands of a young man sitting at a computer.

'Son, read this for me. And I want the dates.'

The young man paused.

'KINGDOM OF THAILAND. Type of Visa: *Tourist*.' He read out some dates, converting them from Gregorian to Persian. They exactly matched Haj Agha's pilgrimage trips. But he had not been in Karbala or Mecca. Or Damascus. Or Mashhad. He had been in Thailand. Wherever that was. She racked her brain to remember history lessons at school, berating herself for never paying attention. As far as she could remember, Hossein's crusade had not ventured to Thailand. Were there Muslims in Thailand? She was not sure. Even if there was a remote Shia shrine in this strange land, one thing was clear: Haj Agha had been telling lies. She tried to pay the translator, but he would not accept her money. She hurried out into the masses swirling around the bazaar, cutting across the backstreets to Vali Asr. This was an emergency. She needed to speak to Mullah Ahmad. For more sensitive matters, Fatemeh would see him in person. She was still not sure exactly what kind of deceit she was dealing with, but it was clear this was not a subject for a four-minute reading on the telephone. She called Mullah Ahmad's mobile and told him she was on her way.

She took the bus the length of Vali Asr. This was her favourite journey in the city, and usually she would enjoy watching the shops and restaurants pass by. But today she was too distracted to notice anything; she prayed under her breath as her mind ran through hundreds of possibilities. She got off at the very end of Vali Asr, where it opens its mouth and spews cars and taxis and buses and people into Tajrish Square. Mullah Ahmad lived in a large apartment on the second floor of a shabby building just off the square. His home was a shrine to mismatching styles and colours: reproduction French Versailles furniture stuffed next to seventies leather sofas; modern Ikea shelves and mass-produced tapestries hung on greying walls. There were the usual Iranian touches: crystal, gilding, marble and chandeliers of varying sizes and sparkle that hung in every room, including the small kitchen; Persian carpets everywhere, hanging on the walls and draped over armchairs.

Mullah Ahmad's wife opened the door in a white flowered chador, under which she was wearing dark blue slacks and a loose knitted sleeveless cardigan over a shirt.

'He told me it was an emergency, I'll get you in next,' she whispered in Fatemeh's ear as she ushered her into the living room, past Mullah Ahmad's teenage son who was wearing Levi's and texting on his iPhone.

Fatemeh was not the only one with a crisis on her hands. A middle-aged socialite with a facelift and a Hermès scarf was snivelling into a tissue. A teenage girl from Shahrak-e Gharb with Chanel sunglasses propped on her head stared sullenly through the net curtains. A wrinkled woman in a black chador was wringing her hands and praying.

When Mullah Ahmad got excited, he had a tendency to shout. As Mullah Ahmad's wife served his waiting clients with tea and assorted Cadbury's Dairy Milk chocolates from a silvery tray, her husband's voice boomed out of his office.

'Why aren't you married? At thirty-nine that is an absolute disaster! Your parents have given you a terrible name and this has obviously affected your whole life. You're going to have to change it straight away!'

It was Fatemeh's turn. Mullah Ahmad was sitting in a gleaming black swivel chair, surrounded by shelves lined with books. Cornices in pastel shades topped the walls of his office. A bleached-out picture of Mecca in the seventies and framed black and white photographs of his ancestors looking glum hung above him, next to a huge poster of the black-turbaned Ayatollah Boroujerdi, a dissident cleric who believed in the separation of religion and politics and who was imprisoned in 2006 for speaking out against the Supreme Leader's absolute power.

Mullah Ahmad was wearing his fine grey robe, his white *amameh* turban and leather slippers. Three chunky silver Islamic rings – one with a large burnt-ochre carnelian, the most important gemstone in Islam, on which was inscribed a verse from the Koran – adorned his long, feminine fingers, giving him a rock-star edge.

'My goodness Fatemeh Khanoum, you've got so fat!' He practically shrieked when he noticed the extra ten kilograms Fatemeh had been lugging round her midriff.

'It's true, I haven't been taking care of myself Haji as I haven't been very happy.'

'A blind person who sees is better than a seeing person who is blind,' said Mullah Ahmad. Mullah Ahmad was not easy to understand, not least because of his thick Azeri Turkic accent and his propensity to break into Koranic verse. His terrible short-term memory did not help matters.

Fatemeh launched into her findings. The details tumbled out in a torrent of dates, holy sites and sobbing.

'As long as I live I will never call him Haj Agha again!' She fished out the evidence from her bag. Mullah Ahmad flicked through Haj Agha's passports.

'But why does he go to Thailand? There are no Shia tombs of our beloved imams, God rest their souls, or of any of their relatives in Thailand, are there Haji?'

Mullah Ahmad was lost for words. Which did not happen often. He knew what men did when they went to Thailand. Only last month one of his flock had confessed to him an addiction to

Thai prostitutes. He had prescribed a strict regimen of prayers, which included reading the *Ayatul Kursi* – the Throne verse in the Koran, believed to protect against evil – five times at dawn and five times at dusk.

'How come you are so unsuccessful in life, for this is truly a terrible husband!' Mullah Ahmad thought that was a good way to ease into telling Fatemeh the truth about what men did in Thailand. He had judged it well. Fatemeh was very pleased with the answer. Not least because it was easy to understand but, more importantly, it was what she had suspected for a long time. She was unsuccessful in life. A loveless marriage, a small apartment in which she would most probably die, a lazy son and a useless son-in-law.

'Haji I don't know, I pray, I give alms to the poor, I do all my Muslim duties. Maybe it is my fault. Mrs Katkhodai's doctor told her that her mental attitude was responsible for her life and that her future was in her own hands.'

'What heresy! A sword in the hands of a drunken slave is less dangerous than science in the hands of the immoral!' he said, breaking into a verse of poetry and a quote from the Koran. Fatemeh squinted as she concentrated on decrypting his words.

'Haji, why has he been going to this country?'

'Fatemeh Khanoum, are you fulfilling your marital duties to your husband?'

'He never wants to do it. I tell you, I am fighting lust the whole time, because he shows no interest.' The mullah shook his head.

'I will not lie to you Fatemeh. There is only one reason why a man would go on so many trips to Thailand. They go for *zanaa-yeh vijeh*.' The mullah was using the euphemism for 'prostitute' that the government had recently adopted: 'special' women.

'I don't understand.'

'Thailand is a country of prostitutes. All the women there are for sale. I have seen this before. You must take immediate action. For this crime is very serious.'

'My husband's been sleeping with whores.' She whispered the words as she hung her head. A conversation with Mullah Ahmad was all it had taken for her life to vanish in front of her eyes. Why had God allowed this to happen to her? Few of the women in her circle talked of infidelity; it was a taboo subject that was only discussed as gossip about other people. Nobody ever admitted it happened to them. She felt stupid for having trusted that Haj Agha had been faithful to her. For having believed he was a Godly person. For having believed his spirituality had driven him to his countless pilgrimages. And most of all she felt stupid for having thrown such lavish parties in his honour, not for having paid his respects to God and the prophets but for having been a sex tourist. Mullah Ahmad could not bring himself to look at her; the pain of others affected him, even if he did not often see it.

'My dear, just as those who are addicted to opium cannot help themselves, your husband is in the same position. He needs your help. Do not forget that Allah is forgiving,' he quoted from the Koran; 'Do not despair of God's mercy; He will forgive you all your sins…For Allah will change evil into good. Allah is most forgiving and merciful.'

Fatemeh did not feel forgiving. She could not help but think of Batool Khanoum and her divorce. Although her *mehrieh* was worth nothing now, and she had no idea how she would be able to survive on her own.

'Haji, does the Koran say I should stay with this man, what do you see?'

Mullah Ahmad usually refused to divine for divorce, but as

this was an emergency case and Fatemeh was a loyal customer, he made an exception. He closed his eyes and whispered a prayer under his breath as he flicked open the holy book. He read out an Arabic verse then translated its meaning for Fatemeh.

'Whatever happens, you must stay with him. You must teach him truth.'

Fatemeh's heart sank. They said the final *salavaat* prayer together: *May God bless the Prophet Mohammad and his family.* She got up to face her husband.

Haj Agha was watching television when she got home. She threw his passports at him.

'You mother-fucking sister-pimping bastard cunt!'

Haj Agha blinked. He had never heard her utter words like that in his life. He blinked again, opened his mouth to speak but no sound came out, so he shut it. Fatemeh screamed as she had never screamed before. Soon enough Haj Agha found his own voice too. He went through the usual cycle of emotions dispensed by the guilty. Anger, denial and counter-accusations. Fatemeh demanded a divorce. She told him she would tell the judge he had been unfaithful, she would use Mullah Ahmad and his passports as evidence. And he could rest assured that the whole neighbourhood would know he had never set foot in the Kingdom of Saudi Arabia in his life. That was when Haj Agha changed tack. He started sobbing and begging for forgiveness. Porn was to blame. It was not his fault. Agha Mehdi had given him a DVD and he had got addicted from the first hit. He respected his wife so much he could not bear to ask her to do some of the things he had seen in the films, that is why he had spared her the humiliation and gone to Thailand, where all the women are whores.

After five weeks Fatemeh forgave him, mostly because she had to. She did not tell a soul as both their reputations would have been ruined. The episode had its upside. Haj Agha now darted around her like a manservant. Somayeh had even noticed how uxorious her father had become and she had wondered, hopefully, if old age wore men down into good husbands.

When Somayeh had told her mother everything, Fatemeh knew then that she was not going to allow the same fate to befall her daughter.

'You must get a divorce,' were the first words that came out of her mouth.

'The shame of it! What will everyone think? Our *aberoo* will be gone, and I'll be all alone, no one will want me.'

'Forget about *aberoo*! I don't give two hoots what people think. Amir-Ali will never change, and you'll regret it. Haj Agha and I will support you, we will all hold our heads up high, you have done nothing wrong.' Somayeh was amazed. She had never heard her mother talk like this. Even more shocking was that Haj Agha had heard every word and he was agreeing with Fatemeh.

'A divorce is the only way you can be happy,' he said with a smile on his face. Even an *estekhareh* by Mullah Ahmad confirmed that divorce was the best option for Somayeh.

Somayeh refused to see Amir-Ali and she refused to talk to him apart from one telephone call to request the divorce. He agreed almost immediately, scared that Somayeh would go to the police, or tell the judge about his stash of porn films, or that he had been unfaithful, even though the latter would be hard to prove as four (Muslim) male witnesses would be required.

By the time word spread of Somayeh's impending divorce, all the neighbourhood, including a long line of relatives, paid her a visit to make sure no salacious detail would be kept hidden. Tact and sensitivity are not highly prized traits in the Meydan, and so everyone offered their advice and opinion. The women were split between those who thought she should divorce Amir-Ali and those who thought she should stay with him. But there was one thing they nearly all agreed on.

'Nobody will want a divorcee with a child. You're ruining your chances of another good marriage, just leave Mona with Zahra and Mohammad,' said Auntie Ameneh. On this point, Somayeh would not relent; she would fight to have her child. By law, Mona could remain with her until she was seven years old or until she remarried, at which point a father would then have full custody rights. But Somayeh knew that Mona impeded Amir-Ali's playboy lifestyle and that his parents were too guilty to request custody.

The judge took pity on Somayeh and the proceedings were over in less than half an hour. She went straight to the *mahzar* notary office to sign and register her divorce papers. The official there had been conducting dozens of marriages on Skype between long-distance lovers; Iranians were getting around strict visa controls without even spending money on air fares for costly weddings, with the groom's only presence in the room being a voice from a laptop.

When Somayeh got home, she dropped to her knees and prayed: *please God, don't let me feel lust.* She feared it would be a long time before she would be married again and she did not want to let God down.

*

It was a bright spring day when Somayeh and her brother Mohammad-Reza walked up Vali Asr, under the green canopy of the sycamore trees. Since she had given to birth Mona, Somayeh rarely got the chance to visit Vali Asr, so she walked slowly, trying to make the journey last. They stopped outside a glitzy furniture boutique that was sandwiched between an office block and an old bakery with bags of flour piled up along its dirty walls; they gazed inside at a giant china cheetah and an eau-de-Nil urn decorated with gold-winged cherubs. They walked past a group of Afghan construction workers in frayed clothes sitting cross-legged on a torn cloth they had laid out on a patch of elevated pavement between the trees and next to the *joob*, eating bread and carrot jam. They looked into Somayeh's favourite clothes shops, and just near Vanak Square they walked into an orphanage. They were here to deliver the fresh chopped meat they were carrying in two plastic bags. It was from a lamb that had been slaughtered a few hours earlier. Somayeh was fulfilling her *nazr* prayer, the prayer she had made that had helped her unlock Amir-Ali's briefcase the year before. Somayeh had God and Imam Zaman to thank for her new life. A life free of Amir-Ali's lies. She had made a promise to God and Imam Zaman to sacrifice a lamb every year for the poor. A promise she would keep until death.

And she did.

THREE

AMIR

Haft-e Tir, midtown Tehran, March 2013

The words punched through the receiver: slow, staccato and deliberate.

'I'm an old friend of your father. I need to meet you.'

Silence. The call was from a strange number; it was not a Tehran code. The voice did not wait for an answer.

'I will see you tomorrow at two o'clock outside the Al Javad mosque in Haft-e Tir. I know what you look like.' It sounded like an order, although there was no menace in the elderly voice. Amir was intrigued.

He arrived early, as was his habit, emerging out of the pyramid-shaped mouth of the Haft-e Tir Square subway station. Haft-e Tir had become one of the first stops on the northbound ascent to wealth and status. Working-class Tehranis who made any money moved here from south Tehran, and so the fabric of Haft-e Tir had become a little coarser than before, a little more religious, but as diverse as ever with its Armenian quarter.

Amir waded into the giant, ten-laned square, walking past the taxis, past the fruit-juice shop and headscarf stands and then slowly past the row of *manteau* shops bursting with custom on the east side of Haft-e Tir. A couple of vans full of *Gasht-e Ershad* morality police kerb-crawled beside the gangs of women who flocked to buy the latest Islamic wear. The morality police scavenged like circling vultures around the square, seeking their prey: young, skinny-jeaned girls in ballet pumps wearing nail varnish and buying bright, tight cloth. The local girls were also out in full force, known as the *Beesto-Panj-e Shahrivar* girls, the pre-revolution name for the square, which was the date that Reza Shah was forced to abdicate and when his son Mohammad Reza took over as King. The girls are ordinary Iranians in most senses – not poor, not rich. From middle- and working-class families. Students, secretaries, office workers, housewives, girlfriends, lovers. They watch satellite TV and have Facebook accounts. But there is nothing ordinary about the way they look. They wear enough make-up to make a drag queen recoil. Eyebrows are usually pencilled or tattooed at fierce ninety-degree angles in the style of Mr Spock. Hair is shades of blonde, stacked menacingly high, like eighteenth-century French aristocrats. A network of scaffolding keeps it aloft, hidden underneath wisps of headscarf, delicately draped across their heads in a thin strip designed to show as much highlighted hair as possible. Noses are rarely real. Shoes are rarely below four inches. It's a look that has spread all over Tehran, but the *Beesto-Panj-e Shahrivar* girls are the experts.

A few women had clocked the *Gasht-e Ershad* rounds and they began to sign to one another surreptitiously, alerting the pack of the imminent attack by raising eyebrows, nodding heads and darting eyes towards the vans. Flogging and imprisonment are unusual, but humiliation, bullying and a permanent black-marked record await those caught and accused of inappropriate dress; as well as a fine, a few hours of morality-education lessons for the victim and the victim's parents.

Even though *Gasht-e Ershad* poses a greater threat to women, Amir always felt nervous around authority and its presence unsettled him. He quickened his pace.

A cross between a fortress and a rocket ship, the Al Javad mosque was Iran's first modernist mosque, true, in all its concrete glory, to the sixties style that plagiarized the ugliest modernist Catholic cathedrals and exported them to unsuspecting Islamic congregations.

Amir stood by the iron gates on the corner of Bakhtiar Alley opposite Bella Shoes, a pre-revolution relic with its seventies sign. He waited. From the other side of Haft-e Tir Square, Ayatollah Mohammad Beheshti stared across at him from his mural, his indignant words painted below his face: LET AMERICA BE ANGRY WITH US AND LET IT DIE FROM ITS ANGER.

The last time Amir had been inside a mosque was over ten years ago, for the funeral of a friend's father. Mosques repelled him; no matter how impressive the architecture, he could not stand them. For Amir they symbolized the hijacking and ruin of the revolution. It was here the gullible were fooled and power-crazed mullahs delivering tittle-tattle sermons manipulated the God-fearing. It was here, on garish Persian carpets, in rooms that stank of sweating feet and cheap rose water, where beautiful verses from the Koran were corrupted. He had, of course, visited the Blue Mosque in Esfahan as a tourist and allowed himself to be overawed by its ravishing beauty, for this was a part of his history, part of a different era that did not belong to what he saw as a new brainwashed generation. The regime's profligate obsession with enshrining every rule and morsel of its religion meant that mosques were multiplying across Tehran. And the more the regime constructed, the emptier they appeared; so many of the younger generation barely went to mosque at all. The government occasionally discussed plans to entice worshippers, such as opening up cultural centres, providing sports facilities and even sewing courses in mosques.

Many of the locals had never taken to the Al Javad mosque, preferring the old, homely mosques they were used to. When the Al Javad established itself as a stronghold of the Basij, the volunteer paramilitary force responsible for duties including internal security and some law enforcement, it attracted the regime supporters.

As Amir watched a few men enter the Al Javad, he realized he had not told a soul about the phone call. That had been easy; he had been a professional keeper of secrets from when he had spoken his first words. He felt a sudden unease. How naive not to have thought this might be a set-up.

He had recently been summoned for an 'interview'. The request – an implicit order – came via a phone call from a private number. Amir had half been expecting the call from *them*. *Ettela'at*. Intelligence. Officers from the feared Ministry of Intelligence monitored and interrogated everyone, from university lecturers to musicians; telephones were tapped, emails intercepted.

Amir had been attending meetings with his activist friends and writing an anonymous blog satirizing politicians and poking fun at the regime. He used proxy servers called VPNs – Virtual Private Networks – to circumvent the government's Internet filter, allowing computers to function as if they were in another country. One was a complementary service provided by the United States government as part of the game to weaken its arch-enemy, comfortably cloaked in the familiar and increasingly meaningless name of freedom and democracy. As fast as the Iranian govern- ment blocked the proxy websites, another one would spring up. Some of his friends refused to download VPNs, saying they belonged to the regime, that this was a conspiracy of entrapment.

He was careful about what he wrote, never daring to stray outside the red lines. Words were picked for their allusive qualities, strung together to create a vague blur of accusations, enough to send a shock of satisfaction through the reader's mind yet exiguous enough in meaning not to rouse the mighty fist of the regime.

There were a few certainties that could knock you off-balance and straight into prison: criticisms of the Supreme Leader, the Prophet and any questioning of God or Islam. Amir's own atheism was one of his most treasured secrets. But there were no rules in this game, when laws could be twisted and manipulated to whatever effect was needed. He scanned his mind for anything he had written that *they* could deem a threat to national security. But it was often the anodyne musings of nobodies like Amir that got them excited – it was easier to pick on a nobody as nobody would notice. It was no use believing the Islamic Republic had bigger fish to fry, because then you wouldn't see them coming for you. The regime always loved a scapegoat: catching them is a favourite pastime of bored, sadistic bureaucrats. The cyber-police, known as FATA, the cyber crime unit of the police force, had swooped on an unknown blogger called Sattar Beheshti. He had written an anonymous blog criticizing the regime for killing protesters in 2009 in the familiar language of Iranian youth, railing against injustice and blaming the Supreme Leader. He was a manual labourer from a working-class, religious family whose blog only got a few dozen views, yet he was still considered to be worth torturing to death.

As Amir was about to turn round, a black Peugeot 405 with tinted windows pulled up beside him. It was too late to run now. The back window slid down to reveal an old, plump man wearing a sharp suit and a crisp, tieless white shirt.

'Salaam Amir. Get in.' His smile disappeared behind the glass as it glided back up.

In the few seconds it took to get into the back seat of the car beside him, Amir began to shake.

'Don't be scared.' His voice as smooth as his clothes; almost soothing. 'It's been a busy time for you kids.' He shook his head knowingly, his bushy, coiffed badger hair bounced gently. The driver spun round on Haft-e Tir and forked left into Modares Highway. 'Let me introduce myself. My name is Ghassem Namazi.' Another generous smile spread across his face as he extended a pale hand. These were the hands of a moneyed member of the elite: soft, silken skin with bright, white nails. 'I'm very pleased to meet you, young man.' Amir was taken aback by his faultless manners. He was so goddam polite. The regime lackeys Amir had met – the technocrats, the intelligence officers, the stooges – were mostly all the same: churlish and uncouth with their bad suits and crude behaviour that matched their second-rate Islamic education. The car was speeding along now, people and buildings melting away as the driver took full advantage of the afternoon lull in traffic. The old man paused, running a hand across his face.

As he came to speak, his head bowed.

'I'm here to ask for your forgiveness.' His eyes were fixed on Amir. There was no hint of sarcasm.

'Do I know you? I don't understand…' Amir croaked.

'You don't know me, but I've known you for years. I've been watching you from afar.'

'Who are you? You said you're a friend of my parents?' The driver's eyes flicked into the rear-view mirror. The old man was breathing deeply, flared nostrils discharging short bursts of heavy, hot air.

Exhale.

Inhale.

'I am the judge who sentenced your mother and father to death.'

Inhale.

'Forgive me.'

Amir rocked back, his gums stretched taut as his mouth extended open like a Rottweiler ready to bite. He had been waiting for this moment for his entire adult life. For years he had fantasized about coming face to face with the man who ordered his parents' execution. He would smash the man's face so hard that blood would pour from his head. He would hear his bones crack. He would kick his groin into a soft pulp. He would watch the pain and the horror contort his face. He would show no mercy.

'Forgive me, forgive,' the old man was whimpering, tears streaming down his face, his fat belly trembling as he sobbed. Amir grimaced with disgust at the old frail man, helpless and pathetic. And disgust at himself, at his impotent fists that were hanging limply by his sides. There was no violent rage. Only blistering pain.

'Let me out of the car,' he could hear himself shouting.

The old man was whispering something, his mouth quivering. But Amir did not want to hear. 'LET ME OUT OF THE CAR.' His face was red and he felt his eyes bulging with the force of his voice. The driver was talking too now, turning round and gesticulating.

'LET ME OUT OF THE FUCKING CAR.' They weren't listening. Amir couldn't breathe. He opened the door. The car swerved as the force of the wind knocked against it. The old man was holding onto him as one of Amir's legs dangled out.

'Stop the car Behnam, stop it, let him go!' The car pulled onto the hard shoulder and Amir stumbled out. Without looking back, he clambered up the steep grassy verge, clawing at the earth with his hands, trampling over the red petunias and pansies. The car had stopped by Taleghani Park, a green elevated expanse sandwiched between roaring motorways. Amir ran into its bowels, among the jacaranda and pine trees, where his sobs were muffled by the distant hum of the cars; where the drug addicts did not notice another lost soul; where lovers concealed in the bushes understood the unspoken language of the hidden.

Amir had not let himself cry about his parents since he had been a little boy. For the next two hours, stupefied by grief, he allowed himself to remember. For the first time in a long time, he felt sorry for himself.

Shiraz, May 1988

Shahla is laughing as she dances to Boney M's 'Ma Baker', her red dress flapping round her legs as her husband Manuchehr spins her around.

Ma Ma Ma Ma, Ma Baker – she never could cry
Ma Ma Ma Ma, Ma Baker – but she knew how to die

Shahla dances with uninhibited abandon, as though no one is watching. And she moves so beautifully, so joyfully, that everyone is *always* watching. Even at six years old Amir knows his mother is captivating, and whenever she dances he feels intensely proud.

Before the dancing is the business of dissent, and the evening started as these gatherings always start. The guests arrive separately, using the back door. It has been like this ever since Peyvand, another leftist comrade, was arrested at a similar meeting. A suspicious neighbour noted a group arriving at the house opposite and called local vigilantes. That was five years ago and Peyvand is still in prison. Since then, the situation has only got worse. Nearly ten years after the revolution, fear and suspicion are the daily currency of life.

A black shroud has fallen over the country. The war with Iraq rages; lives are lost. The revolution fights its enemies within; lives are lost. The lifeblood of the people is sucked dry, they are left limp and afraid. Even the landscape has changed. Antiquities are ripped out, paintings and murals vandalized as remnants of the non-Islamic empire are raped and shredded.

The southern city of Shiraz also looks different: the hillsides, once bright green with undulating vineyards, are a dusty brown, the earth beneath them still recoiling at being torched by the hands of the devout, who swear they will never again allow alcohol to drench this soil.

Like most of the group, Shahla and Manuchehr are not card-carrying members of a political party but they are proud to call themselves *chapis* – leftists. In simple terms, they describe themselves as 'pro-poor and anti-imperialist'. They have, in turn, sympathized with Iran's communist Tudeh Party and the Marxist Fedayin Party. In the last nine years, since the revolution, thousands of political opponents and 'counter-revolutionaries' have been killed. Now, only the brave or foolish continue. Manuchehr and Shahla do not see themselves as either brave or foolish – rather as unimportant in the grander scheme. They never admit this out loud, for to admit this is to acknowledge that they have no real stake in their future, that they are simply powerless armchair activists – although they do allow themselves to take solace in their insignificance when it is remarked on in terms of their protection, for they believe that as long as they are eclipsed by more prominent political players, they are safe. So they continue to fight the system as a matter of principle, as a matter of attempting to right something that, in their minds, has gone terribly wrong.

The group's secret parties happen at least once a month, and are nearly always held at Shahla and Manuchehr's house, as it is the biggest in their small neighbourhood in the north of Shiraz. It is an unlikely group of dissidents, a quixotic mix bred out of revolution and war. Shiraz's intellectual class, which consists mostly of rich, educated Shirazis and a few Marxist-Leninist academics, is now shoulder to shoulder with a handful of fearless middle-class housewives, a group of students, some working-class farmers, two Jews, an Armenian, a few shopkeepers and a devout Muslim. The meetings are an opportunity to be subversive and to kick the machine while it is not looking, from the safety of the living room.

And here they are, Shahla and Manuchehr, huddled with a small group of friends in the kitchen. This is what their lives have become: a brotherhood of secrets, of back entrances and kitchens. They relay messages and share the latest arrests and executions. Somebody unfurls a squashed bundle of dog-eared typed pages, pulled out of underwear. It is the latest communiqué from a *chapi* leader. Somebody else has a photocopy from an illegal political publication.

Finally they discuss what is on everybody's mind – the one issue that Shahla and Manuchehr try to evade. The threats. For the past year they have been receiving anonymous scraps of paper slipped under the door in the dead of night, messages scrawled in childlike, spidery handwriting. The missives are at first vague, but menacing:

WE KNOW WHAT YOU ARE DOING.

But the sender is getting brave. There is a bolder voice:

DISBELIEVERS DESERVE TO DIE.

Manuchehr and Shahla refuse to stop the parties and the secret meetings. Over the past year a few friends have been arrested and imprisoned, yet still the group continues. They tell the group they have not received any notes recently. But they are lying. The truth is that they are scared by the latest message:

WHO WILL LOOK AFTER AMIR WHEN YOU'RE GONE?

This arrived a week ago and Manuchehr immediately stopped his writing. Since he was dismissed from his job as a university history professor he has been working as a journalist for underground left-wing publications; rather, for any publications that dare publish his work.

Amir is shooed out of the room. He is too little to understand the complicated conversations and he flits in and out unnoticed. Amir is told these are illicit meetings and that he must never, ever tell anyone. Manuchehr and Shahla test him; their exaggerated mock questioning, imitating a nosey neighbour, makes him laugh. Aged six, Amir is well versed in the art of lying. He has a ready stockpile of lies perched on the tip of his still-developing tongue, waiting for the cue for them to fall out of his baby mouth and into the ears of adults: grandmother's birthday; a pilgrimage party; a family reunion. The lies are simple and pure and white enough for Amir to happily repeat them with utter conviction.

Food plays an important role and with every new agenda is a new course. Tonight it starts with *dolmeh*, stuffed vine leaves, and slowly moves on to the grand dishes: rich pomegranate, walnut and duck stew; lamb with saffron rice. And then the drinking, bootleg whisky and home-brewed vodka to warm up spirits so dampened by oppression. The need to dance and drink is as great as the need to dissent. The drinking always leads to dancing; eyes closed, trying to find a light in the dark.

Children are never banished in Iranian households when grown-ups play, and Amir wanders around the party being fed and petted. He falls asleep on Manuchehr's lap, cocooned by the safe sounds of music and drinking and talking. Shahla carries him in her arms to his bed and kisses his face as she tucks him under the blanket. But tonight Amir gets bored with the adults, and wanders to the front of the house. He plays with his toy cars in the hallway, in the dark, for the lights here are always off at night so as not to attract attention. He hears rustling by the door. He is curious and walks up to it. There, on the ground, lit up luminous white by the moonrays streaming through the porch windows, is a note. He picks it up and runs into the living room. Everyone freezes at the sight of little Amir holding a note.

'Mummy, look what I found. It was under the door.' They run around, frantically fumbling to turn the music off, collecting the bottles of alcohol. Manuchehr has already crept to the door and back. 'There's nobody there, I checked,' he is whispering. Shahla's best friend takes Amir upstairs. Shahla holds the note. She has still not opened it.

'*What does it say, what does it say*?' Their voices are urgent. She reads out loud, in a sober, matter-of-fact voice: WE'RE COMING TO GET YOU.

Jomhouri Street, downtown Tehran, March 2013

It was dark by the time Amir got home. Without turning on the lights, he slumped on his sofa and stared at the shadows flickering on the wall.

'Where have you been? I've been calling you all afternoon, I was so worried.' Bahar's gentle voice on his mobile.

'I'm sorry darling. Something came up. I'll tell you when I see you.'

She did not press him for more details. She was careful of what she said on the phone, especially since his meeting with *ettela'at*.

Amir fell in love with Bahar the instant he saw her. Within days they were making love. Within a month she was the only outsider who knew Amir's secret. The only person who knew his lies.

Bahar Azimi wore no make-up, which made her all the more striking. She was short and curvy with glossy black curly hair. A warm, round face; big brown eyes, big mouth, big smile and big laugh. She read books; devoured them, one after another. She lived for the arts – theatre, films and music. She worked hard. Money and class did not impress her. She could be evasive but found it hard to lie. She loved to party and get drunk with her friends, she loved Metallica, Radiohead, Zero 7 and Zedbazi, an underground Iranian band that sang about drugs and sex (and who had all left the country). Her friends were relatively new, students she had met at the Islamic Azad University where she had studied art. At first her fellow students suspected she was a *shahrestaan* girl, small-town girl, who had left everything behind for the big smoke; her polite manner and humility did not seem to belong in the city. But soon they realized that she was too proud to be the kind of girl who was ashamed of her roots. And *shahrestaan* girls usually went one of two ways – either wild at their new-found freedom or creeping like mice across this frightening, vast landscape, fearful of stepping into its traps. Bahar Azimi was neither wild nor fearful. She was unexpectedly independent, which made some fearful of *her*. But the arts faculty attracted free spirits and beatniks, the kind of people who embraced Bahar and were intrigued by her individualism. For the first time, Bahar felt she belonged.

Bahar had grown up in a different world from the one which she now inhabited. To be precise, just over five miles farther south of the most southerly end of Vali Asr, on the very outskirts of the city. Shahr-e Rey was already a city when Tehran was just a collection of villages. Parts of it still look the same as they did hundreds of years ago. It is a poor and fiercely conservative place that has been gobbled up by south Tehran. Bahar's parents were strict *namaaz roozeh-ee*, 'prayer and fasting' types, observant Muslims with traditional values. Nearly everyone in Bahar's school came from families who wore the chador; Bahar's parents expected her to wear it. But she refused. She battled with them for the smallest liberties: to sit in a coffee shop, which they deemed unbefitting of a young woman; to not wear *hejab* in front of her male relatives; to chat with ease with local boys. Her parents argued back with even more force: she was jeopardizing the family's honour; *what would the neighbours think?* Her home life was miserable. A couple of other girls at school felt the same as she: none of them was sure where this defiance and independence came from; they were all too poor to have satellite televisions and laptops. It was just the way they had been born. And maybe Bahar would have been forced to conform, if it had not been for a liberal-minded teacher who, recognizing her spark, encouraged her, giving her books to read that revealed the world outside. Gabriel García Márquez's *A Hundred Years of Solitude*; George Orwell's *Nineteen Eighty-Four*. Bahar had two dreams: to get out of Shahr-e Rey and to be financially independent so she would not have to depend on her parents and be forced to live by their rules. Bahar Azimi was a rare, strange creature in Tehran.

Amir had met Bahar at a film club. It was a weekly event

held by a friend who had a projector and a dazzling collection of DVDs. They were delivered to him every month by a middle-aged film-fanatic hawker. He would turn up in a suit carrying a large black holdall stuffed with hundreds of films. Most Tehranis wanted comedy, but he had everything, from forties *film noir* to French art house. He always carried a stash of his two bestsellers that old and young alike requested: *The Godfather* and *Daī Jan Napelon* – 'My Uncle Napoleon' – a classic Iranian television series from the s that had been adapted from a book and was banned after the revolution. The premise of the story is a suspicious fart, and lines from the book and the series had worked their way into everyday vernacular, a favourite being 'going to San Francisco' – a euphemism for having sex. All the hawker's films were 3,000 tomans – one dollar – each. He also sold the latest Hollywood releases, sometimes before they even made it to the cinemas in America and Europe. The copies came from China and Malaysia and were perfect, apart from those that had a FOR YOUR CONSIDERATION message that occasionally flicked up on the screen.

The first thing Bahar noticed about Amir was his smiling eyes above a big, strong nose. His face was soft and delicate, something he tried to disguise with a goatee beard. That night, Amir and Bahar learnt that they seemed to agree on everything, even sharing their favourite film, *The Double Life of Véronique*. They thought Iranian films were overrated and pretentious, apart from Asghar Farhadi's *A Separation*, a gritty, realistic portrait of a disintegrating marriage and class conflicts in Tehran; they laughed at how Western critics were seduced by the heavy-handed symbolism in art house Iranian films.

For their first date they went to the Ta'atr-e Shahr, Tehran City Theatre, on Vali Asr and saw David Mamet's *Oleanna*. It was a special place for Amir; it was one of the few clear memories he had of his father, and his first memory of Tehran. He was five years old and they had walked up Vali Asr, Amir in awe of its enormity. It was the most beautiful road Amir had ever seen, trees like giant soldiers standing to attention. Now the spines of the trees were crooked with age but Amir still felt small under their branches. After the theatre, Amir drove them to a coffee shop owned by the son of a Pole, one of over 100,000 starving Poles released from Soviet captivity and granted sanctuary in Iran during the Second World War. They had laughed when his white Pride, the country's cheapest and best-selling car, would not start. They drank cappuccinos, ate cake and talked for hours. Tentatively they began to share simple truths about each other's lives. They held hands and stared into each other's eyes, unable to do more in public. Afterwards they drove into a dark side street where they kissed for hours.

Little had changed between them since then, even though life had not been easy. Amir had struggled to find a job after university. When times got hard, he worked as a taxi driver, relentlessly chugging through stagnant traffic for little more than blackened snot, aching lungs and a few dollars a day. He finally got a job as a photographer's assistant. The pay was just enough to get by. Bahar worked as a graphic designer and freelanced as an English translator. She had moved straight from university halls of residence to her own apartment, which was unusual for a girl in her early twenties, especially for a girl from Shahr-e Rey. Her parents had been devastated, because women who live on their own have *reputations*. Few landlords would rent to a young, unmarried woman. Many advertisements in the newspapers specified: *Will not rent to single women*. She hated turning up to viewings, in case the landlord was male and would try his luck, which happened often. Some thought she must be a working girl. She now paid 700,000 tomans, just over 200 US dollars a month, for a one-bedroom flat near where Amir lived, in the centre of the city, just where Jomhouri Street is bisected by Vali Asr. Over time, Bahar's parents came to accept their daughter had different ideas for her life; they visited, packing her fridge with never-ending supplies of food. Amir had tried to convince her to live together, but it would have been too risky and a secret too difficult to keep from her parents; they had discussed marriage but Bahar said she was not ready.

Amir did not turn the lights on until Bahar arrived. He wanted to postpone reality for as long as he could. His mouth still felt dry. The old man's face kept appearing in his head. He needed to tell Bahar everything, the only person he could talk to.

She stood at the door beaming. Her smile had a life of its own, as though it were about to burst off her face, her beautiful lips stretched from ear to ear.

'I got it, I got it!' she was squealing with joy.

'Got what?'

'The scholarship!' Amir's throat tightened.

'You're not even smiling.'

'I'm sorry. It's amazing.' The scholarship to an American university had hung over them like a cloud for the past year.

'Just…what does that mean for us?'

'That you'll come with me, stupid.' Bahar grabbed his face in her hands.

'I've told you, I'm not ready.'

She dropped her arms by her sides. 'What do you mean you're not ready? I just don't understand. You say you hate it here, but you're too scared to leave.'

'Bahar, what will I do there? How the hell am I going to get a visa?'

'We can get married.' Bahar's voice was shrinking.

'You're living in a bubble. It's impossible getting a visa these days. And I want to get married because we both want it, not for a visa.'

Bahar began to cry. 'But I don't want to lose you. I won't go.'

'No.' He almost shouted it. Bahar was sobbing now. He held her tight.

'This is your chance. What chance do we have here? I'll come. I promise. I just need time, and I'll save up and I'll get a visa.'

The pizza deliveryman arrived. They barely ate. Bahar broke the silence.

'You said you were going to tell me something…they haven't called again have they?' Amir paused. Bahar was already upset. His news would make her feel guilty. Anyway, what was the point? She was leaving.

'No. Nothing happened. I went walking, up the mountains. I forgot my phone. I just needed to get away.' It was the first time he had lied to Bahar.

Shiraz, June 1988, a month after the party

Amir is playing with Lego in his room when they come. He hears the bang on the door and his parents whispering to each other. He runs out of his bedroom and stands at the top of the stairs, straining to listen. He can hear men's voices.

'There's no need to take them, *I beg you*, just take me,' his father, determined and unbroken. Then silence, apart from his mother's gentle sobs. When the crying stops, she comes upstairs.

'Darling, put on your clothes, we've got to go somewhere.'

'I don't want to go.' Amir is scared. Shahla tenderly strokes his hair, and takes off his pyjamas. 'Where's daddy?'

'He's coming with us, we're all going together. Darling, you never have to be scared when you're with mummy and daddy. You're always safe. We won't let anything bad happen, OK?' Amir nods. The men with the guns march them out into a cool night. The electricity has gone in the street and Amir has never seen his road so dark. Nobody speaks as they climb into the back of the pick-up truck, Amir in his father's arms. Behind curtains, neighbours are watching. Friends or enemies, who can tell?

They are driven straight to Shiraz prison.

Tehran, March 2013

It had been a week since Amir had met the old man; a week since Bahar had told him she was leaving. He had sunk into depression, grappling with it in his sleep. He dreamt of his parents: of being back in prison in Shahla's arms. Of being on his father's shoulders walking up Vali Asr, under the trees. He dreamt the old man was there too, begging Manuchehr for forgiveness. But Manuchehr could not talk, because now his neck was broken, snapped by the noose that hung round it, his feet swinging off the ground.

Shiraz prison, June 1988

The days are hot and the nights are cold. The sour smell of sweat and stale breath. Distant screaming and shrieking. Amir is too little to know that this is the sound of torture.

It has been two weeks since they were brought here. The guard tells them they are being taken to Evin prison in Tehran. Shahla looks shocked. Serious political cases are transferred to Evin. The prisoners here in Shiraz talk about it often enough. Rumours collect in prison like nowhere else she has been; like scarab beetles rolling ever-growing balls of dung, each inmate brings new speculation that swells and feeds them for weeks. *They're going to kill all the prisoners in Evin*, says a monarchist who heard it from his mother's cousin's husband, who works with a man whose son is in the Prime Minister's office. The statement is treated in the same way as all the other rumours, with a mixture of terror and sceptical disbelief. But one thing everyone knows for sure: only serious cases are transferred to Evin prison.

Shahla does not understand how it has come to this. It is all the more galling considering that they had started on the same side; that Manuchehr and Shahla had initially embraced the revolution with passion. They had thought that no one could be worse than the Shah and it was under the Shah's regime that Shahla and Manuchehr had first discovered the political underground and taken solace in subterfuge. The Shah had embarked on eliminating communists and leftists, ever desperate to please the Americans and with a genuine fear of the Soviet Union's threats to Afghanistan. Between 1971 and 1977, over 130 guerrillas and members of armed political groups were executed or tortured to death. Some said over 3,000 political opponents were killed during his reign. The minute the Shah was deposed the leftists and communists surfaced, confident.

Shahla and Manuchehr, with their unshakeable sense of justice, had been full of hope and mesmerized by Khomeini's anti-imperialist, egalitarian talk. Khomeini, the softly spoken, handsome man with modesty as his signature tune. After the shrill fanfare of the Shah and his wife's glaring ostentation, this new tune was a hit. His plain words, calmly preached from underneath thunderous eyebrows, stirred the nation. His slogans daubed on the walls of Tehran had spread, like ivy, across the walls of the nation:

ISLAM REPRESENTS THE SLUM-DWELLERS, NOT THE PALACE-DWELLERS!

THE OPPRESSED OF THE WORLD UNITE!

One by one, for pragmatism, faith or expediency, protesters jumped onto his Islamic bandwagon as it rattled to victory. But memories are short. Iran's tricky relationship with the left had really taken hold in 1960 when the Iraqi Shia cleric and Khomeini's mentor, Ayatollah Hakim, had issued a fatwa forbidding any Shia from joining the Communist Party. Still, the communists and the leftists thought they had a chance. As it turned out, they would have less than a year before being beaten back down. Fear of communism was something that the Islamic dissidents and the Shah had in common.

Shahla and Manuchehr threw themselves into the revolution. Shahla joined Khomeini's literacy campaign, a bedrock of revolutionary zeal (and the foundations of which had been laid down by the Shah). She advanced into the hinterland armed with books, pencils and the thirty-two letters of the Persian alphabet. Some of the villages were eerily quiet. Illiterate village boys make excellent cannon fodder and thousands were sent to the front line to fight in the war with Iraq. Shahla's patience and kindness were not enough. After four years she was sacked, swallowed up by the wave of suspicion that was casually sweeping the country. Manuchehr also fell victim to it, first during the Cultural Revolution when universities were closed for two years and the country was purged of all Western, un-Islamic influences, and then again when he lost his job, accused of being a communist. So their lives continued to unravel.

Jomhouri Street, Tehran, April 2013

In the middle of an afternoon slumber 'private number' flashed up on Amir's phone. He thought it must be *them*, *ettela'at*, on top of everything else. But it was the old man.

'I need to see you. I want to explain.'

Amir hung up. The phone rang again. And again.

'Just leave me alone,' he said listlessly.

Over the next few days the old man called many times, from many different numbers. He even called the home line. Ghassem rang so many times that Amir stopped answering his phone. But the calls continued. So Amir changed his mobile.

He had always longed to know every minute detail of his parents' deaths. He had tried to investigate several times, but the trail had always gone cold, or he had been warned to leave it alone. He was already marked, why draw attention to it? And suddenly here it was, in front of him for the taking. Yet he was not ready to deal with the truth behind his parents' deaths. Amir was also scared. Not just of the truth, but of the old man. He shuddered to think how he had tracked him down.

Within a week, Ghassem was calling Amir's new number. Bahar had noticed the mysterious calls. She thought it was from *ettela'at* and, wanting to protect Amir, she started spending nearly every night at his. They watched films together, in each other's arms, smoking a joint. For Amir, it was painful to have her warm body next to his, knowing that he would soon lose it. They made love with the same intensity as during their courtship – with the hungry longing that time and familiarity mercilessly erode.

On a night when Bahar was staying at her own place, Amir's entryphone buzzed. It was late, past eleven o'clock. He looked out of his front window. It was the old man, hunched and lit up orange by the street light. He was carrying something in his hands. The old man buzzed again. He looked up to Amir's window and Amir was too late to duck his head.

'Just let me in. I won't be long.' He was craning his slack neck, his soft voice struggling against gravity and the pane of glass.

Amir threw the window open.

'Can't you take a hint? You've done enough harm already.' He did not realize it, but he was shouting. 'Aren't you satisfied that you said your piece? Just go.'

'You haven't given me a chance…to explain…to try…' The shaky voice was barely audible above Amir's.

'What the hell's going on out there?' a neighbour yelled, 'he's an old man, show some respect! And keep it down!' Amir raced down the stairs, fists clenched. Threw open the front door. The old man hardly flinched. Sad and tired and ashen from guilt and age. Again Amir's rage receded, leaving a burning resentment in its place, that this old man was denying him his hate.

Ghassem was holding a gift-wrapped box. On the ground by his side, an enormous tin of oil and a sack of rice. 'I've got a gold watch for you and some essentials you may need, I know you live alone.'

'I'm not a fucking earthquake victim!' Amir hissed, trying to keep his voice low.

From his inside suit pocket the old man produced a cheque-book. 'I just want to help. You've struggled enough in life because of what I did. Here's twenty million tomans, it's nothing.'

'I would never take your blood money for as long as I live. You think you can buy me with a cheque and a tin of oil? Is that what it costs to assuage your guilt? Is that what my parents are worth?'

'I'm sorry, I didn't meant it that way, I just want to do the right thing.'

'Can you bring my parents back? If you can bring my parents back, then I'll consider forgiving you.' He slammed the door in the old man's face.

Back in his apartment, he turned off the lights and edged towards the window. The old man had left his gifts by the door and was now walking up the alley, towards the main road, unsteady on his legs.

Amir did not hear from Ghassem again that week, and life resumed as normal. Bahar was getting ready for her trip. Amir threw himself back into his work. He updated his blog, with renewed energy.

Evin prison, Tehran, August 1988

Shahla and Amir have still not seen Manuchehr, not even when the three of them are transferred to Evin. A few days after they arrive, the initial shock thaws, exposing Shahla's anger. But she is certain they will be released soon. Theirs is not a serious case. They are not official members of any party, something she reminds her interrogators at every opportunity. 'If your intelligence is so great, then surely you know that!'

Amir misses his father and does not like this new world full of women squashed together, the heat intensifying the smell of sweat, cheap soap and milky breasts. He has made a friend, Maryam, but she is older and does not always want to play. He has a tantrum. Manuchehr had promised him a toy truck. He stamps his little foot on the ground and shouts louder and louder. The women stare in silence. Maryam watches him from the bunk bed with her mother, both looking at him with their sad eyes. His mother pleads with a guard through a tiny hatch in the door.

'He misses his father, that's all – please let him see his father, little boys can't be without their daddies.' At the word 'daddy', Amir starts to wail, throwing himself on the floor with drama and flourish. And then everyone looks up as they hear the jangle of keys working its way down, until the door is opened.

'Just. This. Once.' says the woman in the green uniform, her unsmiling face hidden by her cap. Amir wipes his wet eyes, embarrassed at the scene he has caused. Shahla hugs him and whispers in his ear before taking him to the threshold. And then Amir is on the other side, his wet face blasted dry by an icy airstream. He is led along endless corridors of sparkling white tiles under flickering yellow strip lights. He can hear the squeak of rubber soles on the floor above the hum of the air conditioning. Then more keys jangle, more banging on doors. He is led into a room full of men, they shout his father's name and nudge him towards the back where he is wrapped up in his father's hot, familiar arms. Giggling together, Amir nuzzles his face in his father's neck, breathing in his musky smell. They play, father and son, for what seems like hours.

'As soon as we're out, the first thing I'm going to do is to buy you that truck.'

Jomhouri Street, Tehran, April 2013

Amir had spent most of his life avoiding subversion and staying away from anything vaguely political. But moving to Tehran for university changed that. He was drawn to the buzz of the underground student movement. It was barely organized, and mostly consisted of a handful of dissidents giving impassioned speeches in their bedrooms to a rapt audience of less than five.

In the run-up to the presidential elections in 2009, he had joined his university friends at their old haunt, Café Prague, west of Vali Asr. The café was close to the campus and a popular meeting place for students, activists, artists, intellectuals and hipsters. Here couples would date, friends would gossip, poets would read their work and everyone else discussed politics over endless teas, coffees and cheese sandwiches. Conversations were often heated. To vote or not to vote, that was always the question. The Boycotters would fail to convince the Voters that their votes gave the regime legitimacy. The Voters said change was possible; it was in their hands. They would discuss the lost years of reform under the old President, Mohammad Khatami, who had served from 1997 to 2005 and was a hero to so many. Amir and his friends would noisily argue that they had all been blinded by Khatami's petty reforms: headscarves slipped back and a few more films were made, but they all seemed to forget this man was a coward. They reminded anyone who cared to listen that Khatami had condemned the anti-government protesters in 1999, denouncing the protesters and accusing them of being led by 'evil elements'; and he was decidedly quiet whenever students and dissidents were rounded up and arrested. Not forgetting that Khatami was ungracious and bitter to boot: when the human rights lawyer Shirin Ebadi won the Nobel Peace Prize he sniped that it was not a very important award. As for the reforms, Amir would say, everyone in Iran knows where the real power lies, and that is in the hands of one man alone, Ayatollah Ali Khamenei, the Supreme Leader. Talk would then turn to Mir Hossein Mousavi, the man whom Khatami made way for, the new great prospect of the reformists. Amir hated him and was unexpectedly mute on the subject. *He's our only hope!* his friends would cry, and his face would go blank with a look that he had honed over years – dead eyes that gave nothing away.

Amir and his friends finally got the chance to go public with their politics when mass protests erupted after the contested result. The mood in the streets was euphoric. Standing in an ocean of hope and joy, Amir was overwhelmed with a happiness that he had not known since before his parents' death. He started filming everything on his mobile phone, as so many others did. Footage from the first few days showed Tehranis of all hues, of all classes and ages standing side by side. You could see thousands chanting, demanding a re-election; none of them believed Ahmadinejad had won again. They flashed peace signs and smiled for the cameras; families were there too and some had brought their children to join the crowds. At times it looked more like a celebration than a protest. You could see the excitement; kids were laughing and running and holding each other, ordinary human expressions of exuberance that are not often glimpsed on the streets of Tehran. People charged down Vali Asr; a river of bodies beneath the trees. Amir was ecstatic at being part of the collective consciousness. But as the days wore on, the looks on people's faces started to change. Fear crept in. So did the riot police and the Basij militia. Amir began wearing a bandanna tied in front of his face and dark glasses to conceal his identity; the mass protests gave way to mass arrests. These ordinary young Iranians scared the regime.

Amir had gathered with his friends where Vali Asr Street meets Beheshti Street. The crowd was huge. A young woman had brought her wheelchair-bound mother; there were labourers, rich kids, students, housewives. And they were all shouting, 'REFERENDUM! REFERENDUM!'

Amir held up his little camera and captured girls blowing kisses. Then the shouts turned to their saviour, the man they wanted in power, Mir Hossein Mousavi. 'MOUSAVI – MOUSAVI!' The crowd was roaring.

No one knew where the shots came from, and at first no one was even sure they were shots. Suddenly everyone was running and screaming. More shots. Amir started to run. He almost stumbled; at his feet was a young man, blood trickling out of his ear and oozing out of his head. His friends were trying to pick him up and drag him away.

That was the moment when Amir felt the need to honour his parents' courage with his own. Writing a blog and attending activist meetings was the first step.

The group consisted of journalists, bloggers, human rights lawyers, film directors and members of the women's rights movement. Tonight they had arranged to meet at Amir's house, as he had the lowest profile. Some of them were convinced their houses were bugged. They all whispered in their cars, and only if there was music blasting. Not long ago, they used to meet in cafés where the owners often joined in. But the café owners had been ordered to install cameras, the contents of which would be available to the police – or any other authority – if they so requested. Café Prague, their old haunt, had refused to install them and instead shut down.

The 2013 presidential elections were only a couple of months away and there had been the expected crackdown. In the last few months, more than a dozen journalists had been imprisoned in Evin, accused of having 'foreign contacts' who were friends and colleagues who had left for London, to work at BBC Persian.

As his friends began to arrive, Amir opened a plastic petrol can filled with *aragh sagee*, vodka moonshine that he had bought from his black-market booze seller Edvin, a ponytailed Armenian with muscly arms from years of lugging around boxes of bottles. Edvin did excellent business. He sold to everyone from civil servants to rich kids, and sales of wine in north Tehran had rocketed; most of it was the ubiquitous François Dulac plonk, but once a year he would sell some of his uncle's delicious home-made wine. Making it was not risky for them, as being Armenian they are Christians, and so are allowed to produce alcohol for their own consumption.

Amir poured the drinks and they all started taking out the batteries of their mobile phones, having heard that their conversations can be tapped even when phones are turned off. Fereshteh, one of the journalists, read a text message she had been sent by Ershad, the Ministry of Culture and Islamic Guidance: WE REMIND ALL JOURNALISTS THAT SPIES ARE IN OUR MIDST, AND THOSE FRATERNIZING WITH THE BRITISH WILL BE CONSIDERED SPIES.

'They've been going into overdrive with their messages recently. Our editor gets a phone call every day, either from intelligence or from the Ministry,' said Bita, who worked as a reporter on a reformist newspaper that had been shut down countless times over the years. Recently, the papers had been receiving faxes and phone calls almost nightly with instructions on what was to be censored. Bita said intelligence was checking the entire contents of the paper before it was published.

'Nourizad's written another letter. Here we go again. When is he going to give up, they don't even care about his letters any more,' said Behzad, a civil engineer by day, blogger by night and Amir's closest friend.

Mohammad Nourizad, an established film-maker and former journalist for the staunchly conservative regime mouthpiece, the

Kayhan newspaper (whose director is appointed by Khamenei, the Supreme Leader), was once a favoured lackey of the Supreme Leader, his unctuous fawning causing some dissidents to snigger that he was a member of the Leader's inner harem. But the protests changed everything; he wrote an outrageously brave, scathing letter to Khamenei, daring to criticize him and urging him to apologize to his people. Seventy days in solitary confinement did not manage to shut him up. Neither did interrogations and abuse. After 170 days in prison, he came out fighting, the only way he knew how: writing letters. No matter how much pressure the government put on him, he kept bouncing back. The letters never stopped, despite death threats. So the regime had taken to ignoring him. It was a good tactic, even if it was not meant as one, for soon people lost interest in his letters, frustrated at their lack of reaction. It was just another letter that would not change a thing.

'And Khazali's on another hunger strike, we've had a really hard time getting to him,' said Mana, the human rights lawyer, who had seen several of her colleagues imprisoned in the last two years.

Mehdi Khazali was one of the government's most ardent critics. A mild-mannered ophthalmologist who attended writing clubs and poetry readings, he was also an Islamic scholar and a committed blogger. Most controversially, he happened to be the son of one of the most right-wing, powerful and faithful clerics of the regime. Ayatollah Khazali had the exalted honour of being a member of the Assembly of Experts, a group of clerics charged with monitoring the Supreme Leader, and with the authority to dismiss him. The Ayatollah publicly denounced his son, who was sucked into a cycle of beatings and imprisonment. Meanwhile the Ayatollah's younger son released a pop video. Such is life in Tehran.

Mana updated the group on another round of arrests of Baha'is, a religious minority in Iran that the state considers heretics. Despite the government declaring that Baha'is are not discriminated against, they are excluded from much of public life, including not being able to go to university, to have government jobs or be involved in politics.

The friends drank and talked and shared information until the early hours. Bahar arrived halfway through. She was not political, but she loved the idea of resistance, and always wanted to hear the group's news. She had noticed that meetings were different now. More serious and contained, not like the ones they had at university when they would finish their sessions with riotous parties dancing to techno and popping ecstasy pills into their mouths.

Evin prison, Tehran, August 1988

Amir squeezes his little nose under the crack of the door, pressing his cheek down hard on the dirty tiled floor. Maryam is next to him, doing the same, their foreheads touching as they wriggle their bodies into place. A rush of ice-cold air tingles Amir's skin. Bliss. He closes his eyes and sticks out his tongue, trying to reach into the jet stream of air conditioning that shoots along the corridor outside. It is the height of a scorching summer and the overcrowded cell heats up like a kiln. The hot, sticky air in the room fuses Amir's clothes to his skin and he is covered with big, fat droplets of sweat, making the sensation of cool air on his face all the more delicious. This is his favourite thing to do here. He and Maryam lie in silence, fingers and faces wedged under the door, panting softly, until one of the women spots them.

'If they open the door, they won't see you and you'll get hurt! They'll tread all over you and you'll break your necks and never be able to walk again!' is the usual cry, expressed with the exaggerated alarm employed by Iranian mothers. But Shahla never exaggerates anything. Amir has noticed she is not as strict in here. She is softer, more forgiving. When he and Maryam are told off, he runs into Shahla's outstretched arms and she smiles. 'My love, my beautiful boy. Did you feel the cold air? Are you cooler now my angel?'

Amir still dreams of those moments crammed in the gap under the door, stealing slivers of chill from the slipstream of cold air outside. In moments of panic and stress, he shuts his eyes and transports himself back there, marvelling at the irony that a memory from Evin prison is what pacifies him.

Jomhouri Street, Tehran, April 2013

Amir had just returned from work when the old man called. It was the day after the meeting.

'You should be more careful. Inviting a lawyer round who is being followed twenty-four hours a day, with a load of journalists and a known blogger. It isn't the brightest thing to do. People will start to wonder what you are up to. What with the elections coming up, you know it's a sensitive time. Not forgetting your parents' record, it doesn't look good. And then not even I will be able to help you.' The voice sounded stronger than before, more authoritative. Amir had no words left for the old man.

'Are you still there?'

'Who are you? How do you know these things?' This was the first time Amir had not shouted.

'I'm an old man who wants to explain.'

Amir put the phone down. But the old man had finally got the boy's attention, as he suspected he would.

Ghassem Namazi had the blood of quite a few of his people on his hands and it needed washing off. The onset of guilt had coincided with his decrepitude. There were few signs from Ghassem's outward appearance that this was a man made of flesh and blood. His skin was tinged grey, his eyes were unflinching. His pursed mouth barely moved when he spoke in his quiet monotone voice, carefully crafted to conceal any show of emotion. This immutability was to be expected of a man of Ghassem's standing, of a man who spent years working as a judge in the Revolutionary Court of the Islamic Republic of Iran. Ghassem and his colleagues were man-made myrmidons of the machine; dispassion was lauded by the regime.

But somewhere along the line there was a shift. Many of the judges changed, as Ghassem had changed. At the beginning they had believed in their work, dispensing God's justice. They were serving their country and standing up for the dispossessed. But it was no longer about Islamic Revolutionary principles. It was now about money and power.

Ghassem had worked hard to cultivate his urbane exterior, for he was from peasant stock. For generations they had ploughed the land in the fertile plains of Varamin, south of Tehran. The Shah had overlooked these peasants and that was one of his greatest mistakes. The villagers did not complain when plunged into darkness in the winter, nor did they complain when their precious supply of fresh water ran out during the torpid summer months. They had lived more or less the same way for centuries. While the world around them was changing their belief in God was inflexible, and so when an uprising began in the name of God and the poor, they dutifully followed. Generations of monarchs had kept them alive but had not given them much more than a hand-to-mouth existence. They glimpsed new possibilities.

Ghassem was the youngest son, and by the time he was born his mother had already given birth to all the farmhands that her husband would need. Ghassem's father wanted more for his youngest than a life of subsistence. The decision was made to send him to a religious seminary in Tehran. He studied under the tutelage of a well-known, firebrand cleric who was impressed by this sharp peasant boy who had witnessed the drudgery of village life and had realized God and the Koran were his only chances to step up the ladder. The cleric made sure that by the time the revolution happened, Ghassem was ready.

Soon after the revolution, the regime realized it had an ever-increasing caseload but its judges knew nothing of Islamic law. Most of the judges presiding in courts were remnants of the Shah's rule; they had simply removed their ties, grown beards and renounced the king, like snakes shedding their skin to reveal new scales. They did brisk business: between the revolution in 1979 and June 1981, revolutionary courts executed nearly 500 opponents of the regime. In 1983, clerics were drafted into the judiciary to enforce *mojazat*, punishment under Koranic law. Ghassem was one of them.

His ascent was swift. In 1988 he was assigned to a special court in Evin, set up for the cleansing of *moharebs*, enemies of God, and *mortads*, apostates. Ayatollah Khomeini had given a secret order to execute all prisoners who remained opposed to the Islamic regime. Trials were brisk, sometimes with only one question used to determine the accused's innocence, such as 'Do you pray?' or 'Are you a Muslim?' and 'Do you believe in

Heaven and Hell?' Some of the questions confused the panicking prisoners, who knew their answers would mean the difference between life and death. When asked: 'When you were growing up, did your father pray, fast and read the Holy Koran?' they would lie, and answer in the affirmative, not knowing that if they had responded truthfully, with a 'no', they then could not have been held accountable for their un-Islamic views and they would have escaped execution, which happened there and then.

It was easy work. During a few months over the summer of 1988, over 3,000 – and maybe over 5,000, for nobody is really sure – Iranians were either hanged or shot by firing squad. Ghassem was rewarded handsomely for his bloodletting and was given a residence at the top of Vali Asr, in Tajrish.

Ghassem witnessed this new Islamic jurisprudence during his first year as a judge. A few years before he started signing count- less death warrants, he joined a crowd of a few hundred people gathered in a courtyard at Evin prison. In the middle of them a man and two women were half buried in the ground. They had been found guilty, by another cleric, of adultery and moral turpi- tude. They had been given their death rites, their bodies washed and ready for the grave and encased in white shrouds. The living corpses were placed upright in dug-out ditches, the man up to his waist and the women up to their breasts. The law states that if the accused manages to wriggle out of the holes and escape, they must be allowed to walk free (if they have admitted their crime) – an impossible task for women, who have no way of using their arms to prise themselves out. This discrimination is justified in the name of decency, for as the victims are ready for burial they are naked underneath, so if the stones rip open the material, breasts may be revealed and that would be a sin for them *all*.

Ghassem felt nothing when he threw his first stone. He felt

nothing when the first burst of blood soaked the white muslin cloth, spreading its red tentacles across it like hundreds of rivulets. This was justice. The law also states that spectators guilty of the same crime are forbidden from throwing stones. Everyone wanted to be seen throwing stones. How could he not join in?

Evin prison, Tehran, September 1988

Days in prison are identical; Shahla, Manuchehr and Amir are suspended in time. Today is like any other day. Amir is playing with Maryam while the mothers sleep. It is dawn. There is the jangle of keys, which signals the arrival of a guard. It is either a new prisoner, or an inmate being taken away for another interrogation. This is part of the routine. The guard steps into the room.

'Shahla Azadi. Come with me.' The guard fixes her stare on the wall as Shahla gives Amir a hug and tells him she will be back in a little while. And because this is not an irregular occurrence, Amir barely notices. He continues to play with Maryam.

Half an hour or several hours later – it is impossible to remember how long – the whole room erupts into crying. 'Oh God. Oh God!' Maryam's mother almost shouts the words. Then a deep, rasping sob. The women cluster around each other. Amir and Maryam are shaken out of their imaginary world by human howling. Maryam runs to her mother and Amir looks for Shahla. But Shahla is not there. Amir feels more alone than he has ever felt in his entire little life. Maryam runs back to him. He jumps up, a tiny creature in the corner of a room.

'Don't you know why they're crying?'

'No, what's happened? Where's mummy?'

'She's dead. They just killed her. They hanged her with a rope.'

And that is how Amir learns of his mother's execution.

He remembers crying. Remembers being held by adults. Nobody knows what to say to a six-year-old boy whose mother has just been executed.

An hour later, he is escorted out of the prison. A guard opens the gates and stands with him, this child with skinny legs poking out of his shorts. Amir does not know that the guard, an eighteen-year-old on his military service, has witnessed the executions and his face is now streaked with tears. The guard cannot bear to look at Amir, the quivering little bird holding onto his hand.

Amir sees his grandfather and uncle running towards him, their faces pale. His grandfather is shaking. 'Where's daddy?' Amir remembers this is all he said when he saw them. Those were the last words Amir spoke for two years. His uncle Fariborz breaks down, sobbing into Amir's neck. Amir has never seen a grown man cry. With it he understands: his father has been killed as well.

Karim Khan-e Zand Street, Tehran, April 2013

Amir needed to warn his friends of what the old man had told him. He sent a coded text message to Behzad. *I'm watching football, it's a great game.* Which meant: *Meet me by the bookshop.*

The bookshop was on Karim Khan-e Zand Street, one in a line of bookshops that Amir and Bahar spent hours in. Over the last few years some had been shut down or raided, one had its windows smashed. The owner had been holding literary nights and poetry readings in the shop, which had attracted artists, writers and human rights activists. The *edareyeh amaaken*, the security services in charge of public spaces, had issued warnings. When the owner of the bookshop complained, a judiciary representative turned up with a lorry and cleared the shelves of all the books.

In the window was a black and white poster of Woody Allen next to a stack of books about his films. The bestsellers were nearly always the self-help books. This particular bookshop prided itself on its more highbrow collection, and their surprise hit of the year was by Florence Scovel Shinn, an American born in the nineteenth century who wrote about metaphysical spirituality. *The Seven Habits of Highly Successful People – Powerful Lessons in Personal Change* came a close second. As with most bookshops in the city, in the fiction department nobody could outsell Haruki Murakami and Kazuo Ishiguro.

Behzad turned up looking frantic. They started to walk towards Vali Asr. Behzad told Amir that Mana had been arrested. And that *they* had been in touch with him. *They* knew about their meetings. *They* had called Amir a 'known blogger'. Amir did not ask for too many details, for they were talking the cautious language of dissidents. 'Clean everything. Get rid of your Facebook. And we've both got to get rid of our useless fucking blogs. They can read anything that's on your hard disc, so get rid of your laptop.'

They walked all the way to the end of the road, turning on to Vali Asr Square, where the great road charges through it in an eruption of noise, fumes, traffic and people. Behzad flagged down one of the shared taxis that drive up and down Vali Asr picking up and dropping off passengers along the way. Amir took a bus south, getting off outside a billiard hall on the junction of Jomhouri Street.

As soon as he entered the flat his phone rang. Amir knew it would be the old man.

'They're closing in on your friends. I think you should let me in.'

'Don't tell me you're outside?'

'Yes.'

The old man was a master manipulator. He was getting his way.

It took a while for the old man to make it up the stairs. Amir responded to his greeting of Salaam and led him to the sofa. It unsettled him that he was treating the old man as if he was just that, an old man, and not the killer who had signed his parents' death warrant.

The old man sat down and sighed heavily, looking around the tiny apartment. Then he said nothing. Just sat there with his head bowed.

'I need some explanations. How do you know everything? Am I in danger?'

The old man finally looked up. His eyes were moist. 'I can find things out. You know I can't tell you how. I advise you to stop your blog and your meetings because I have no power, there is nothing I can do if you get arrested. And you're headed in that direction.'

'I don't want your help. I just want you out of my life.'

'I'm begging you to allow me to explain.'

Amir said nothing.

'We believed what we were doing was the right thing. We believed your parents were enemies of God. We were surviving too, we were under attack. I did as I was told. I lost my way because I was lying to myself, lying to the world, and above all I was lying to God. He will judge me, I know that. I want to make this right, and I need your forgiveness.'

'You're just scared of God and of judgement day now you're old and death's not so far away, that's why you want my forgiveness.

You have no idea of the suffering you caused. I still feel ashamed, can you believe that? The pain will never leave. You have to live with your pain the way I have to live with mine.'

'My guilt and my regrets have eaten me alive for years now, believe me. I am suffering.'

'Let *me* tell *you* about regret – do you know what the biggest regret of my life is? That I didn't hug my mother for longer the last time I ever saw her. How is *that* for regret?'

The old man fell to his knees. Amir could not stand to look at him, and he could not stand for him to see the tears that were now streaming down his own face.

'I beg your forgiveness, I beg your forgiveness.' The old man repeated the words over and over, like a mantra. His suffering did not make Amir feel better. The old man was struggling to stay upright on his knees. Wearily, Amir got up and helped him to his feet.

'I don't hate you; it's past that. But I can never forgive you.'

Pasteur Street, Tehran, 1989

It is Amir's first trip since the executions. Baba Bozorg – granddad – pummels a decrepit orange BMW through the desert; his tight clench of the wheel does not loosen. No matter how far they seem to drive, sand, rocks and mountains remain framed in the windows like a painting. Baba Bozorg talks occasionally, mindful that his grandson is still mute with loss. Amir listens, but is simply unable to reply, wishing instead to exist in his own world, where Shahla and Manuchehr are still alive.

Baba Bozorg is unusually optimistic. He is now the only person who talks about Shahla and Manuchehr. At home Shahla and Manuchehr are never mentioned, except when his grand-mother tells Amir his parents are coming home soon. That makes everyone angry, apart from Amir. She is hushed up. The whole episode becomes just that – an episode. This is survival. The executions have marked the family out, have branded them as possible traitors and so they must distance themselves from this episode for protection.

When they reach the city Baba Bozorg roars up Vali Asr, spluttering against the traffic until they turn into a side street and park the car. Amir helps Baba Bozorg set up the tent they have brought. They pitch it as near as they can get to the Prime Minister's office without being told to clear off. The guards are unsure how to react to this incongruous sight of an impeccably suited gentleman and his dumb grandson.

'Young man, we're not going anywhere. We are here to see the Prime Minister, and we are not leaving until we see him. Even if it takes 1,000 days,' Baba Bozorg booms at them whenever they get near.

With the tent pitched, Baba Bozorg strides up to the guards. 'Now if you could let us know where the nearest *hammam* is, we could really do with a wash.'

'Yes sir,' they reply respectfully, Baba Bozorg's tall stature and natural authority forcing them into capitulation. Amir feels proud to be with Baba Bozorg when he sees how the guards react to him. Baba Bozorg is his hero. But Baba Bozorg can hear the pity in the guards' voices, that such a dignified man has been reduced to sleeping in a tent.

In the morning, a guard brings tea; word has spread of the migrant visitors sleeping rough in search of hot showers and justice. Baba Bozorg has brought two folding chairs on which they sit and play backgammon as they wait. Most of the time,

Baba Bozorg's eyes are fixed on the road ahead. His son tried to persuade him to grow some Islamic stubble, the sign of a regime supporter (imitating the bearded Prophet is almost a requirement). Baba Bozorg refused. Anyway, his elegant demeanour does not lend itself well to the fundamentalist look. Of course, he is not wearing a tie, which he always does at home. Sales of ties were banned just after the revolution, and even though it is not illegal to wear them, they are seen as symbols of Western imperialism.

There had been no funeral. No grave. No bodies. Shahla and Manuchehr had vanished into the hidden recesses of the regime. It refused to release any information, apart from the brutal details of the killing. Baba Bozorg has dedicated his life to finding his daughter's body. He has written hundreds of letters, made hundreds of telephone calls. He has visited every government office, flying and sometimes driving over ten hours from Shiraz to Tehran, to sit for days in waiting rooms stuffed with people just to make appointments with incompetent secretaries. At the mention of Shahla's name doors close, telephone calls and letters are unanswered. But still he persists; his anger only intensifies. The more he begs, the more they seem to revel in denying him. Finally he has had enough of wasting time with the lackeys and the tea-makers and the paper-pushers and the petty officials with their ill-fitting suits and unkempt appearances. He has come to speak to the man who was in charge when his daughter was executed. He is going to the top.

For three nights they sleep here, waking at dawn. They keep watch during the day and in the evening they stroll the streets, always heading for Vali Asr where they have a *chelo kabab* in Nayeb Restaurant. On the fourth day they spot him. He is in a white Mercedes. A mane of thick black hair, a full beard and square-framed glasses emerge. Baba Bozorg jumps up and Amir runs behind him.

'Your honour, we have been patiently waiting for three days to talk to you. If you could be so kind as to give us a minute of your time, we would be most grateful.' Polite and firm. The man turns round, and is about to walk away as his eyes rest on Amir. 'We just want to know where my daughter is buried. Where his mother is buried.' He nods to Amir. 'That little boy needs to know where his beloved mother and father are. Please, we beg you, most humbly, with respect, from the bottom of our hearts. We are desperate. Please don't punish us any more than we have all already been punished.' Proud voice starts to tremble. 'She is called Shahla Azadi and her husband is Manuchehr Nikbakht. They were hanged in September 1988 in Evin prison. I have been to every office in the country. I have written every letter that I can write. I just want to say goodbye to my little girl.'

And without even missing a beat, the man blinks into his thick glasses as he taps Baba Bozorg on the shoulder. A dismissive, contemptuous tap. 'No. I will not tell you. Because they did wrong. Your daughter did wrong.' He looks Amir in the eye. A dismissive, contemptuous look. And with that the man turns.

The man is the Prime Minister, Mir Hossein Mousavi, under whose rule the executions happened. Amir feels salty tears on his cheeks. Baba Bozorg slumps to the ground. The guards pretend not to notice. The Islamic Republic has no mercy. Baba Bozorg never writes another letter, or makes another phone call or visits another office again.

The Prime Minister does not know it yet, but he is about to lose his office as a new constitution scraps his role. Mousavi will slip away from politics until he emerges just over twenty years later, as the figurehead and hero of the reformist movement.

He will be a beacon of democracy and freedom, his name will be chanted by thousands, by some who are prepared to die for him. He will eventually be arrested himself, and placed under house arrest, for speaking out against the crushing of protesters. The bloodletting during his time will be forgotten and forgiven. Mousavi will say he did not know of the killings.

The mass deaths served their purpose: they struck fear into the hearts of thousands. No more kitchen meetings, no more parties. Back home, Baba Bozorg is too afraid to send Amir to a child psychologist in case the psychologist is an informer. Amir moves in with his uncle and his wife, and assumes a new identity; *amoo*, uncle, is now *baba*, father. A little sister is born. Amir finds his voice and starts attending a new school where he also finds a best friend, Afshin. The two boys are inseparable. It does not take long before Amir confides to him: *They killed my parents. They hanged them in prison.* Amir never sees Afshin again; he does not return to school and his parents lodge a complaint with the headmistress. She calls Amir into her office. 'You should feel ashamed of yourself, putting us all in danger!' She is apoplectic. 'If you ever speak of your parents again, you will never be allowed back here and you will be a sad, lonely little boy, all on his own.' Amir never speaks about his parents again. Not until he meets Bahar.

It is long after Baba Bozorg's death that the regime shows mercy and reveals where his daughter's body lies. Shahla and Manuchehr are together, dumped in a crude trench that is their grave, squeezed in with thousands of others on top of them and below them and next to them. There is no mark, no stone, no sign that this is where their bones lie. It is as though they never existed. But it turns out the wasteland where Shahla and Manuchehr are buried has a name – *Lanatabad*, Land of the Damned.

Jomhouri Street, Tehran, November 2013

As Bahar disappeared through airport security, Amir wished he had told her about Ghassem. No one knew about the old man; with Bahar gone, Amir's history went back to being a shameful secret.

At first, Amir spoke to Bahar every few days, but as her life changed, they began to grow apart and the phone calls became more infrequent. A few months after her departure, he had saved enough money to travel to Turkey to apply for a US visa. His application was rejected. He promised himself that he would tell Bahar about the old man when he saw her next.

Amir felt an isolation he had not experienced since his parents' deaths. After the old man's warning, the group stopped contacting each other. There were more arrests. Bita was sentenced to five years' imprisonment, on charges of membership of the Committee of Human Rights Reporters, acts against national security and disseminating misinformation about the system. The *Filternet*, as everyone now called it, was slowed right down. Presidential elections came around again; the Voters and the Boycotters argued the same arguments they had four years earlier.

A new cycle of life began when, in June 2013, Rouhani was voted in. People were jubilant at the prospect of a President who was pushing for relations with the West. Amir and his friends emerged as emboldened and as hopeful as they had been under Khatami. The atmosphere felt freer than before, ordinary people on the streets seemed less depressed. Even those who had given up activism during Ahmadinejad's years came back out. Now they were angling for small changes; none of them wanted an Arab Spring-style revolution, the very thought of it terrified them;

they were afraid of Iran going the same way as Libya, Syria and Egypt – too fearful after the protests of 2009. They were also still too bruised and jaded by their parents' experience to think that a revolution could work. *Yavaash yavaas*, slowly slowly, is what they said.

The old man had turned up at the flat shortly after Bahar's departure. Amir was too broken to argue and let him in without resistance. The old man sat on the sofa and began to cry; Amir did not know what to do, so offered him a glass of black tea. The old man tried to talk, but Amir shut him up.

The old man's visits became one of the constants in Amir's life. They were always the same: sitting in silence, opposite each other, drinking tea. Amir and the old man who killed his parents. And every time, just before he got up to leave, the old man would ask the same question: 'Will you forgive me?'

And every time Amir would give the same reply: 'No.'

FOUR

BIJAN

Around Makhsous Street and Gomrok, south Tehran

The police chief had insisted on meeting in the park. It crossed Bijan's mind that this might be a sting; it was, to say the least, an odd choice. The Chief knew well enough that without back-up he would not be safe. Bijan had told him that even *he* might not be able to protect him. And Bijan had a busy day ahead, no time for extra drama; but the Chief had been adamant.

The park near where Bijan lived in the south of the city was where all the local small-time gangsters, pretenders, dealers, hooligans and thieves hung out. Even now that the air had begun to crackle with winter's crisp, cold breeze, they still gathered here, to hustle for work, to rob, to get stoned and to socialize. Only when the first spidery crusts of ice covered the shrivelled grass would they retreat to the tea houses and hidden opium dens nearby. The park was the kind of place Bijan avoided. Not because he was scared; far from it. He knew all the reprobates in this neighbourhood, it was *his* patch after all. But he had moved on from them, from these careless, lazy, in-and-out-of-jail drunks and addicts who had about as much nous as a three-year-old child. The one thing they did all have was an indefatigable fondness for violence and a fierce glint in their eyes, the basic qualities needed to keep them in business. They were an uncomfortable reminder of where Bijan had come from and of who he used to be.

The Chief was waiting for him on the corner of the road, under the white sky that had been streaked pale yellow by December's low, watery sun. His smile was so broad his lips looked like they might crack. It was the smug smile of the powerful and on seeing it Bijan had an instinctive urge to smack it off his face. The Chief began to strut through the park, chest puffed out, legs swinging high, as though he was on parade. Bijan had to stifle a laugh. *They're going to eat him alive*, he thought. But instead they started jumping to attention. The local heroin dealer clamped his hand to his forehead in a salute: 'Hello sir!' Even the addicts on the bench stood up and bowed their heads towards the Chief, deferentially touching their hearts. They shuffled out of the shadows of the trees, peeled themselves off the grass where they liked to gather in circles on their haunches, and they each came and paid their respects. The Chief looked at Bijan, his grin even bigger than before.

'You looked surprised!' The Chief was good at faux naif.

'What the fuck have you done to these poor bastards?'

The Chief giggled like a schoolboy. 'I took care of them. Since they've stopped listening to you, I thought I'd teach them a lesson.'

Muggings in the area had become uncontrollable. There were only so many official figures the Chief could successfully fudge without raising suspicions. Everyone knew the boys in the park were responsible, and that once upon a time those boys had been under Bijan's control. But Bijan had insisted this was no longer his beat. He was involved in more sophisticated operations these days, which the Chief respected him for.

'I suppose I'm going to have to pay you for this service.' Bijan was almost laughing – he had never seen anything like it.

'Work doesn't come for free! Now, how about a quick toke in the tea house where we can sort out business, eh?'

Bijan heard the story later; he got it out of a sixteen-year-old kid who had started selling *sheesheh*, crystal meth, in the park. The Chief had decided to teach these boys a lesson. He had gathered ten officers and local *basijis*, volunteer militiamen. Good boys he trusted. They had stormed the park, swooping on over a dozen of them. The guys had not been scared at first; when their lookouts had seen the cops coming they had simply hidden their drugs and weapons as they always did. They had even smirked at the approaching unit. 'Hello ladies, what can we do for you today?' one of the layabouts had said, imitating a camp rent boy. That is when the smirking stopped. The Chief's men rounded them up and marched them to the edge of the park, lined them up under the shade of the willow trees and pointed guns to their heads. The Chief watched as one of his men produced a glass bottle; the gang were held down as the cold, dirty vessel was thrust up each of their anuses. Every single one of them was raped. Some were silent; some screamed in pain. All were left humiliated and bleeding.

The tea house was a long, narrow, dingy room with bare light-bulbs hanging from the ceiling. A row of small tables was pushed up against the grey tiled walls and beside a silver samovar, blue and green glass hookah pipes were lined up on the floor. A patchwork of old banknotes from the Pahlavi reign was displayed under the glass top of a wooden desk by the entrance; here sat the owner, a big man with a comically large moustache and a tattooed hand that swung jade *tasbih* rosary beads between gigantic fingers. On the wall was a poster of Imam Ali with a lion at his feet; hanging inside the door, a sign: *No entry for drug addicts and those under the age of* 18.

The regulars raised their arms and nodded as Bijan and the Chief took their usual spot at the back. The talk was of a stabbing that had happened in the tea house a few years earlier.

'So your boys found Behrouz last night?' a young mechanic shouted out to the Chief.

'Nothing gets past you fishwives.'

'The Kurd told me.'

'I don't know how the Kurd does it, I suppose you know too?' the Chief was asking Bijan.

'With a little help from your boys.' They both laughed. Bijan began stirring the strong black tea that had been smacked in front of him. The news about Behrouz was the best Bijan had heard in a while.

Behrouz, a local fraudster, had knifed Hooman to death in a fight over a heroin deal. Hooman was one of Bijan's closest childhood friends and the manager of his car-washing company. The regulars had barricaded Behrouz in the tea house until the police had arrived. Behrouz was given the death penalty. Hooman's brothers received *diyeh*, blood money, for the murder, which is worked out at the current market value of either 100 camels, 200 cows or 1,000 sheep: 114 million tomans (about 30,000 US dollars), although if Hooman had been killed during the holy months his life would have been worth thirty per cent more. When Behrouz asked for a pardon, as was his legal right, Hooman's brothers agreed and told the court that they forgave Behrouz and that he should be spared execution and a lengthy prison sentence. But they had not forgiven him. They simply wanted the satisfaction of killing him themselves. They only had to wait a few years. Just three hours after Behrouz was released from prison, Hooman's brothers nailed him to a wall, slashing his throat. They smoked a cigarette as they watched the blood leak out of him.

'Chief, is it true they got Astollah?' a toothless man near the door was asking. Astollah was a big-time booze merchant who lived nearby. *They*, as always, meant *ettela'at*, intelligence. Stories abounded of dealers and smugglers caught by the security services and forced to be turncoats, spying on their own and informing on their customers.

'I got to tell my boys to keep their mouths shut, there's more gossip in here than a beauty parlour.'

Astollah had been shifting thousands of litres of alcohol a year. There is no corner of the city where booze is not bought and sold. Vodka and whisky are the bestsellers. Most of the alcohol comes from Erbil in Iraq where a bottle of Smirnoff costs six US dollars; Astollah could flog it in Tehran for thirty. He had been caught before, but had always paid his way out of lashes and a prison sentence.

'What else you got for us Chief?' asked a sixty-year-old strongman, who still travelled the country in black trousers and a vest, a leather band tied round his head, lifting improbable weights and dragging cars with his teeth. The Chief threw his hands in the air in mock exasperation, but really he loved the attention and enjoyed being the purveyor of the latest news and scandal.

'We got a mullah the other day, you know, the one that's got his face on posters all over Vali Asr.'

'Let me guess, little boys?' asked the mechanic.

'Little girls. Made one of them pregnant,' said the Chief. 'I bet you a million tomans nothing will happen to him. This is the third time he's been in. That bastard has got some friends in high places, I tell you.'

The caretaker of a mosque had discovered that a visiting cleric had been raping his two daughters in the room where the family lived; his fourteen-year-old had become pregnant. The police had been sympathetic but had told him there was nothing they could do. The cleric was untouchable. The caretaker went to see editors of magazines and newspapers, begging them to take on his case. They were all too scared. Then the cleric was caught with another child. And another. The police had finally agreed to have him arrested; but still they had little hope he would be charged.

'Who was responsible for the mosque incident?' Now the Chief wanted information.

'Why Chief, is he in trouble?'

'The opposite – I want to pat him on the back.'

The local mosque's congregation had dwindled to only a handful of faithful in recent years. Bijan hated going to the mosque, and it pained him to go into its adjoining *hosseinieh*, the congregation hall used for gatherings and religious ceremonies, which he did at least a few times a week to buy the best (and cheapest) *khoresht-e ghormeh sabzi* in the whole of Tehran, a rich, deep-green stew of herbs, dried limes, kidney beans and lamb. In an effort to drum up interest, the mosque had started broadcasting its dawn *azan* from an amplifier cranked up to full volume, through a made-in-China loudspeaker bolted to the side of the minaret, cheap plastic parts rattling away. The noise had been deafening and there were dozens of complaints. It would have been half tolerable if the muezzin did not sound like a cat being skinned alive. For someone with such a bad voice, he delivered his off-key shrieks with more confidence than Pavarotti. Even the Chief had complained. The mosque refused to turn the sound down, so the locals, some of whom had never stepped inside a mosque, began to complain in person. The man responsible for the *azan* revamp was a vindictive mullah who took great pleasure in causing a stir and waking this lazy community out of its torpor. 'You can't turn down God's message,' was the stern reply. Nothing could change his mind, not even a ribbon-tied box of his favourite golden, sticky, deep-fried *goosh-e-fil* pastry, delivered to him by an exasperated housewife.

Early the previous morning, a young man with four children and impeccable aim shot the speaker from his living-room window with an air rifle. 'That coward of a mullah won't be turning up that music again,' he had said to his wife as he placed the rifle back in its hiding place in a hole behind the sink. So far, the mullah had not dared.

Bijan and the Chief had an easy familiarity; they had both grown up in the area, an urban inner-city south Tehrani neighbourhood west of Vali Asr, not far from Monirieh Square. For decades the place had had a reputation for being a rough, crime-riddled hood, but slowly it cleaned up its act, on the surface at least. There were no obvious signs of poverty, as there were less than two miles away on Shoosh Street; the drug addicts stuck to the parks here and kept out of the way; the poorer families still had tight networks around them and so they were not yet lost to the city. Apartment blocks were built. New residents moved in, prices rose. But the same kind of people ruled these streets; they had simply retreated farther underground. Every now and then, the area's real colour would reveal itself. The last time was a gang fight over territory; a rival group from across the motorway thundered into a small street, clubs in hands, smashing every car window on their way. The police were called but did not turn up until the rampage was over; they never got involved in turf wars.

In the clutch of alleys where Bijan and the Chief lived, every other house was involved in crime, some way or other. Drugs, guns, black-market goods, knocked-off DVDs. It was just the way it was, the way it had always been. It was as though they were a tribe apart from everyone else. The community was neither religious nor particularly educated and most of them could not stand the regime. Pragmatism ran in their blood; they understood the power of money in this city, and the fact that it could buy them into the middle classes. Some who made money moved north, to stylish apartments in Shahrak-e Gharb and Sa'adat Abad. But not all of them wanted to hike up Vali Asr. There was a freedom they had on these streets that was missing in north Tehran. The people ruled here and stuck together. It was not the same as the high-rise living in the more salubrious parts, where everyone was hidden indoors or trapped in cars.

After the war with Iraq, thousands of Iranians travelled to Japan, and it was there that Bijan and the Chief really got to know each other, in their early twenties. They had both returned from the front lines to a jobless country shattered by war. Visa restrictions for Iranians had been lifted by Japan in the early 1970s following the world oil crisis. Japan's economy had been almost entirely dependent on imported oil and was hit hard; it needed to ingratiate itself with Middle Eastern nations and distance itself from American foreign policy. By the late 1980s, Japan's economy had peaked and Iranians were eager and willing to provide cheap manual labour. They did the work the Japanese were not willing to do, known as the '3K' jobs, because they were *kitanai* (dirty), *kitsui* (difficult) and *kurushii* (painful). When visas become compulsory for Iranian citizens, they simply stayed on and the police turned a blind eye. At one point, 500 Iranians were going to Japan every week and thousands were overstaying their visas. Most of them worked on construction sites, returning home with money, contacts and wild tales of womanizing. But before long, men like the Chief became involved in scams that were more lucrative, more fun and not so '3 K'. The Chief made his money in counterfeit phone cards. When seedier possibilities emerged, hundreds of boys from around the hood flew over; the Japanese underworld throbbed with Iranian crooks and pimps barging in on the action. Bijan was enlisted as a footsoldier in the yakuza, Japan's own mafia. It was here that he met many of the men he would later hire, tough guys pumped up on steroids and hulking tree-trunk-necked wrestlers – men who were used to the rough, knife-wielding ways of south Tehran streets. The yakuza snapped up these south Tehrani thugs, deploying them as their heavies; Bijan and the boys liked to say the Japanese police were more scared of the Iranians than they were of the yakuza. Both Bijan and the Chief were deported from Japan in one of the crackdowns on illegal immigrants. The Chief's uncle was in the police force and made sure his favourite nephew was given a job and that his records were cleared of all trace of his Japan jaunt; people knew what hard-nosed goons like the Chief got up to in the Land of the Rising Sun.

Bijan slid a stack of greens across the table, the Chief's monthly hush money. The cloudy water in the hookah pipe purred as it bubbled up. He drew in a mouthful of smoke.

'They're going to raid Chahar Dongeh soon. Don't have any details yet,' said the Chief.

'Shit. How long d'you think I've got?'

'At least a week.'

Bijan took out another wad of notes from his jacket pocket. 'Much obliged.'

Bijan had moved on to drugs and he had set up a meth lab in

a disused warehouse in Chahar Dongeh, a small, ragged industrial town just south of Tehran. As the country's economy was flailing in the wake of stricter sanctions, the illegal drugs trade was booming. Sanctions were not new to Iran; they started when the US froze Iran's assets during the hostage crisis over thirty years ago. The Europeans soon joined in, punishing Iran for its nuclear enrichment programme (which it has always maintained is for peaceful energy purposes). Oil exports were slashed to a third, and as sanctions triggered inflation, the poor and vulnerable were predictably affected. The price of some foods more than doubled in a year; staples like Tabrizi feta cheese, fruit and meat became unaffordable for so many. But the price of drugs had barely changed. Iran's meth empire was expanding at an astonishing rate. It was easy and cheap; the chemical needed to make crystal meth was legal and, as the Islamic Republic was one of the highest importers of the chemical in the world, there was lots of the stuff around. The head of the anti-narcotics unit had just declared that Iran was the fifth-highest consumer of crystal meth in the world. Bijan's operation was growing by the day.

In Iran, *sheesheh* has become the most popular drug after opium, heroin coming in a close third, not least because *sheesheh* is cheap – a gram costs about five US dollars. Bijan's dealers in Tehran sold *sheesheh* to all types, including rich girls who used it to keep their weight down and trainers who bought it for their athletes. A champion wrestler had been banned for life after having tested positive for D-methamphetamine.

Bijan was now sending some of his guys to sell in Malaysia and Thailand. The average price of meth pills in Malaysia was at least fives times more than in Iran, and Iranian meth labs and dealers were setting up shop all over Asia – a move Bijan was considering.

When Bijan started to make good money, he realized he needed a legitimate business, a front. He opened a car wash that had a surprisingly high turnover. If any of his friends hit hard times, he sent them to work at the car wash. It was the perfect cover. Bijan knew he had to be careful. The government was fighting its crystal meth problem with vigour. The previous year, Tehran's governor had announced that 145 crystal meth labs in Tehran had been busted; by the first three months of this year, the number was already at seventy-seven. The authorities also claimed to be arresting thirty drug dealers and addicts every hour.

Now he had been tipped off by the Chief, Bijan would shut everything down for a few weeks and start up again somewhere else. He needed to see the Kurd in Gomrok, but first he would stop off to see his best friend Kambiz.

Early-morning rush hour had smeared the air with thick smog; it hung low, obscuring the city that rose up behind Bijan and stretched out in front of him. The pollution was so bad this morning that schools had been closed.

He walked along a litter-strewn road, past a homeless junkie in a red coat rifling through an overflowing bin. Kambiz was sitting in his glass-fronted office, full of old furniture, bags of rice and knocked-off silverware. He was leaning back in his chair behind his paper-scattered desk, feet up, watching a small television attached to the wall opposite him; *Jumong* was playing, a South Korean drama series about one of the ancient kingdoms of Korea that had been a nationwide sensation.

'You lazy bastard, when you going to actually do some work?'

Kambiz jumped up, laughing, 'At least I haven't turned into a fat old bastard.' He pinched Bijan's stomach. The best friends could not have looked more different: Kambiz was muscular with slicked-back hair and always wore a suit. Bijan had a big belly, a balding head and always wore T-shirt, jeans and trainers.

After Japan, Kambiz worked for the Kurd before getting in with some human-traffickers, arranging Iranians to be transported all over the world. He found the work depressing, and, crucially, the profit margins were getting smaller. He then got involved in the kidnap and ransom game, targeting rich businessmen. Nobody knew exactly how many people were getting kidnapped, because more often than not the victim's family were too scared to call the police and only too willing to hand over mounds of cash for the speedy release of their loved one (another plus point). One group had made a million US dollars on one businessman alone.

Bijan had never been tempted by the kidnapping business, and he was not averse to lecturing Kambiz on the immorality of taking someone's freedom. When Kambiz argued with him, reminding him that the guns and the drugs Bijan sold were robbing people of their lives, Bijan would start shouting in self-righteous rage, defending his work. Kambiz would laugh hysterically; he enjoyed winding Bijan up. 'You're a tart with a heart but no goddam brain!' he would say to him.

'You sorted out the mess?' asked Bijan.

'No, and it ain't looking good.' Kambiz was shaking his head.

For the last few weeks, Kambiz's group had been holding a middle-aged carpet merchant hostage, chained to a radiator in the basement of a building that belonged to Kambiz's uncle. The carpet seller's family were not paying up; instead they kept trying to negotiate the price down. Kambiz was scared it was a police ploy, that they were biding their time.

Bijan gave Kambiz the news about the impending raid in Chahar Dongeh as Kambiz's nephew had started working in the meth lab.

'I'll tell him to stay away. Send my love to the Kurd.' The men hugged and Bijan stepped back onto the road. He bought a newspaper from a kiosk to check the pollution levels, which were reported daily. Today there were no figures. The previous evening, the Supreme National Security Council had sent a fax to every newspaper in Tehran banning them from disclosing the pollution levels for the next two months of *Azar*, December, and *Dey*, January, when the toxins in the air were at their most concentrated, winter's cloud cover not allowing the pollution to escape. Journalists had been warned: *Siah-namaaee nakoneed.* Do not blacken the Islamic Republic.

Tehran's pollution seems to worsen every year. Not only are there too many cars, but the sloping valley with mountains on each side is a perfect trap for the fumes and smoke. Because the country has limited capacity to refine its own oil and petrol imports have been hit by sanctions, cars in Tehran run on low-quality, poorly refined fuel.

Bijan waded into the filthy air. He walked past a wall daubed with graffiti: FUCK was scrawled in English, and beside it in Persian: IN MEMORY OF JAPAN. Two teenagers in hoodies with long black 'emo' haircuts stood in a doorway selling bags of *sheesheh*. He turned into Gomrok, where his criminal career had begun. During the Shah's time, the bordellos of the red-light district of Shahr-e No had stood here, next door to one of the city's most exclusive cabaret clubs, Shoukoufeh-ye-No. The area had brimmed with underworld bosses, pimps, pickpockets and revellers. Like many men of his time, Bijan's father liked to recall how he lost his virginity to a Shahr-e No prostitute. After the revolution, the brothels were bulldozed and burnt down and some of the working girls were executed. But Gomrok had retained an edge; an undercurrent of illegal activity still surged through the road, even if it had officially gone legit. Now motor-bike showrooms have replaced many of the original shops on

Gomrok, but a batch still remain, a long parade mostly selling army surplus goods. They are stuffed with gas masks, desert boots, gloves, Russian army uniforms and rucksacks with MADE IN KNOXVILLE, USA labels. Some of them sell second-hand trainers and shoes, freshly stolen from outside mosques while the owners are busy praying.

A dozen shovels were propped up in front of the Kurd's shop; they had last been used to dig trenches during the war with Iraq. Between white and black hard hats, yellow wellington boots and a stack of traffic cones, the Kurd was sitting on a three-legged stool. He was a short, small man with a silken white beard and pale crinkled skin; he wore a khaki parka and a skullcap on his head. A gas stove was burning in the middle of the shop for heat, in the back a chicken was clucking. The shop smelt of cigarettes and lamb *kabab*, two of Bijan's favourite smells.

'Hello sunshine, how you doing?' Bijan kissed the Kurd on the cheeks. The Kurd hugged him and gave him a glass of strong black tea.

When Bijan was kicked out of Japan, Kambiz had sent him to see the Kurd. The Kurd had a network of nephews and cousins who smuggled guns over from Iraq, but as they had become increasingly involved in fighting the Turkish government with the Kurdistan Workers' Party, known as the PKK, the Kurd started hiring new gun-runners. It was dangerous work – the penalty for smuggling illegal firearms is death – but the money was excellent. Bijan's family had known the Kurd all their lives. Everyone trusted the Kurd and Bijan was known to be trustworthy. He started making monthly visits to Baneh, a town in Iranian Kurdistan, not far from the border with Iraq. Sometimes he travelled on horses or mules across the mountains, other times he was hidden in the back of trucks. He would return to

Tehran with all kinds of weapons and bury them in his mother's garden, where the Kurd would send buyers. Mostly they were drug lords and gangsters, but there was the occasional bent cop and *basiji* gone wild.

'I heard what happened to Behrouz last night,' said Bijan.

'Bet you haven't heard about the Farshad boy though,' the Kurd chuckled. He always knew the news before anyone else did.

'Don't tell me they already got him?'

'Yep. The cops found his body a few hours ago. They'd chopped off his dick and shoved it in his mouth.' Bijan grimaced. 'Any of the Radan boys been arrested yet?'

'No, and they won't be. Everyone knows Behrouz deserved it.'

The Radans were a band of ten brothers who had all followed the family tradition of selling opium, which now costs 3,600,000 to five million tomans a kilo, depending on quality (about 1,200 US dollars to just over 1,600 dollars). As well as having close ties to several high-ranking policemen, the Radan brothers had links with influential Baluchi tribal elders in Sistan and Baluchestan, the wild-east province that borders Afghanistan and Pakistan. Twice a year the Radans would drive through the desert, load up a truck with giant slabs of opium and bring it back to the city. They had begun selling to a small-time dealer called Farshad who had grown up in the neighbourhood. Bijan remembered playing football with him as a kid. Farshad was a good goalie but a sloppy dealer, leaving a litter of evidence behind him. But his real downfall was greed. He had evaded paying off the necessary officials on whose radar he had flashed up. What made it worse was that he was not arrested on his own patch, but in the suburbs of Tehran Pars, in the east of the city. Farshad only had a small amount of drugs on him, so the police agreed to cut him a deal if he gave them some big names; he promptly grassed on the Radan brothers. Based on the information Farshad gave, two of the Radan brothers were given death sentences. Farshad had chosen to forget their rule. When dealing with the police, the boys had one rule: the No Rule. In Iran, the 'no' gesture is a backward tilt of the head. With the No Rule, you had to imagine the tip of a sword was touching your chin as you were being questioned. If you said yes, your head would fall on the sword.

'The Chief told me they're going to raid Chahar Dongeh. He says we've got a week. He doesn't know any more than that, but the boys have to go underground. I've been to see Kambiz, he says hello.'

'Love that kid. I'll send word to the others.' Neither the Kurd nor Bijan ever used their mobile phones or emails for serious business.

'I'm going to go there today. Make sure everything's out and clear.'

'They may be watching it already. I worry about you.'

'Don't worry *amoo*, you know how careful I am. Let them watch. There'll be nothing to see and everyone's sweet.'

Bijan's father had died when he was thirteen; the Kurd treated him like a son. Now that Bijan was making good money, he made sure the Kurd and his family were looked after.

'In case the heat is on, we should hide the next consignment, it's due tonight,' said the Kurd.

'What you got?'

'A dozen Colts.' The Kurd had been shifting military stock and industrial equipment for thirty years; but the real money he made was from illegal arms sales. He could sell a Colt for anything from one and a half to two million tomans. A hitman along with a Colt cost ten million tomans, but the Kurd had never been involved in that part of it. If customers ever asked him, he shrugged his shoulders. But, like everyone else involved in this business, he knew who did it; a few of them hung out at the tea house.

'No problem *amoo*, tell them to take it to *maman*'s house.'

Bijan's mobile rang. It was Asal.

'The women still got you by the balls.' The Kurd winked.

'Just the way I like it!'

The Kurd tried to shove some notes into Bijan's hand, but he refused, kissing him on the head.

Bijan was late for Asal and she would not be happy. He did not have time to go home and pick up his car, so he stepped out onto the road to flag down a taxi. The pollution was getting worse as the day wore on. The acrid smell of old petrol and regurgitated car fumes burnt his lungs. Everyone's organs were struggling to digest the poisonous particles that stuck to the city; they were praying for a breeze to nudge the dangerous fog out of the valley.

Bijan had been seeing Asal for over a year, after she had brought her car to be cleaned at the car wash. She had a small waist, enormous breasts and was wearing crimson lipstick. He had asked her out on the spot, in the only way he knew how: 'Listen gorgeous, I'm not good at smooth talking, but I love the way you look. I want to take you out. Everyone in the neighbourhood knows me, you'll be totally safe. Give me a chance.' He cracked a few jokes and then stood smiling at her – a huge, warm smile with a lustful look in his eyes. Asal was flattered and disarmed by his openness. Over dinner at the Azari Café, a traditional restaurant in the tented garden of an old building on the southernmost end of Vali Asr, where the brick walls were covered in black and white photos of wrestling champions, he rubbed her thigh under the table as a group of musicians played classical Persian music. After their meal they reclined on a cushioned bed, smoking from a hookah pipe and staring at each other. 'Sweetheart, I'll cut to the chase. I'm a horny guy. I'd love to have you in my life. I just need to be looked after a few times a week and in return I'll look after you for as long as you want me.' Asal agreed straight away. She had been widowed in her early twenties when her husband had died in a car crash, leaving her with a small son and no money. Her family were poor. Her job as a dentist's receptionist did not pay the bills. Her marriage prospects were dire. They had sex that night and Bijan knew he had made the right choice. She was desperate to please him; it was the best sex he had ever had. Soon after, he housed her and her child in a small apartment he bought just off Imam Khomeini Street. Asal fell in love with Bijan quickly. She spent much of the money he gave her on lingerie and expensive foods to cook for him. After enduring six months of marriage hints, Bijan finally told Asal the truth: he was married with three children. Asal was devastated. But not angry enough to end the relationship. Bijan was finally honest with her. 'I'll never leave my wife; but as long as I have blood running through these veins, I will look after you.'

Bijan was as cunning and sly at evading detection by his wife as he was by the police. He had two mobiles, one for his wife and one for Asal. He made sure Asal never found out his home address, and did not let her mix with his friends. Bijan's wife was his childhood sweetheart. It was a marriage of love, but sex with her had always been dull. The older she got, the fatter she got, and the less attractive Bijan found her. He had never been faithful to her. It was as simple as that. But he adored her. He was respectful enough to carefully guard his indiscretions. Three times a week he would see Asal in the afternoon. Bijan loved films and sometimes he would take her to the Mellat Cinema multiplex. Bijan prided himself on appreciating the subtleties and artistic vision of Iranian cinema. He watched everything by Abbas Kiarostami, although he preferred comedies, like Kamal Tabrizi's *Marmoulak*, 'The Lizard', about a convict who escapes from prison by dressing up as a mullah. But Hollywood films were his favourite. He had seen *Titanic* a dozen times. Bijan had even once found out about auditions that were held in his area, and had got a small talking part as a local gangster. He had taken all the boys to see it on the big screen; they teased him for years afterwards, nicknaming him Mr Hollywood.

Bijan and Asal usually headed straight for the bedroom when he visited; afterwards they would eat in front of an episode of *Miss Marple* on television. But today Asal opened the door with swollen red eyes and smudged make-up.

Just before Asal met Bijan, she had been having sex with a married dentist at the practice where she worked. She abhorred the man, but he had forced her, threatening to have her sacked unless she slept with him. Asal had barely enough money to survive as it was, and jobs for women like her were scarce. He took advantage of her for a year, in between his appointments. He had left the practice just before Asal had met Bijan, but last night he had called her to say he was returning to his old job, and that he was looking forward to seeing her.

Bijan was raging. Asal tried to calm him. She knew what Bijan did for a living and the kind of people he associated with; she did not want to get Bijan in trouble or the dentist killed. Bijan extracted all the information he needed, as he always did, and gave Kambiz a call. Kambiz said he would put two of his boys on the case straight away.

*

There was still Chahar Dongeh to sort out. Bijan was relieved to be driving out of Tehran and away from the bad air that had left him with burning eyes and a stinging throat. He put a DVD of Persian music into the car stereo for the journey, and he started shouting out the words to an anti-regime rap song that was pounding out of the speakers. A group called Anonymous Sinners had used a sample of a haunting chant from one of Iran's most famous war songs, an ode to a brave volunteer fighter of the Iran–Iraq war, Mohammad Jahan-Ara. He had commanded the defence and recapture of the south-western city of Khorramshahr in an epic battle. Jahan-Ara had pushed back Saddam Hussein's army with a ragtag of untrained boys and men, and had been one of the last soldiers to leave the city before it fell to the Iraqis. But Jahan-Ara did not live to see the city's liberation, and the song was in his honour, lamenting his death, sung in the Ashura *sinezani*, rhythmic chest-beating style: *Mammad, if only you had lived to see the city is free!* Now Anonymous Sinners told Mammad how proud he would have been had he lived: *there's no prostitution, no drugs, press freedom, food and jobs, oil money for everyone, people are so happy they never complain…*and so the list went sarcastically on, making sure Mammad knew he was better off dead.

As Bijan drove farther south, the city's buildings slowly receded into rubbish-strewn arable land; thousands of plastic bags bobbed along the dirt into the horizon. It was as though the city had vomited out its guts and they had landed here; car factories, gas tanks, water tanks, wasteland bordered by barbed-wire fences and Portakabins flashed past. On a small patch of scrubland beside the motorway, a family had laid out a *sofreh*, picnic blanket, and were eating *abgoosht*, a hearty peasant dish of meat, beans and potatoes; nothing could get in the way of an Iranian and a picnic, not even six lanes of roaring traffic.

There were a few miles of respite when nature reclaimed the land, where wheat fields, walnut and fir trees stretched out ahead; orchards of apples, cherries and pears and carpets of mint, coriander and basil; until the squalor of urban life rose up again from the ground as Bijan entered Chahar Dongeh. Dilapidated buildings, pitted roads and mounds of rocky earth surrounded him. In the centre of town a huge billboard loomed overhead with a message from the government: IF YOU SUPPORT THE SUPREME LEADER YOUR COUNTRY WILL NOT COME TO HARM.

He drove down a lonely, shabby road where a few old men in rags were carting rubbish in wheelbarrows and giant trolleys, to be sifted and sold. Some carefully displayed their detritus on the ground. A group of Afghan workers with bandannas tied round their heads mooched past. Bijan got out of his car to buy some pomegranates from a man in a seventies flying jacket who was selling them out of the back of his pick-up truck. Six tired, worn sofas bundled on vans wobbled past them. Bijan always tried to do some shopping when he came to Chahar Dongeh; everything was cheaper here, including the drugs and women. The grocery shops still sold opium as if it were milk.

As Bijan opened his car door to get back in, he saw them walking towards him, two *basijis*. He whacked the door shut so hard the car rocked. It was a while since he had played the tough guy; he had missed it. There was nobody he hated more than small-town *basijis*. He stared straight at them

'That T-shirt is illegal!' one of them screamed. Bijan was wearing his favourite T-shirt; white with the letters 'USA' emblazoned on the front and back. Bijan's dream was one day to live in America.

'It's apostasy!' screamed the other.

This is going to be fun, thought Bijan.

'You have to burn your T-shirt right now, in front of us!'

'Listen closely you pair of illiterate faggots.' Bijan took a step towards the boys. 'If you want to burn my T-shirt, first I suggest you go to the store at the end of this road and burn every single packet of USA-made Winston cigarettes in there. Then, when you're done, I suggest you go to Karaj dam, which provides us all with electricity. And guess what? You'll find Morrison of the USA made it, so you'll have to burn that down too. Next, may I suggest a visit to the airport where you can burn the Boeings, the F-4s, the F-5s and the F-14s. Guess why? Oh yes, they're from the US of A. Once you've burnt all of them, then you can come and pour gasoline right over my body and burn the T-shirt from off my FUCKING BACK!' The boys were edging away. They knew a real thug when they saw one.

'You're crazy, he's fucking crazy.'

'Yeh, I'm fucking crazy. Next time I see you, I'll rip your fucking testicles off,' Bijan laughed as they turned on their heels.

He drove for another ten minutes through the wretched streets. He spotted his first lookout, who nodded. He could see the warehouse ahead, in the corner of a derelict plot of land the size of two football pitches. They had an excellent safety record and produced high-purity, good-quality meth. He only used a handful of people he knew and paid them well. He was proud of his operation. As he parked the car, another lookout walked towards him.

'Sir, everything's already been cleared. We got word this afternoon.' The warehouse was spotless. The Kurd was always one step ahead. Bijan tipped the lookout and smiled as he got back into his car.

Tehran's yellow lights were glimmering in the distance. He put in a CD of his favourite underground music, turned up the stereo and rapped along to a song by Hichkas:

> *This is Tehran*
> *A city that tempts you till it saps your soul*
> *And makes you see you were always meant to be*
> *Nothing more than dirt*

As he entered the city, Kambiz rang and told him to drive to a road off Pirouzi Street, in the east of town. When Bijan arrived, Kambiz's boys were waiting on a motorbike. One of them was an ex-soldier who also moonlighted doing night shifts as armed security for a crime syndicate that sold drugs under a motorway flyover in north Tehran. They would act as lookouts and protection as the dealers traded on a lay-by. It was a busy spot where two motorways converged, so there was a constant stream of customers; two o'clock in the morning was peak time.

When Kambiz's boys saw Bijan, they walked up to a small, two-storey house and knocked on the front door. The dentist opened it. They dragged him onto the street and started beating him. They broke both the dentist's arms and knocked out four of his teeth. Bijan watched from his car, all his nervous tension melting away. On his drive home, he called his wife and told her to stop cooking and leave the kids with his mother; tonight he was taking her for supper to Café Azeri on Vali Asr.

FIVE

LEYLA

Imam Khomeini Street, south Tehran, Motahari Street
(Takht-e Tavous), midtown and Sa'adat Abad, north Tehran

Leyla was on her knees. Her hands gripped the edge of the brown velvet sofa. She flicked her hair over her back and arched her round bottom upwards. Taymour dropped his iPhone slightly as he started to pound faster. The small tea glasses on the side table chinked as the sofa rocked against it. On cue, Leyla started to moan loudly. Taymour grabbed her hair, pulling back her head. Then it was over. A few seconds of silence before the electricity meter on the wall clicked it away. Taymour threw her a towel and Leyla wiped herself down and put on her clothes. And so began Leyla's career as a porn actress.

In truth, she was a prostitute who made home sex movies, but in her mind she was a porn actress. That is because making home-made porn changed Leyla's life. She no longer felt like a prostitute; she was an actress, she told herself. And, more importantly, she was earning three times the money she could get from turning tricks. The grainy film she made with Taymour was an underground hit. Which meant she was a step nearer to fulfilling her dreams – of giving up hooking and setting up a happy home with a rich husband.

Leyla grew up a lower-middle-class kid in a middle-class

neighbourhood in north-west Tehran. Her childhood was like thousands of others. Her mother was a secretary. Her father was an administrator in a bank who worked as a chauffeur to supplement the family income. If there was extra money, holidays were spent in a cheap chalet in Babolsar, a resort town on the Caspian coast. At the weekend, on Fridays, they picnicked in Park-e Mellat on Vali Asr.

Leyla was still a little child when her parents began to despise each other. It had dawned on Leyla's mother that her husband would never amount to much, and that life would always consist of juggling their debts to stay afloat. It had dawned on Leyla's father that his sex life would never recover after Leyla's birth. He also realized there was a direct relation between the passage of time and nagging; the older his wife got, the more she nagged and belittled him. The few happy moments gave way to arguments and bitterness. They both took lovers. Leyla's older sister escaped by marrying a doctor and moving out of the city, to the wealthy manicured suburbs of Lavasan. The doctor's parents had tried to talk their son out of marrying beneath him, the daughter of a driver, but he had stood firm. To everyone's relief, Leyla's parents finally divorced when she was sixteen. Her parents soon both remarried, her father to a jealous young wife who forbade him from keeping in touch with his family.

By that time Leyla had fallen in love with a wild boy rebel. Babak was a year older and a teenage girl's dream. He had a rap group, a nose job and wore his Versace sunglasses even when it was dark. He had once deejayed at an underground rave in a car park, and still rode the wave of the fame that episode had brought him. Leyla and Babak had met at the food court in the Jaam-e Jam shopping centre on the north of Vali Asr, where gangs of teenage boys and girls flirted, swapped numbers and drank milkshakes after school. Their pairing was inevitable; Leyla was the prettiest girl of her year. She looked like she had been dipped in caramel: honey-highlighted hair, toffee-dyed eyebrows and a gold tan. She spent most summers sunbathing at her local public swimming pool, slathering baby oil that she spiked with coffee granules, tea and chillies (a secret recipe that ensured maximum tanning) over her body. As soon as the autumn months began to suck the bronzed colour from her skin, she slathered herself with fake tan instead.

The first time they had sex was in Babak's father's car. The second time was in her bedroom when her mother had gone to check out the Hyperstar supermarket Carrefour that had opened in the west of the city. They fell in love the way teenagers do, with a dramatic intensity that masked any lack of substance. They had enough in common that mattered to teenagers in their circle: a love of parties, irrepressible vanity and an unquenchable need for conspicuous consumption. Clothes were from Sisley and Diesel on Africa Boulevard (which they all still called by its pre-revolution name of Jordan Street), Debenhams on Vali Asr, or bought from the upmarket shopping malls in Shahrak-e Gharb. The girls spent a fortune on make-up, the boys on cars, souping up their Peugeots. They would meet at Niayesh Highway to race them at four in the morning when the roads were empty; every once in a while there would be a fatal accident, but a few weeks later they would be back. All of them spent money on cosmetic surgery; a nose job was *de rigueur*.

A year after they met, Leyla and Babak got married. Neither of them had wanted marriage at such a young age, but it was the only way they could live together and act as a normal couple without being judged or arrested. It was also a way for Leyla to build a new life away from the miserable home she had grown up in. Leyla's parents had never been interested in their children, and although her mother tried to talk her out of marrying young, Leyla was stubborn and in love. Babak's parents had always spoilt him and told him he could have anything he wanted; this now included a wife.

Babak's father made enough money from a pizza delivery business to be able to look after his family. He paid Babak and Leyla's rent for a small apartment in Vanak, north Tehran. Babak wanted to become a pop star, but he did not have the right connections or the talent. When the allowance from his father vanished, Babak borrowed money to start an auto-glass business. It failed, as did every other business he touched. He was better at partying than making money, so they danced at the weekends and smoked *sheesheh*. By now Leyla was working as a secretary and was paying off Babak's debts. Resentment quickly found its way into their lives. They started to fight. Once Babak whacked Leyla so hard he gave her a black eye. She ran to the police. They sent her home; they had enough on their plates without a moaning housewife dragging her dirty laundry through the station.

Less than a year later it was all over. Leyla had come home to find Babak having sex with his cousin in their bed. She could have put up with the occasional fist fight and verbal abuse. But she had been a friend of Babak's cousin and the betrayal was too much to bear.

Babak refused to give Leyla a divorce. Her *mehrieh* prenuptial agreement had been set at 1,500 gold coins, an ostentatious show of wealth rather than a real indicator of what Babak's family were prepared to pay. Babak made it clear that if Leyla wanted a divorce, she would have to forgo her *mehrieh*. They threatened each other with court action and accusations that could get both of them thrown in prison, until Leyla could take no more. She left with nothing. By now she was no longer speaking to her mother. Rent had nearly tripled in one year alone. Leyla could not afford north Tehran, or the northern suburbs where she had grown up. Her best friend, Parisa, suggested looking farther south; it was where she had first rented a place after her own marriage ended. Leyla sold her jewellery and used the money for a deposit on a small studio flat near Imam Khomeini Street, which cost her 600,000 tomans a month. She heard the whispers immediately after she moved in. That she was a whore and a husband-stealer. Within a month, two married men had already asked her for sex. The words had been branded on her like an indelible stain.

In Tehran complaining is a way of life. And Tehranis make excellent complainers. The rich complain about Western policies affecting their businesses, the poor complain about the rising price of food, drug addicts complain of the wildly fluctuating purity of smack that could end their lives with a single hit. And everyone complains about the traffic, pollution, parking spaces, queue-jumping, inflation and politics. Every year there is more to complain about, more to be miserable about. Complaining ambushes conversations – a constant reminder of all that is rotten.

The day after Leyla's boss complained about sanctions, he slashed her pay by over a third. Overnight her salary went from 800,000 tomans a month to just 500,000. Overnight she could no longer afford her shoebox of an apartment. Leyla was forced to call her mother, who told her to call her father. Leyla's father felt guilty for having neglected his children and he gave her half the cash he had in his account, but that was only one million tomans, barely enough to get by for a couple of months. Leyla could move farther south where the rents were cheaper, but the thought of living near Shoosh, the road at the end of Vali Asr, scared her. People were too different there. If her neighbours in Imam Khomeini questioned her morals for being a single divorcee in fashionable clothes, she could not bear to think what would happen to her in Shoosh. She called Parisa, one of the only women she knew who lived on her own, and asked if she could stay with her while she decided what to do.

Parisa was a *palang*, a panther, the nickname given to women who dressed like her. A suitable moniker, for *palangs* looked as though they could pounce at any moment and claw at you with their acrylic talons. They were a step up from the *Beesto-Panj-e Shahrivar* girls, more petulant and more overtly sexual. The look was nineties porn star: blonde hair, skin pumped with Botox, biscuit-coloured tans and engorged lips that had either borne the brunt of a syringe full of collagen or whose outside rim had been stabbed by lip liner. They wore Perspex stripper-style shoes in the summer and thigh-length boots in winter, always visible under their short, belted *manteaus* that flapped open. They shared the same love of cosmetic surgery as other Tehranis, but they favoured implants and liposuction along with the requisite nose job. Ten years ago *palangs* were confined to north Tehran, but now they were everywhere, blow-up dolls teetering around town, prowling among the poor and wealthy alike. They could even be spotted grinding their six-inch stilettos into the streets of south Tehran.

Parisa had grown up in Tehran Pars, a working-class suburb in the east of the city, and had progressed to a small flat in Sa'adat Abad, a middle-class, north-western neighbourhood encircled by motorways, west of Vali Asr. Because of the Allameh Tabatabai University, locals were used to students and to renting *khuneh mojaradi*, homes for single people. It was an up-and-coming area, filled with upwardly mobile Tehranis, many of whom had climbed their way out of working-class suburbs. The recent surge in *dolati*, government workers, and self-made businessmen rich from the construction boom had pushed up the price of rents; even a few Porsches had made their way onto Sa'adat Abad's streets, the poorer show-offs resorting to leasing Dodges in Dubai and driving them over. Neighbours held different ideologies and politics, but they shared the same ambitions.

Parisa spent her days tattooing eyebrows and administering 'Hollywood' and 'Brazilian' bikini waxes in a beauty salon that had, for a while, offered *sheesheh* as a slimming aid. She earned more than Leyla, but still not enough to cover her rent and expenses. She had told Leyla that her parents helped her, but that was a lie. Her parents had no money to give. After a week of late-night conversations in which the girls updated each other about men and swapped stories of their miserable childhoods, Parisa revealed her secret. She had been working as a private lap dancer to pay the bills and cover her cosmetic procedures, her most recent being cheek and chin implants. She offered Leyla a gig. It would be dancing at a party at the weekend. They would make 50,000 tomans each, not including tips.

'Oh my God. Do I have to take off my clothes?'

'If you flash your tits you'll get a bigger tip, and if you make it look like the films and wear sexy underwear, they'll pay us at least double. They're good guys, we'll be safe. It's like going to a party.'

The party was for a group of middle-aged *bazaari* men in suits who were celebrating a birthday. They knocked back vodka shots and drank neat Ballantine's whisky at the kitchen bar. What the men lacked in charm, they made up for in humour. They were bawdy and fun, bantering with the girls and throwing around innuendos and jokes about sex and mullahs: 'After a mullah finishes a long sermon on the merits of the *hejab*, a woman approaches him and says: "I'm so pious, I wear my headscarf even inside my own house – how will I be rewarded?" The mullah replies: "God will give you the keys to paradise." A second woman approaches him and says: "I want you to know I wear my chador inside my house." The mullah tells her: "You too will be given the keys to paradise." A third woman comes forward and says: "I don't bother with any of it in my home." The mullah says to her: "Here are the keys to *my* house!"'

When everyone was drunk, they moved into the living room. Chairs lined the walls and flashing disco lights had been set up. The girls started to dance to Iranian pop songs interspersed with Euro-hits and Beyoncé. The men cheered when the girls took off their tops. The rest happened naturally. Parisa was right, it felt like just another party, only speeded up. Parisa disappeared into a room with one of the men – another secret she had not told Leyla. The girls left just before dawn, Leyla clutching an envelope stuffed with money.

Hung-over and drinking coffee the next afternoon, Parisa and Leyla dissected the details of the night, laughing at the men's crude jokes. Leyla finally asked what she had wanted to know since they had left the party.

'How did you get into that?'

'Can't you guess?'

'Not the *street*?'

'Of course. That's the only way to build up your own client list. It doesn't take long.' Leyla silently stirred sugar into her latte, watching the milky-brown swirl. She looked up at Parisa.

'Where?'

'Takht-e Tavous Street. You'll be fine, I promise. You'll meet some nice girls down there.'

Leyla was not surprised by the location. Nor was she particularly surprised to learn that Parisa had been paying her rent by streetwalking.

It is impossible to escape sex in Tehran. Everybody knows that the streets are full of working girls. Prostitutes are part of the landscape, blending in with everything else. Pornographic photos are blue-toothed across the city, strangers send obscene images to strangers sitting opposite them on the underground, or in a café, or passing in the streets. Internet chat rooms and social sites are full of hook-ups and file shares for sex. Triple X porn channels are beamed in by satellite, the channels unlocked for a premium price by black-market television technicians. The regime valiantly goes into battle against sex. It is obsessed by how its people are having it and whom they are having it with. Lawmakers and scholars devote hours to discussing sex, philosophizing sex, condemning sex, sentencing sex. Mullahs issue countless fatwas on it; some have become the stuff of legend. One of the nation's favourites astounded with its specificity. Issued shortly after the revolution, it was a hypothetical scenario raised on television by a cleric called Ayatollah Gilani: *If you are a young man sleeping in your bedroom and your aunt is sleeping in the bedroom directly below, and there's an earthquake and the floor collapses, causing you to fall directly on top of her, and if you should both be naked, and you happen to have an erection, and you happen to land on her so that you unintentionally penetrate her, would the child of such an encounter be legitimate or a bastard?*

Prostitution is so ubiquitous on the streets – with the average age of girls starting out only sixteen – that the authorities are wringing their hands at what to do. The Interior Ministry has suggested rounding the women up and taking them to a specially designated camp where they can be 'reformed'.

*

Leyla took a bus to just over halfway down Vali Asr. Here, splintering east, is a criss-cross of main roads that eventually feeds into downtown Tehran, leading south to the bazaar. This is where the city's heart starts to really beat. Older residents remember how, sixty years ago, before the masses began their northbound migration up the social ladder, it used to be the refined north – suburban and underpopulated. Now the city rages on its streets and in its alleys. Takht-e Tavous, 'Peacock Throne' Street, had been renamed Motahari Street after the revolution, in memory of the cleric Morteza Motahari, a disciple of Khomeini who was assassinated by a member of the fundamentalist Islamic Forqan group in 1979. The street still clings on to its old identity, and many call it by its old name.

For once, Leyla was thankful for the traffic, even though the summer sun singed metal and made the bus feel like a furnace. The stink of foul body odour mixed with the reek of choking exhausts and burnt tyres that wafted through the open windows. Yet Leyla wished the journey would never end. It was not the act itself that terrified her, but everything that went with it. Where to stand; what to say; how to look inconspicuous yet obvious enough to actually make money. Her biggest fear was getting caught. The humiliation would be far worse than any physical punishment.

When she stepped onto Vali Asr, she almost turned back to the bus stop. But as she looked across the road, towards Takht-e Tavous, she saw them: girls staggered along the street in the spot Parisa had told her. Leyla crossed the corner of Vali Asr and Takht-e Tavous, past Bank Melli, and positioned herself near a huge billboard poster. This month's message was not from a fashion retailer, but from the government. It was an attempt to tackle the interminable bitching and grumbling of its people. Big white letters were stamped out as friendly advice underneath a picture of a white house: LET'S NOT SPEND SO MUCH TIME DISCUSSING SOCIETY'S PROBLEMS IN OUR HOMES.

There were about a dozen other girls standing there. They were attractive and dressed in trendy *manteaus*, some with rolled-up jeans and trainers looking like students, some with sparkly eyeshadow looking like they were about to go clubbing. After her lap-dancing experience, Leyla had glimpsed hope for the first time since she had moved out of her parents' home; this new optimism eased her nerves. Parisa had told her that she would not have to work the streets for long; after a few months prettier girls would get enough repeat customers to be able to work from home, which is what had happened to Parisa.

Leyla had worried that someone she knew might spot her, but she realized that Parisa was right – they just looked like thousands of other girls standing on the streets of the city hailing a cab. In many ways, they were no different. There were a handful of students funding university degrees, three women whose blue-collar jobs were not enough to pay the rent and feed the children, a few girls who had fled abuse and broken homes and two girls who wanted to buy iPhones and designer clothes. Leyla was amazed some of the girls looked so respectable. One of them even had a fake Louis Vuitton handbag.

Cars slowed down as they reached the women; taxi drivers tried to figure out if they were girls wanting a ride and customers tried to figure out if they were girls looking for business. The girls did the same, working out if the cars were taxis or punters. With the country plunged in an economic crisis, there were as many rogue taxis operating these days as legal ones – desperate men, and even women, who had lost jobs and were supplementing paltry incomes by driving around the city looking to give somebody a ride for a few hundred tomans. Everyone looked the same. It was impossible to tell who was a punter and who was a prostitute. Transactions were brisk; a glance to see if the goods were worth it; a few stabs of conversation shot out through an open window. The price of flesh had also risen, in line with inflation, and the girls were charging more than six months ago. It was different on the streets here from south Tehran, where drug addicts still charged just a few thousand tomans for sex, their world dictated by opiate production in Afghanistan, a world largely untouched by the realities of sanctions and internal economics.

A man in his thirties in a white 4x4 Nissan Murano was Leyla's first customer. They had sex in his flat in the Saman building in Vanak. Afterwards he took her number and told her he had never seen such a pretty prostitute. She did not feel dirty or degraded. Just scared of God – a feeling that would sour nearly every encounter she would have.

Leyla quickly learnt the rules of the street: go with your instinct. Do not get in a car with more than two men. And, she had been told, if you get raped, too bad. The girls sometimes chatted to each other, about boyfriends and music, and they shared warnings, either about clients or the police. The police knew most of the girls on their beat. Some of the officers knew them as intimately as the punters. In 2008, Tehran's police chief, Reza Zarei, had been caught in a brothel, reportedly with six naked women. Zarei had been in charge of a programme to fight indecent behaviour.

A blow job was usually all it took to buy freedom. If the police were feeling randy they would swoop for an arrest, sometimes demanding full sex, but the Takht-e Tavous girls almost always refused.

'I'd rather be stoned to death than have to fuck you, your wife must be a blind cripple!' one of them had screamed as she was handcuffed and dragged to the police station. She was imprisoned for three months and got ninety-two lashes. The officers thought these uptown girls pugnacious. They were feisty, unlike the fear-addled heroin and *sheesheh* addicts in south Tehran who accepted the whippings and rapes with the particular resignation found among the abused and dispossessed. In south Tehran, sex with a cop usually happened there and then, in alleyways and under motorway bridges. Blackmail would be enforced in twos; one officer would be on the lookout while the other had his turn. On Takht-e Tavous, the girls moved faster and talked faster, their wits undiminished by malnutrition and cheap drugs. Unlike their counterparts in the south of the city, these girls had an inkling of the ever-changing face of the law and, more importantly, of its flexibility. It was almost impossible for the police to prove the girls were conducting any business other than agreeing on a price for a taxi ride. But they would still arrest the girls and threaten them with the legal punishment for sex outside marriage, which was up to 100 lashes and, in the case of adultery, execution. The green-uniformed cops lavishly dispensed shame, hauling parents into the police station for sessions of humiliation.

The girls were armed with their own means of protection. When bribery did not work, some would produce folded *sigheh* papers from their handbags. *Sigheh* is a temporary marriage approved by both God and the state, between a man (who can already be married) and a woman (who cannot), and can be as short as a few minutes or as long as ninety-nine years. It is Shia pragmatism at its vital best, ensuring that even a quickie can be given an Islamic seal of approval and sanctified in the eyes of the Lord. A crooked mullah in Haft-e Tir had been peddling fake ecclesiastical documents; he would issue *sigheh* contracts for 600,000 tomans a pop (about 200 US dollars), complete with an official stamp. In an emergency, the girls simply had to fill in the man's name. The *sigheh* papers were valid for six months, renewable at a discounted rate of fifty dollars. By law, in most cases a *sigheh* did not require official registration, but the girls did not want to take any chances. Every few years a debate would rage about *sigheh*. There was the obvious charge against it: that it was the ultimate in clerical hypocrisy. Women's rights groups would also complain, for like so much in the Islamic Republic the benefits were weighted towards the men who, unlike the women, could already be married; could have as many temporary wives as they wanted and could end the *sigheh* at any time. The former President and powerful politician Akbar Hashemi Rafsanjani had once led the way in advocating it during a sermon but with the caveat that it should not encourage Iranians to be 'promiscuous like the Westerners'. Thousands came to parliament to protest. Another cleric had even proposed licensed brothels, with a mullah on hand to perform temporary marriage rites, so that transgressing Tehranis would be able to act out their lust in a religiously appropriate way. The plan never got off the ground.

Leyla had been working Takht-e Tavous for less than a month when the raids began. The first time, they approached from behind, hurtling the wrong way down the one-way street. There were four of them, fluff-stubbled teenagers revving up their motorbikes, crazed by their virginity and obsessed with love for the Prophet. Everyone knew the Basij Islamic vigilantes were the ones to watch out for. They took girls straight to the station, and not before a beating. On occasion even some of *them* could be bought; mostly for aggressive, angry sex that left the girls bruised and depressed. But this group of *basijis* had discovered the police were ignoring the whores on Takht-e Tavous and they were incensed, determined to mete out justice themselves. They rounded the girls into a tight, frightened swarm. When they got close, one the girls offered a blow job and was rewarded with a shower of stinging slaps in her face. A skinny, pale-faced boy drew a truncheon from an inside pocket of a Russian combat jacket a size too small for him. They ordered the girls into the back of a van and Leyla felt the thudding soles of their boots kicking their backs as they got in. Leyla and the girls were locked in a police cell with a group of uptown north Tehrani revellers who had been caught with alcohol, and a thirty-two-year-old woman who had been seen kissing a man. It transpired the man was her husband, but they would not let her go until her parents turned up with her marriage certificate. Meanwhile her husband had also been thrown into a cell. They were all kept overnight. Leyla's mother had refused to come down and be humiliated; she thought it must be the usual charge of bad *hejab*. Leyla was ordered to appear in court.

Leyla was scared. She had never been in front of a judge before. The courts were in a grey concrete slab of a building that could have been any municipal building in any developing country of the world. In the rows of offices that lined its long corridors, bored secretaries and bureaucrats shuffled paper and played solitaire on old computers, oblivious to the chaos around them. The crowds spun in and out of their offices, grasping their *parvandehs*, case files – little more than a few pieces of A4 paper with illegible notes, dates and names scribbled on them. They bustled from office to office. They waited on plastic chairs. They crouched on the floor and leant against walls. Mostly they queue-jumped.

It was early morning, peak hour for the disgruntled and the accused. The usual fracas of sobbing and swearing and begging echoed up and down the packed stone staircase. Prostitutes, adulterers, fraudsters and drug addicts screamed insults at whoever would listen; their language was filthier than anything Leyla had heard on the streets.

A map of Tehran hung on the wall in the judge's room next to the obligatory framed photograph of the black-turbaned Supreme Leader, with his white beard and glasses, the black background giving the image an iconic edge. On the judge's desk was a framed three-dimensional piece of gold calligraphy of the word *Allah*. The judge was short and well groomed. Despite his age and height, he had a debonair manner about him. He did not bother looking up when Leyla was escorted to her seat opposite him. To the judge, all the girls looked the same. Shameful. It was impossible to tell who was a real fornicator and who was not, and he did not really care. So he just booked them all, lest he got caught out missing any real culprits by accident, which would be worse than condemning an innocent girl. The judge had lost his appetite for dispensing justice. There was no point in even opening Leyla's file. He delivered the sentence with a sigh: ninety-two lashes.

'Have you ever been lashed, sir, for doing something you shouldn't have done?' The judge looked up for the first time. Girls usually shouted back at him and caused a scene. He was not used to having his authority questioned in such a personal way. He studied Leyla. This bronzed, dyed-blonde beauty. And watched as she was marched away.

An office with a brown plywood desk and net curtains doubled as a whipping chamber. Leyla was told to sit on her knees, propped up against a wall.

The guidelines for flogging had been set by Ayatollah Mahmoud Hashemi Shahroudi, a politician and former head of the judiciary. Ayatollah Bayat Zanjani also issued a fatwa on flogging. Between them, they had the punishment well covered. Sexual contact without penetration called for more vigorous flogging than that for alcohol consumption. Pimping and giving false testimony got off more lightly, quite literally, with the severity of the lashes to be less than for boozing and heavy petting. The face, head and genitals are out of bounds. Men must be standing, women sitting down. The whipping must be done with a leather-bound whip, one metre long and no thicker than one and a half centimetres. Hands and feet can only be tied if they are going to get in the way and result in the genitals, head or face being accidentally whipped. The flogging must be done in moderate temperature – not too hot or too cold. Lashes must be evenly distributed.

The flogger had been ordered to whip Leyla with the Koran wedged under his armpit, to ensure he would not be able to raise his arm above his head and lash down with his full might. But he had a particular dislike for loose women, the scourge and ruin of the Islamic Republic. He had heard, often enough, clerics on the radio and the television blaming immoral women for the deterioration of society, for spreading adultery and even for earthquakes and the state of the economy. These women needed a good thrashing and, like many civil servants, he liked to bend the rules. He had devised a contraption to deal with situations like this: a sling. He had attached a small copy of the Koran to a sling that he strapped across his shoulder, satisfying his legal obligation while giving his arm full manoeuvring power. A weedy, sinewy man, he did not look like he would have much power in his skinny arms, but he did. As he thrashed the leather whip down on Leyla's back, she could see from the corner of her eyes the Koran flailing around under his armpit, its pages flapping open.

Leyla had thought her two layers of clothing would provide protection, but the leather strap sliced open her skin like a razor blade. She could not lie supine for a week afterwards. The red, raw welts turned into black, crusty bruises that covered every inch of her back. It was bad for business.

It was not long before Leyla was back in the same building, in the same room before the same judge. This time she had refused to have sex with a policeman. When the cop had booked her she had threatened to lodge a complaint with the judge. The cop had laughed scathingly, making a show of putting on his Ray-Ban Aviator sunglasses. By now it was impossible to know what Leyla was thinking. She had learnt to disguise signs of laughter, hurt and fear on her face that would only expose her to abuse. Her stony countenance and her beauty worked against her as much as they protected her. The police would see her expressionless face as arrogance that should be knocked down. They needed to feel pity in order to show mercy. And if her looks did not soften them, they saw it as something to be used.

Leyla was not as scared as before. One of the working girls she knew had paid someone to take her lashes. Leyla had already struck a deal with an addict she found loitering outside the court-room charging 2,000 tomans per lash; the addict was splitting the money fifty-fifty with the duty flogger.

'Repeat offender. Ninety-nine lashes and a month in prison,' said the judge.

'I'll tell you the real reason I'm here. I refused to have sex with a policeman. He wants to blackmail me and I won't do it. How does that fit in with your laws?'

The judge gestured to his secretary, who then whispered to a group sitting on chairs at the back of the room to leave. The secretary closed the door behind them.

'You know you can be punished for what you're telling me.' The judge's tone was more relaxed now his audience was gone.

'For telling you the truth? Yes, I know, funny isn't it?' Leyla shrugged her shoulders. The judge was silent for a while. Watching her. Leyla leant back in her chair.

'I couldn't lie on my back for weeks after I was flogged.' She narrowed her eyes and cocked her head sideways. The judge raised an eyebrow.

'I appreciate that you've been honest with me. You know I can help you,' he said.

'I'm assuming you don't mean by bringing the policeman to justice?' Leyla smiled. The judge flicked his head upwards, the Iranian nod for 'no'.

'I will have your file destroyed, so you don't exist.'

That is how Leyla's affair with the judge began.

Leyla was not working when Takht-e Tavous was raided again. This time it was the police, embarrassed that the *basijis*' raid had exposed their indifference. They were determined to make a show of it, to prove they were doing their job. A few of the girls were imprisoned. One turned out to be only fourteen years old, forced onto the streets by her drug-addict parents. Her case was taken up by a human rights lawyer who managed to place her in the care of a charity that helped 'runaway girls'. It was a never-ending cycle, a cat-and-mouse game between the authorities and prostitutes. The net would close in on the girls; a round of arrests and convictions would begin; all would go quiet. Then they would appear again, proliferating in the city as though nothing had happened. Most of the girls never returned to Takht-e Tavous after the police raid. They decamped four roads farther north, to a shopping mall on Gandhi Street. The girls were diversifying, and the police struggled to keep up.

The cyberpolice, launched in 2011 to fight Internet crimes and protect 'national and religious identity', are cottoning on to what many have known for years: Facebook is teeming with Iranian prostitutes. There are hundreds, maybe thousands of girls working through social network sites. They are easy enough to find; the user just has to pick a random Iranian girl's name and add the word 'whore' after it. Maryam *jendeh*, Azadeh *jendeh*, Roxanna *jendeh*…they are all there. Pictures of the goods on sale beside lists of services offered in the 'About me' section: threesomes, anal and *lez* sex for women. There are step-by-step instructions on how to buy, which usually involve topping up pay-as-you-go phone credit before arranging a rendezvous.

Some of the girls in Leyla's group were on Facebook, but were terrified after the head of the cyberpolice announced a crackdown on the Internet and Facebook pages that promoted pornography and prostitution. The girls had heard that undercover agents were posing as customers, and the customers had been scared off by rumours that some of the profiles were honey traps planted by the government. After news of the last raid, Leyla, like the other girls, stopped working on Takht-e Tavous and moved to the shopping mall. It was an ugly marble and stone building with boutique-lined arcades. The girls drank freshly squeezed melon juice in the basement next to the food stands where teenagers hung out. If they spotted men on the prowl, all it usually took was a look. Sometimes they picked out leather handbags and expensive clothes with their punters shuffling behind them, looking more like browbeaten boyfriends than seedy clients.

*

A middle-aged man with a paunch and spectacles opened the door; a heavy waft of frankincense floated out. At first Leyla thought he must be an assistant, as he looked more like a tired office worker than a sorcerer. She had booked an appointment to see a witch doctor who was a favourite of the ladies who frequented Parisa's beauty salon. He was known for his potent spells and warding off the evil eye, working out of his apartment in a scruffy block in downtown Vali Asr. Leyla was not an observant Muslim, but she believed in God, the Prophet and the imams. That is why she feared holy retribution for what she was doing.

The man led Leyla to a living room decorated with multicoloured remnants of material draped over the windows, evil eyes hanging from the walls, a gigantic silver hand of Fatima next to the television, and joss sticks burning on every available surface. Past a dirty kitchen, Leyla could see a satellite dish propped up on a balcony blackened by pollution. The sorcerer sat at a small Indian hand-carved table, to his right a burning candle and a copy of the Koran, to his left a pestle and mortar and dozens of jars filled with coloured powders and herbs.

'I've heard you cast spells for protection. I need protection because I'm a sinner.'

'We are all sinners. You must tell me exactly who you need protecting against.'

'God. I'm afraid of judgement day.'

'God will forgive you. You need protection from people around you who wish you harm. Many people wish you harm, I can see it.' He lit the candle and began grinding a potion together while uttering a prayer. He mixed in some water and told Leyla to drink. It tasted of turmeric and dust. He charged her 100,000 tomans.

'I can only guarantee protection for six months,' he said as he ushered her out of the door.

Leyla also enrolled in *erfan*, spirituality, classes in an office building one block north of the witch doctor. The teacher was a handsome, long-bearded Sufi scholar in a white kurta. His speciality was Gnosticism. Most of the students were uptowners and Leyla felt a little out of place, even though the teacher treated her no differently. They tackled metaphysical issues and read poetry. But Leyla could find no answers to her own questions and felt no nearer to being pardoned by God.

Word of her looks had spread and she was in demand. It was rare for a girl as pretty as Leyla to work in public for very long. She had amassed a dedicated following, enough never to work the streets or the shopping malls again. During her short time on Takht-e Tavous, Leyla had earned a year's salary as a secretary, as well as a new wardrobe. She had moved out of Parisa's flat and rented her own place a few roads away in Sa'adat Abad.

One of her first regular customers after the judge was the rich owner of an upmarket jewellery shop on Vali Asr. He had been referred to Leyla by a friend who had picked her up on Takht-e Tavous. He could not believe his luck. He kept Leyla to himself for as long as he could, without submitting to his impulse to show her off and share her. They would meet every Tuesday at three o'clock for half an hour at an empty office he owned on Fatemi Street. It was after one of these sessions that he told Leyla he had a new client for her, a very special man who required absolute discretion.

Leyla walked past a long row of Mercedes Benz cars and past two armed bodyguards as she entered the spectacular domed lobby of a high-rise apartment block in Kamranieh. This was prime north Tehran property, and at 15,000 US dollars a square metre it was bricks and mortar designed for businessmen, politicians and the moneyed upper classes. The latter preferred not to live here because of the proliferation of regime stooges and industrialists, whose chador-clad wives and whose habit of leaving their shoes outside the thick wood doors screamed *nouveau riche*. The building was a study in the kind of vulgarity only the rich can afford: an excess of marble and sparkling gold, faux Renaissance murals and columns topped with ornate Grecian flourishes. Residents included a foreign diplomat, the spoilt child of a famous politician and two members of parliament. But the bodyguards were not for them. They provided round-the-clock protection for a well-known cleric who also happened to be Leyla's newest customer.

Leyla had not been given a name, only instructions to tell the liveried porter that the resident of the twenty-third floor was expecting her. The porter was an old, tiny, white-skinned *Rashti* northerner who was paid handsomely by at least half the residents of the block to keep his mouth shut.

'Salaam Khanoum, you are as beautiful as I heard,' said the cleric as he opened the door, bowing his head deferentially to Leyla. Everything about him was elegant; even now, dressed in the white *gabaa* undergarments worn beneath the robes, he looked refined (in his religious regalia he looked almost dapper). He was tall, with a lean body, and wore expensive spectacles. His beard was perfectly trimmed.

The cleric took Leyla's *manteau* and headscarf and led her through an enormous reception room stuffed with imitation rococo furniture and intricately carved dark wooden chairs covered in gold brocade. In a bedroom with drawn curtains, they sat on the edge of the bed.

'My dear, do you say your prayers?'

'No sir, my family isn't religious.'

'Are you a believer?'

'I love God and the Prophet, *God rest his soul*, with all my heart. I think the imams are amazing. I'm a very spiritual person, sir.'

'Good, very good. But doing this kind of work you must take extra care to remain untainted in God's eyes.' Leyla nodded. This was not the first time she had been lectured by a customer, but instead of getting angry, she was listening intently.

'Have you ever been temporarily married – done a *sigheh*?'

'No, sir.' Leyla was too ashamed to tell the cleric that in her handbag she always carried the fake *sigheh* paper she had bought from the bent mullah.

'My girl, as long as relations between a man and a woman are sanctified in God's eyes, they are not immoral. It is imperative that you learn the *sigheh* prayer. God is forgiving. It is not too late to save yourself.'

The cleric read out the words in Arabic and then translated them into Persian for her to understand: *I marry you for a specific amount of time and for a specific mehrieh.*

Leyla and the cleric repeated the words in Arabic together, and then she uttered them one more time on her own.

'Now we are not sinning.' The cleric patted Leyla's leg and smiled. He took off his glasses and his rings and turned off the side light before undressing in the dark. They sank into the memory-foam mattress. Afterwards, for the first time, Leyla did not fear a reprisal from God.

The cleric became a regular and they would meet every week. He was polite and attentive. He bought her gifts, nearly always cheap, ugly underwear – bright red crotchless knickers, scratchy lace teddies, hold-ups and see-through baby-doll nighties. Leyla would give them to Parisa, who would sell them at the beauty salon. After sex, they would drink tea on the balcony with the entire city splayed out in front of them, thousands of concrete tower blocks receding into the smog, to the west the tall spire of Milad Tower, Tehran's tallest building, which from a distance looked like a seventies alien spaceship atop a gigantic spike. On days when the pollution was not so dense, they could see all the way to the mountains that cradled the south of the city.

As he grew to trust Leyla, the cleric would confide in her about his troubles: ungrateful children and a bitter wife who refused to have sex. He serenaded Leyla with his favourite verses from the Koran, about paradise and beautiful gardens that await the righteous:

> *Rivers of milk*
> *Of which the taste*
> *Never changes; rivers*
> *Of wine, a joy*
> *To those who drink;*
> *And rivers of honey*
> *Pure and clear.*

Leyla would learn them off by heart, which pleased the cleric; she showed far more diligence than any of the spotty teenagers that he taught. She became fond of him, this sage father figure. He had awakened her spiritual senses in a way her *erfan* classes had not, and taught her how to keep her work on the right side of the Lord. There were no endless discussions on morals, no philosophical questions where there were no real answers. Instead there were ethereal words of righteousness and divinity straight from the Prophet's mouth. And Leyla never again had sex without whispering the *sigheh* prayer under her breath.

*

The first time the judge heard her say it, he had laughed out loud.

'Oh I'm so glad you said the *sigheh* dear girl, because I had been worried what we were doing was wrong. Now I can rest in peace!'

'But if clerics say it makes it OK in the eyes of God, how can you argue with that?'

'Quite right, who are we to argue with the justice of the clerics?'

Over thirty years as a vassal of the Islamic Republic had rewarded the judge with a droll sense of humour, as well as disillusionment at how the revolution had turned out. He had seen many men he trusted and loved, who had fought shoulder to shoulder with him on the streets of Tehran and then in its courts, chewed up and spat out by the system. Good men, some of them the very architects of the Islamic Republic, were now either imprisoned or under house arrest for daring to criticize the regime and the Supreme Leader. The judge had made a decision early on: the regime was like a child he had created and it was almost impossible to turn your back on your own blood. He also knew that being an enemy of the state would be his ruin.

The judge did not pay Leyla to begin with, according to their arrangement. He liked it the way nearly all her clients did: doggy-style. After that, Leyla became the judge's concubine; he had never had sex with such an exquisite woman. He paid her rent and had her on twenty-four-hour standby. Whenever he could make excuses to his wife, he hurried to her apartment. He bought her gifts, including an expensive carpet she picked out herself from Solomon Carpet on Vali Asr. She feared he was falling in love with her.

*

Leyla was beginning to feel a sense of accomplishment. She had a roster of respectable clients and the money was rolling in. She was no longer just surviving; she was living. She figured that within a few years she could open her own beauty salon, a good earner in a city where, no matter how severe the economic downturn, women always found the money to beautify themselves.

She soon revised her calculation down to a year. When Taymour first saw Leyla, he wanted to film sex with her. Leyla refused. She had a strict policy: she would allow anonymous photographs for extra money, but she would never be filmed. Taymour would not give up. He was a thirty-year-old software designer who lived in a small apartment with his parents in the east of the city and he was addicted to porn. Taymour was desperate to make his own; he wanted it to look good and Leyla was the prettiest girl he had ever met. He offered her so much money that Leyla finally agreed, on condition that he would not show her face and that she would approve the final result.

Taymour liked the look of amateur porn. It turned him on. The seedier, the more real, the better. The Internet had sucked most of the money out of the under-the-counter porn market in Tehran in recent years. But uploading and downloading videos that could be traced was a risky business. Taymour preferred DVDs. In any case, during elections or protests the authorities would grind Internet connections down to an excruciatingly slow speed to dissuade use altogether. In these times, it was back to the good old days of underground porn bought and sold on the streets. Taymour had been told that there were a handful of kiosks and computer shops near downtown Toopkhaneh Square that sold porn. Hawkers stood on the square and whispered *super*, the Persian word for a porn film, out of the side of their mouths at potential customers. It was pot luck; as many people got ripped off buying blank DVDs as those who got the real grainy, blurred thing. Through trial and error, Taymour had found a reliable dealer. He was an old hand, a suave, middle-aged man with a mountain of jet-black hair in dark jeans, loafers and a smart jumper.

'Listen mate, don't fuck around, it's like being caught with a truckload of heroin. Death sentence,' he had said to Taymour as he sucked hard on a cigarette and made a hanging noose gesture with his left hand.

'Home-grown stuff is hard to find. I got a shitload of foreign, but home-grown is going to cost you more.' Every time the Internet was slowed down, the dealer was inundated with requests for local porn. Not the blonde, foreign girls, but beautiful, dusky Iranians. Some wanted to see them in their headscarves and chadors, others wanted to see the young and beautiful having fun. Taymour bought everything the dealer had; clips that had been sent to international porn sites and had been filed under the 'amateur' section; girls who had been filmed without their knowledge, girls who were seen shouting instructions not to film their faces. But there were also girls who did show their faces, who smiled at the camera. A few even waved. There were girls flashing their breasts in the backs of taxis driving through packed traffic. One couple was having sex in a park. Another was in the back of a car. These were young people taking deadly risks.

Sex is an act of rebellion in Tehran. A form of protest. Only in sex do many of the younger generation feel truly free. They have ultimate control over their bodies, if nothing else in their lives, and they have made them weapons of revolt. It is a backlash against years of sexual repression; in the process of having to continually lie and hide natural desires, the sense of ordinary sexual behaviour and its values is being lost.

Taymour played his porn collection for Leyla. She had watched foreign porn with clients before, and it looked much slicker than the fumbling on the screen in front of her. She knew she could do it better. They filmed it in Leyla's apartment, because Taymour lived with his parents. Leyla charged double for home visits; she would make men wait outside until she sent a text, then they would come in through the basement car park to ensure they would not be spotted by neighbours; she paid the Afghan caretaker to act as lookout.

Leyla made Taymour listen to her *sigheh* prayer before they started filming. Taymour was thrilled with the results: every glistening crevice and prickle of shaving rash was sharp and clear, even Leyla thought it looked good. He called it *Tehran Nights* and made a load of copies. He handed them out to his friends and even sold one to his DVD seller. A week later, Leyla's porn film was everywhere. The touts standing in downtown Tehran and on Vali Asr Square, outside Ghods Cinema, were flogging unmarked CD copies of it for six US dollars a pop – twice the amount as for a classic series of *Benny Hill* and even more than *Desperate Housewives* and *Lost*. It was also the underground bestseller at the various electrical shops scattered through the city that ran lucrative side businesses in stolen mobiles and black-market goods. Even the marble-floored, air-conditioned stationery boutique on the northern reaches of Vali Asr, renowned for its under-the-counter Hollywood blockbusters, had already sold fifty copies of *Tehran Nights*. The DVD would be fished out from behind a drawer that was concealed, not in a back room but under a glass cabinet where a handful of top-of-the-range fake Mont Blanc pens were carefully displayed.

Taymour's friends wanted their own sex tapes. Leyla was in business. She was charging 1,000 US dollars and upwards. The guys liked to outdo each other. She filmed on a high-rise balcony, in the back of a car, in a park and in the mountains. Most connoisseurs of local porn soon recognized the round bottom, the soft girlie voice and the big full lips as the same girl who had spread her legs so adroitly in *Tehran Nights* and, by now, *Housewife from Shiraz*. But only a handful of people knew her real identity, for the camera never went past Leyla's mouth, which was either smiling, parted in an elongated moan, or, more usually, stretched over an erect penis.

Kayvan was one of Tehran's *bacheh pooldars*, rich kids. He wore Rolex watches that he bought on Vali Asr. He lived in a mansion with Roman pillars at the entrance and peacocks strutting in the garden. In the summer he had pool parties. In the winter he skied in Shemshak, forty-five minutes north of Tehran, where he would drink under-the-counter vodka and tonics and eat wild boar at a hip café. After the skiing season he would retreat to Dubai, the Mecca for holidaying Iranians. There he would hire breathtakingly beautiful Russian hookers.

His father imported a famous brand of American printer with a regime-approved licence. Despite sanctions, most government offices were still buying the latest models. A deal brokered with a member of the Revolutionary Guards, the most powerful force in the country and directly answerable to the Supreme Leader, meant the printers surged into the country with the same velocity as before, through a port that also welcomed shipments of alcohol and drugs.

Kayvan's best friend was Behfar, whose father had made a fortune in food manufacturing. International sanctions had been excellent for business; even though prices of basic produce had shot up, demand was higher than ever; the whole family prayed for an eternal stalemate. Behfar's father was a canny operator and had made some powerful allies in the regime, donating extravagant gifts and money for election campaigns. He had also built a spectacular mosque on Vali Asr. There was a rumour that the Supreme Leader had told him he never had to pay another penny in tax again for his services to the nation.

Kayvan and his friends were bored and idle trust-fund kids, all in their early twenties. Their fathers' bank accounts injected their congenital arrogance with an uninhibited confidence. The money gave them a degree of immunity, for they had learnt they could buy their way through most red tape and sticky situations. The women were as abundant as the allowances from their fathers. Cruising in his Porsche, or in Behfar's Bugatti in the tangle of roads in his stomping ground, Fereshteh, it would take less than ten minutes to pick up a giggling teenager. He had timed it. Some would be in it for a flirt, some for sex. Nearly all, he suspected, were after a husband. But he had a particular liking for whores. The girls he used were the uptown variety, pretty girls who only wore branded goods and who cost top whack, 500 US dollars a night and upwards. He had slept with every single high-class 'escort' signed to an agency with an impressive client list that ran out of a small office in Gheytarieh. Not all the girls he picked up were working girls, like the ones he met in the upmarket coffee shops; but there was a tacit agreement that they expected a shopping trip to the Valentino Red boutique in the Modern Elahiyeh Shopping Center if they were to open their legs. They were so Barbie-doll perfect, it was a fair deal.

After Kayvan watched one of Leyla's films, he tracked her down through friends of friends. He wanted a piece of the action.

He captured their first film together on his iPad for his own personal collection. He decided she was the best whore he had ever met. Unlike most of the girls he hung out with, Leyla was straight-talking and direct. There was no game-playing, none of the baby-voiced faux coyness favoured by so many Tehrani girls. Kayvan started parading her everywhere with him – parties in north Tehran, luxurious chalets in the mountains. At a rave in the ski resort of Shemshak, Leyla danced as a sea of luminous white eyeballs bobbed around her, the revellers' coloured contact lenses picked out by the UV disco lights. The super-rich kids were a mixed-up lot; it was hard to tell who was the son of a *bazaari*, who was the son of a *dolati*, government worker, and who was old money. Sophistication could be bought for the price of a Western education and a passing knowledge of art.

Leyla had never imagined she would experience life at the top of Tehrani society. Her need to better herself combined with her beauty had catapulted her northwards, reaching the pinnacle for every Tehrani working girl, which was as an escort to the uptown playboy circle. She dropped her regular clients like the cleric and the judge. And Kayvan no longer paid her in cash; instead he bought her whatever she wanted. It was easy to pretend she was his girlfriend.

Tehran Nights eventually made its way to the offices of the cyberpolice. It had been picked up during a house raid and lain hidden under a pile of written statements on a police officer's desk for a few weeks. The DVD was unmarked and the officer was about to throw it in the bin when he thought it might be his copy of *The Bling Ring* that he had lent a colleague. He pushed it into his laptop and Leyla's jiggling breasts appeared. The officer thought it looked quite tame compared to the porn he liked to watch. He gave the DVD to his sergeant, who handed it to the cyberpolice.

The fight against porn was a losing battle. The clerics were worried. The government was worried. Porn had even been discussed in parliament. A new bill was introduced that updated the law, enforcing stricter punishments, which included being found a corrupter of the earth, an executionable offence. Sex tapes were leaking out, and the cyberpolice needed to act. When the private sex tape of a soap star, Zahra Amir Ebrahimi, had exploded across the whole country, more than 100,000 DVD copies were sold on the black market. The regime was caught in a tricky situation; the actress was adored and it would not look good to come down too hard. She had also made her name by playing the pious lead character in a soap opera called *Narges*; she was the face of virtue and purity on state television. A celebrity sex tape was not the image the Islamic Republic of Iran Broadcasting (IRIB) had hoped for. Ebrahimi left the country and never returned.

Even the threat of execution had done little to deter the fornicators. The courts had sentenced two people to death for running porn sites; one of them, an Iranian-born Canadian computer programmer called Saeed Malekpour, had his death sentence reduced to life imprisonment for 'designing and moderating adult-content websites' which went hand in hand with insulting the sanctity of Islam.

The cyberpolice pored over hours and hours of porn films. They needed a conviction, but finding the culprits was almost impossible. The officers watched *Tehran Nights* several times; it looked like another amateur porn video but classier.

*

A girl in a catsuit with blonde pixie-cropped hair was gyrating with an Amazonian beauty wearing a sheaf of a dress slashed to her navel. Around them a group were popping ecstasy pills in each other's mouths as they danced in front of a DJ spinning house tunes from his booth. Two famous actors were on the sofa with a group who were chopping out lines of cocaine on a glass table. The house belonged to a returned exile, notorious for her wild parties. She was an interior designer and her home was a homage to gothic style: pointed arches, black and red walls, heavy velvet curtains and six-foot wrought-iron candelabra.

Leyla was about to take off her *manteau* when the hostess sprang on Kayvan.

'Get that fucking *jendeh* out of my house. How many times have I told you before about bringing those girls here?' She dragged Kayvan to the kitchen. Leyla stood on her own, her headscarf round her shoulders. She was unmoved by the attack, but was surprised that the hostess could tell she was a *jendeh*. Leyla had thought she was now assimilated well into the north Tehran set, but the hostess had trained eyes. Kayvan returned.

'Sorry babe, I'll get you a cab home.'

This was the first time he had abandoned her.

'You said we were going to a party tonight – together?'

'I know, but you heard her. House rules, what can I say. I'll call you next week.'

'You fucking arsehole.'

That night Leyla decided to leave Iran, to start a life where no one knew her.

Leyla had always thought that marrying above her station was the only way that she could better herself, just as her sister had done. The sex films had given her an independence she never thought she would have, but it was not enough. She wanted a husband; she wanted love and a family like everyone else. Partying with Kayvan had been fun, but she had been wrong about him and her own naivety surprised her. It was obvious really: they were all happy to fuck her and even to be seen with her, but no rich kid with high-society friends would marry a whore. Even the most outwardly urbane guys who seemed so sophisticated and, well, Western, wanted to marry virgins – or at least upper-class girls who knew how to play virtuous.

Parisa had reached the same conclusion and was now working as a prostitute in Dubai, where Iranian flesh was some of the most expensive on the market (Chinese and then African the cheapest). Parisa was now earning nearly 1,000 US dollars a night, and she was not half as striking as Leyla.

Recently Leyla had been listening obsessively to Dr Farhang Holakouee, a Los Angeles-based celebrity agony uncle with a daily radio call-in show; his popularity had peaked a few years ago, but Leyla still tuned in. His callers were mostly Iranians living in the United States. No subject was off-limits and he tackled them all with a no-nonsense manner, doling out sensible counsel with stern impatience. Housewives and professionals from all parts of the city downloaded his show and bought his DVDs on the black market. He was anti-regime, secular and modern, and he understood the damaged Iranian psyche. He spoke of cycles of behaviour, of taking control, of cause and effect, of responsibility for your actions. A caller had phoned in to ask if changing your life was really possible: *of course it is possible, first you have to face reality and then you must know that your future is in your own hands.*

Leyla knew what to do. She would save up in Dubai and then start anew in the USA. She lay awake all night, overwhelmed with this sudden urge to leave Tehran.

*

They came for her at six o'clock in the morning, her head still full of the plans she was making to join Parisa. She shook with fear when they put her in the back of the police car. This time she knew it was more serious.

The officers in the cyberpolice unit had whooped with excitement when they noticed a box in the corner of the screen with a serial number on it. It was Leyla's electricity meter. It had taken a matter of hours for them to track her down.

She was taken straight to Evin. There was no police station, no courtroom, no lawyer. On the way, she had frantically called the judge's number. No answer. The line was dead. She managed to send two texts before they confiscated her phone, one to Kayvan and one to the judge. *I NEED HELP. POLICE HAVE GOT ME.*

Neither of them replied. Kayvan had got scared and deleted all signs of her existence from his life. The judge had died.

Most of her cellmates were either working girls or women who had been found guilty of other moral crimes, such as adultery. The sex workers were from the streets, and at first Leyla found it hard to identify with them. She had worked hard to eliminate the memories of her Takht-e Tavous streetwalking days from her mind. Many of the girls took drugs and often fights broke out between them. Leyla won them over with gossip about her film star clients and details of lavish parties. She sold herself as the glamorous porn star headed for Dubai – what they could all be. She even comforted the women by teaching them the beautiful passages from the Koran that the cleric had taught her. The women shared with her their own stories of bouncing in and out of prison and reassured her she would be freed in no more than a few months.

Leyla was told she would be assigned a lawyer, and that she could call her family. Her mother sobbed down the phone and said she could not bear to visit her in prison through shame. She told Leyla to call her when she was released.

But she was not in prison long.

It was a beautiful spring dawn when Leyla was hanged.

SIX

MORTEZA

Imam Zadeh Hassan, south-west Tehran

There was blood everywhere. It was smeared over faces and streaking down necks. A sticky film of it glistened viscous pink on chests; in places it had clotted deep red in tufts of hair. From each lash more droplets spurting outwards in a ruby mist.

Morteza was standing at the back of the room, clutching a chain in his hand.

'Ya Hossein!' He was chanting the imam's name as he watched his comrades. Forty of them were thrashing chains down on their bare backs in perfect synchronization to a hypnotic electro-techno beat.

'Ya Hossein!'

They were in a *hosseinieh*, the hall next to the mosque, in the south-west suburbs where Morteza had grown up. The doors were locked and the curtains were pulled. The room had been turned into a dark, dank box, lit by a few bare yellow lightbulbs on the dirty tangled wires hanging from the low ceiling. The room was fetid with sweat, blood and rose water. To his right Morteza could see Abdul slashing his head with a *ghameh*, a big dagger. Blood was seeping out in waves; his eyes were half shut, ecstatic with pain.

'Ya Hossein!'

One voice led them all, rising above their cries, hovering somewhere between a groan and a sublime soprano. Morteza stared at the singer on the small stage, head tilted back as if singing to God himself. It was the first time in all these years that he had really studied him. He was a bearded man in his thirties with steel-rimmed glasses and a green scarf tied round his head, Bruce Springsteen-style. A special-effect reverb on the microphone produced an ecclesiastical echo that looped over the rhythmic throb.

'Ya! *Ya...Ya...Ya...*'

'Hossein! *Hossein...Hossein...Hossein...*'

'Ya Hossein.' Morteza repeated the words in a flat whisper.

It was Ashura, the ten-day festival in the Islamic holy month of Muharram that commemorates the martyrdom of the Prophet's grandson, Imam Hossein, who was killed with seventy-two others at the battle of Karbala in 680. But this was a secret Ashura, hidden from view ever since the state banned bloodletting during the ceremonies, deeming it barbarous and fanatical. A hard-core minority ignored the edict, believing that some things are strictly between a man and his God and none of the state's business. Violent self-flagellation where blood is a sign of love for Hossein was part of their culture, a tradition that their fathers' fathers' fathers had practised. These rituals simply disappeared underground, in guarded *hosseiniehs* and back rooms across the country. Illegality stamped the gatherings with added importance, binding the men closer together, brothers in arms. Morteza had been a part of this ritual for years, hearing the same songs in the same rooms.

'*Hossein went to Karbala...*' The singer broke into a sob that the microphone regurgitated and spat back out, sending the sound spinning across the room: *wah wah wah wah.*

In the next breath he was deliriously upbeat, as though a different man had taken over.

'Come on everybody, let's hear it louder! Let's put a little more into it!' The singer now sounded like a holiday camp leader whipping up the crowd. A reminder of the forgotten sob was still reverberating as he spoke: *wah wah wah...*

The men responded, jumping up now as they whipped their backs, bellowing the words as an incantation until they were all gripped in a trance.

'Hossein! Hossein! Hossein! Hossein! Hossein!'

For the first time in his life, Morteza did not join in. He just stood there, surveying the spectacle as though he had never seen it before. His comrades looked strangely like the north Tehran ravers they abhorred, lost to the rhythm of a drum, in a haze of adrenalin and cortisone instead of ecstasy and alcohol. For the first time, he found the singer's mock sobs ridiculous. Morteza realized that even the real tears he conjured up every year were not really for God or Imam Hossein, but for himself.

Morteza dropped his chain and fetched his coat. His friends tried to stop him leaving.

'What's happened? What's got into you?' They barred his exit. Morteza said nothing as he pushed through them and walked upstairs and out into the late afternoon light. On the street an official, more sedate public Ashura was on show: rows of men in black shirts softly tapping themselves with blunt chains, eyes on the women, who were more interested in the quality of the self-flagellators than the self-flagellation. A sanitized version of the real thing. Morteza weaved through the crowds, and when he had nearly overtaken the parade, he turned round and took a last look. He shook his head and walked away, knowing what had to be done.

*

Morteza was born a disappointment. When the midwife had pulled him out of his mother she had slapped his wrinkled face and all that had come out of his tiny pink lips was a feeble whimper. 'You've got yourself a weakling. This boy's not built for this world,' she had said as she placed him on his mother's breast. Morteza groped around for her teat, and even when it was shoved into his mouth he lacked the strength to suck out enough milk.

The men in his family were built short, wide and strong. Stocky, fat babies that became strapping boys whose robust bodies rarely allowed illness to invade. Morteza's pretty, delicate features never filled out and his slight frame only got leaner and longer. The women in the family cooed over him, drawn by his beauty – deliciously long eyelashes and a perfect, heart-shaped face. Morteza spent most of his childhood clinging to his mother's chador.

The revolution was the making of the Kazemis. The family had been plagued by poverty, a hereditary curse passed down from generation to generation. Imam Khomeini changed their fate. They had always been deeply religious and not just because they were *seyeds*, the honorific title used to identify direct descendants of the Prophet. They attended the mosque a few times a week and they never missed Friday prayers. When a newcomer to the neighbourhood erected a satellite dish on the roof, Morteza's mother Khadijeh went straight to the head of the Basij unit in the local mosque and reported it. The dish was destroyed a few hours later by a policeman and two young *basijis*, who warned the owner that next time they would destroy him too.

The family home was a small brick house, in a row of identical brick houses in Imam Zadeh Hassan, run-down, ugly suburbs in the south-west of the city where the only well-kept buildings were mosques, and where cars were either white Prides or dented and rusted pick-up trucks, the backs of which were as often filled with families as with produce. Five of them – Morteza, his parents Khadijeh and Kazem, and Kazem's parents – lived and slept in two rooms, one of the bedrooms doubling up as the main living room during the day. It had small, high windows with dirty lace curtains that were rarely parted. The walls were bare, greying and flaky. Persian floor cushions lined the room and in the corner was a dark plywood desk. It was crammed with most of their possessions: a television, a computer, a bottle of perfume, a magnifying mirror, a pair of tweezers, toothpaste and a big blue tub of Nivea cream. Underneath the desk, bed sheets and blankets were neatly rolled. A makeshift kitchen had been erected in the hallway, where Khadijeh cooked on a camping stove next to a fridge with a lopsided door that rattled loudly into the night.

Many of Morteza's uncles were original *Hezbollahis* who had formed little battalions during the revolution and fought against the unbelievers, leftists and the monarchists. People like the Kazemis were remunerated with jobs and respect. It allowed them to be proud once more of the strict religious control they exerted over their lives and their women. The revolution also unwittingly brought about more equality between the classes – for the first time in the history of the Kazemis, female members were allowed to be educated beyond primary school, safe in the knowledge that they would not be corrupted under an Islamic education system. A stream of distant relatives from a farming village in central Iran, from where the Kazemis hailed, poured into Tehran. The family found strength in numbers. An uncle who had excelled at spying for the Islamic Revolutionaries, liberally denouncing neighbours and inculpating dissenters, was swiftly rewarded with a position in a newly established Ministry. Nepotism was another bonus, and before long several more Kazemis were installed as clerical assistants, cleaners and even office managers. Despite the new-found power and income, unlike Somayeh's clan, the Kazemis were not friends with people who did not share their political and religious beliefs – especially not those who were making the climb to higher class and looser morals. They isolated themselves against outsiders who brandished invasive influences, and that was a crucial tactic in their survival.

War also served the Kazemis well. Morteza was just a baby when his two teenage brothers, Ali and Hadi, were sent to fight against Iraq. They had joined the Basij as volunteer militiamen. It was near the end of the internecine war when Khadijeh had paid a forger in downtown Toopkhaneh Square to falsify Ali's birth certificate. With the stroke of a pen Ali was bestowed another three years, going from an underage fifteen years old to a fit and fighting man of eighteen. Sending her son as a child soldier to war was Khadijeh's way of showing her gratitude and love to Saint Khomeini and God. Ali and Hadi were immediately drafted to the front line, where they survived for nearly a year, watching their friends die around them, some during notorious 'human wave' attacks. The tactics were suicidal: charging into incoming artillery and wading into minefields in order to clear them, encouraged by the promise of the glory of martyrdom and virgins in paradise.

Ali was finally hit by a rocket; miraculously he survived long enough to pick up his debris-encrusted entrails from the ground, push them back in his ripped stomach and whisper the death rites before his blood went cold. Less than a week later Hadi was killed; his body was never found. Stories of the brothers' bravery emerged after their deaths and grew ever more impressive with time: both boys had relentlessly and fearlessly charged towards the enemy, dodging bullets and bombs, dragging comrades to safety, killing dozens of the enemy with no more than an AK-47 in their hands, *Allah Akbar* on their tongues and Khomeini in their hearts. They were war heroes. With two of those in the family, the position of the Kazemis in the new Islamic order was instantly bumped up a few more notches. Photographs of Ali and Hadi were displayed around the house and on the walls of local businesses in the neighbourhood.

The fringe benefits of martyrdom were also reaped by those left behind. Morteza's father gave up his job as an office cleaner and, with the help of a foundation set up for families of martyrs, he opened a cab company, licences for which were favoured to families of martyrs and disabled war veterans.

The pride of their martyrdom did not lessen the pain of Hadi's and Ali's deaths for the family, nor did the passage of time. And the more time passed, the more obvious it became that Morteza was the opposite of his brave brothers. As a little boy he liked to play on his own, or with his aunties. His favourite game was when they would dress him up as a Persian prince and paint his nails red; when his father Kazem found out, he slapped him across the face even though he was only five years old.

Morteza had recognized his father's disdain for him early on, which soon morphed into revulsion. By the time he was ten, Kazem had begun regularly whipping his son with his belt. At nights Morteza would hear his father sobbing and shouting at Khadijeh, 'I had two sons in this life and because of you, I now have none.'

More than anything, Morteza wished he was more like his brothers. Khadijeh spoke of them incessantly; she hoped that igniting jealousy in her son with stories of their bravery would goad him into behaving more like them – local bully boys who were scared of nothing. Morteza tried hard to emulate them, playing football in the alley outside the house as they had. He persevered, despite being mocked for his irrational fear of the ball. He hung out with the neighbourhood boys after school. He began to wear Hadi's and Ali's old clothes, musty and two sizes too big for him, desperate that their essence would be transferred into him through the fraying cotton. Even if his parents could not see it, Morteza was the most determined, tenacious child ever to have been born to a Kazemi.

A group of boys had gathered in the lobby of the mosque; Morteza stood alone beside them, his pointed leather shoes shining from the slick of vegetable oil he had used to polish them. His new white shirt was so stiff it looked as if it was made of cardboard. Khadijeh was near the entrance, shouting out to him and waving her hands, urging him to queue-jump as all the other boys were doing. But Morteza was getting pushed farther back.

The mosque was at the centre of the community; it was as much a social club as it was a spiritual retreat. Worshippers arrived well before prayers to catch up with friends and gossip. The mosque fed and clothed the poor in the holy months and at *norooz*, New Year. It lent money to struggling families and helped with the cost of marriages. Morteza's local mosque was also a Basij headquarters.

Khadijeh had tried to dissuade him from joining the *Basij-e Mostazafin*, the 'Mobilization of the Oppressed' voluntary militia. Even though it was her deepest wish that he should be a member, she did not think he was up to it – this meek and frail twelve-year-old with a languid walk, all long limbs and skinny buttocks, who would cry at the slightest provocation. Morteza had insisted. Being a *basiji* would make him a respected man equal to his heroic brothers. Khadijeh had finally relented, not least because the family was struggling to survive. With Morteza a member, it would mean he would be fed and taken care of at least once a week.

Morteza's father Kazem had always enjoyed an occasional toke of opium, but after the death of his sons he began smoking more. Soon his state pension, Khadijeh's jewellery and the money they received from the *Bonyad-e Shahid* martyrs' fund foundation was being used to feed his addiction. When that ran out, he sold his barely functioning cab business. Most of his day was spent pipe in hand, bent over a small *manghal* or brazier, sifting white-hot coals with iron tongs. When he was not smoking, he was shouting, either at Khadijeh or Morteza.

After the boys were registered they were led into a classroom in the adjoining *hosseinieh*. The mosque's caretaker, Gholam, a bent, wiry man in faded cream pyjamas, darted across the room, broom in hand, making last-minute adjustments. Nobody ever saw Gholam stand still. Between making tea, sweeping floors, cleaning shoes, washing carpets, praying, bleaching loos, buying groceries and watering plants, he ostentatiously prostrated himself to those he deemed of higher rank, which was everyone. He was from a long line of illiterate caretakers; he had guarded and tended the mosque since he was sixteen years old, taking over from his elderly father. Now he lived in a small room off the lobby of the mosque with his wife and two young daughters.

Gholam hushed the boys as he scampered out. The Commander strode in. He had a suitably militaristic gait and a stony glare. The Commander was wearing the non-uniform uniform of a

Basij leader: a pair of large-pocketed khaki military trousers and a loose-hanging shirt. No emblems on display or badges indicating rank. All brothers are equal in the Basij. A grey beard concealed miserly thin lips and a forest of hair was stacked on his head like a compost heap, rising as high as his stomach ballooned out in front of him, a solid bulk of fat and flesh.

'Salaam-on Alaykom! You are the army of our future. You represent the Islamic Republic of Iran. We are here to serve God and our prophet – God rest his soul. We will serve the Supreme Leader against infidels, the West and Zionism. Death to Israel!'

'Death to Israel!' The children, who were all around the same age as Morteza, parroted back the rallying call, but only a few of them knew what Zionism was, or why Iran considered the West the enemy.

The Ahmadi twins punched their fists in the air. They were sons of a diehard former *Hezbollahi* leader who had taught his children to burn the American flag and shout 'Death to America!' as a party trick when they were four years old. Haji Ahmadi had been one of the first to join the Basij in 1980, when Khomeini had envisioned a magnificent people's militia that was twenty million strong. In the early days they were simply volunteers used as a security force to help the Revolutionary Guards; they were also sent to fight Baluchi, Kurdish and Turkmen separatists. When war broke out, they were herded to the front lines. Haji Ahmadi survived with shrapnel in his legs and an invigorated passion for the Islamic Republic that he siphoned into the post-war tasks that *basijis* like him excelled at: policing vice, enforcing virtue and crushing protest. Haji Ahmadi was disappointed at what the Basij had become – more youth centre than fighting force. He would give his life to the Supreme Leader and he expected his sons to do the same.

The Commander marched towards the boys, shouting at them to stand in front of their desks. He inspected his new charges. He hovered over each one so closely that his belly brushed against their bony-ribbed chests. A warm, wet burst of the Commander's breath snorted out of his nostrils and was expelled against Morteza's face as he moved down the line. He stopped at a louche-looking kid, perhaps sensing a subversive spirit in the wild, black eyes that confidently met his gaze. Ebrahim – Ebbie for short – was handsome, even in dirty clothes and with holes in his shoes. He had a sensual swagger and an innate intelligence that life on the street had sharpened to lightning-quick wit. From the age of eight he had been working as a porter in the bazaar and had been playing backgammon in tea houses for money. When he was not gambling or skiving from school, he was lying his way out of trouble. His father beat him for no reason; if he misbehaved, he was made to sleep outside on the road. The Commander stared at him.

'Stand up STRAIGHT!' Ebbie stamped his feet together and saluted the Commander with a flourish, shouting out, 'Yes sir!' The Commander was too vain to notice that Ebbie was mocking him.

The Commander also took his time over the next boy. Mehran's parents had persuaded him not to wear his new trainers, for it gave him a Western, *balaa-shahri*, uptown air that did not go down well with the Basij. Even without the trainers the signs were there, in the extra inch in length of his hair, in the closer fit of his check shirt and in the glint of a gold chain half hidden under his vest. Mehran's mother had been cleaning houses in north Tehran for ten years, exposing her children to a lifestyle they could only dream about. She had persuaded Mehran to join the Basij for the same reason that Ebbie and at least half the group had joined: the perks. The Basij laid on extracurricular activities that few families in the neighbourhood could afford. The boys would have free access to the local swimming pool, free use of a football pitch, day trips out of the city to tourism hot spots and even the possibility of a stay in a summer camp. They would also get occasional free meals, low-interest loans, preferential treatment by government organizations and – thanks to a specially designated quota of forty per cent for Basij students that overlooked poor grades – a vastly increased chance of getting into university. Time spent serving in the Basij would also be knocked off compulsory military service. For these boys, the Basij was part Islamic Boy Scouts club and part Freemasons. If they showed devotion and hard work, they could even hope for a regular wage. Few underprivileged families would miss the opportunity of joining the Basij.

These motivations were kept quiet. Everyone knew about each other's drug habits, incomes, debts, quarrels and marital problems. But any liberal outlooks that might have crept into their world were ferociously shielded from view. Nobody knew that Mehran's mother worked as a cleaner and maid in north Tehran where she would serve alcohol at dinner parties, that her sons did not pray, or that Ebbie's family thought religion was a waste of time.

While many religious, *sonati*, traditional families were accepting that issues like divorce and protest against the state were new realities of modern city life, true *basiji* or *Hezbollahi* families held tightly on to values they saw as being intrinsically part of their religion. Even Mehran's mother knew her own boundaries. Divorce within this community was still seen as bringing shame upon a family. A woman who considered divorce was simply brandishing her wantonness, no matter how unfaithful her husband was. Mehran's mother still whispered the taboo word *talaagh*, divorce, even though half her employers were divorcees.

Abdul was the son of a bus driver whose father was the head of the Basij unit of bus drivers. The unit, like many of the professional Basij units that had been established, was seen by non-Basij supporters as countering the unions in an effort to weaken them. Abdul had learnt not to look women in the eye and never to shake a woman's hand in order to protect himself from lustful feelings. He already knew most of the Koran off by heart. For Abdul's family, joining the Basij was about loyalty and *khedmat*, duty to serve, a chance to pledge allegiance to the state and to benefit society. It was a way of doing good. Majid, the son of a local mullah, was less staunch in his view of Islam, but had been brought up to believe a man's worth was based on how scrupulously he defended God and good morals. The Basij was a perfect platform to fulfil his religious obligations. For boys like the Ahmadi twins, being a *basiji* was also about reputation and power. The Basij attracted as many thugs and religious fanatics as it did bored, idle boys from impoverished families. Baton in hand and a motorbike between their thighs, these teenagers' dedication to the Islamic Republic made them perfect enforcers. They were the ones who struck fear in people's hearts.

When the Commander was satisfied the boys were adequately intimidated, he set them a task. They would learn five passages from the Koran to be recited at a weekly meeting.

'Please sir, when do we get our guns?' The Ahmadi twins nearly always spoke together. Haji Ahmadi, who was standing with folded arms in the doorway, laughed proudly.

'Patience, dear boys. Work hard, show your true colours and you can reach the top and maybe one day be a commander like me.' The Commander stalked away, leaving them on their own. Ebbie broke the silence, looking to Morteza who he sensed would be an appreciative audience. 'I forgot to congratulate the Commander.'

'What for?'

'Because he's clearly nine months pregnant and expecting any day!' The boys howled with laughter. Even serious Abdul suppressed a smile.

'Show some respect,' hissed the Ahmadi twins.

'Relax, we'll get you some guns soon and then maybe you won't behave as though you've got rods up your arses.' The twins stood up, growling.

'Is he your uncle or something? Why are you so upset?'

'You can't talk like that about a commander of the Basij!'

'And you can't talk to me wearing such ugly trousers, did your granny make them?' With that, Ebbie darted out of the room before the Ahmadis had a chance to catch him.

On the way home, Morteza saw Ebbie kicking a deflated football with some street urchins. 'Aren't you scared of the Ahmadi twins? They may tell the Commander and you'll be in trouble.'

'I like trouble. Anyway, just watch, the Ahmadi twins will be eating out of my hand soon.'

Morteza smiled.

'So did your parents make you join the Basij?' Ebbie asked.

Morteza repeated words he had heard since he was born. 'I want to serve God and my country. It's our duty. And if we go to war, I'll fight just as my brothers did.'

'What, and end up six feet under in a war we won't even have won? Anyway, I hate to break it to you, but you wouldn't last five minutes, you couldn't carry a can of cola to the front line, never mind a gun.'

Morteza launched at Ebbie, pounding his fists into his chest. Ebbie did not flinch.

'Hey man, I'm sorry. I deserve all the punches you throw. I was only teasing you. I think you're cool. It's the tough guys like the twins who are the idiots.' Ebbie fished out a handful of fluff-covered raisins from his pocket as a peace offering. Morteza chewed on a few before speaking. 'So why did you join then?'

'My mum's a terrible cook,' Ebbie deadpanned. Morteza began to laugh.

The following week the boys waited outside the Commander's office. Morteza was the first to be summoned inside. He began the recital in his mellifluous voice, '*Those who oppose (the commands of) Allah...*'

'I can't hear you. Stand here boy.' The Commander gestured to Morteza from behind his desk.

He started again, '*Those who oppose (the commands of) Allah, And His Messenger will be, Humbled to dust; as were, Those before them: for We...*'

The Commander stood up and walked towards Morteza, who backed away. The Commander did not stop advancing until Morteza was up against the wall. The Commander's stomach pressed hard against Morteza's chest. Morteza's voice grew louder, '*Have already sent down, Clear Signs. And the Unbelievers, (Will have) a humiliating, Chastisement...*' The Commander clenched his buttocks as he ground his pelvis into Morteza. Morteza continued to recite, eyes on the floor, '*On the Day that, Allah will raise them, All up (again) and tell them, Of their deeds (which), Allah has reckoned and, Which they forgot, For Allah is Witness, To all things...*'

When the Commander started to pant, Morteza began to cry. He was struggling to get the words out. The Commander stopped, a look of surprise on his face.

'The path to God is always painful, but why are you crying? Is your spiritual connection with Him making you feel uncomfortable?'

'No sir.'

'It is a sin to cry when speaking God's words. You'd better have a good excuse for this crying?'

'I'm sorry. I'm so sorry.'

'I will forgive you but only because you have learnt your homework. You must not be scared by the spiritual awakening that happens in us when we are at one with God. Do you understand me? Or shall I tell your parents about this?'

'I understand you. Please don't tell my parents.' The Commander nodded. Morteza felt overwhelming relief and gratitude to him for showing such leniency.

Ebbie was called in next. The Commander took the longest with him. Ebbie emerged silent and sullen.

Within a few months, Morteza was madly in love. He thought he would accept a grisly death in exchange for Ebbie taking him in his arms. It was not the first time Morteza had been in love with a boy. To his parents' shock, he had repeatedly exposed his erect penis to his cousin Jaffar when he was seven. They did not realize that, at that young age, Morteza had felt the first pangs of sexual desire towards a boy.

Ebbie knew it. Yet he was unperturbed. He revelled in the attention. He was used to the eccentrics and oddballs that were vomited up on the streets. The bulk of Ebbie's education had been in the company of labourers, black-market traders, street kids and prostitutes. They had filled his mind with all that was possible; it did not matter to him if it was condemned. His uncle was a part-time transvestite who wandered the streets in a dress and lipstick; some people thought he was mad and left him alone, others spat on him. Ebbie accepted Morteza without question or judgement. Because of this, Morteza came to trust him more than he had trusted anybody else. Ebbie was the only one who knew that Morteza picked and dried flowers as a secret hobby, or that he liked to touch silk chadors in the bazaar.

The changes happened quickly. Far quicker than Morteza could ever have imagined. For the first time in his life, he began to feel accepted. His uncles now patted him on the back. The local baker, a member of the Basij unit of bakers, served him and other *basijis* before anyone else. When he entered secondary school, his teachers made the *basiji* boys classroom monitors. When enrolment for the Basij took place at school, Morteza was asked to help.

He was experiencing the pride and power of respect, and it was because he was a part of something big and powerful. The Commander said there were millions of Basij members across the land. In reality, nobody really knew how many of them there were, but they had units in schools, universities, mosques, factories, state institutions and private businesses. They were in towns and villages and even tribes in all corners of the country. They were everywhere.

Morteza's own views were not changing so much as being formed for the first time. The lectures were having an effect. Islamic scholars thundered about the dangers of moral decay, titillating the boys with enough morsels of lascivious detail to keep them interested and entrusting them with enough responsibility to keep them excited. The boys were wide-eyed with pride when they were told that they were guardians of their citizens' virtue. A local mullah enraged them with stirring tales of class inequality, underpinning the threat against the Islamic Republic of Western-imported promiscuity.

The majesty and romance of war were instilled in regular lectures by heroic veterans who had fought on the front lines against Iraq. The boys were electrified, and left desperate to fire futuristic weapons straight out of films and experience the purest love they would ever encounter, that of brothers in combat. They were shown videos of Basij training camps. Over a pumping soundtrack, men in fatigues bounded over mountain terrains, bombs exploding around them as they fired their automatic weapons. Afterwards, the boys would be reminded of the invincibility of the Basij force. If they were to be slain in honourable action, they would be venerated for the indisputable glory that awaited them in death. The highest service a Basij could give was to sacrifice his life in war. It was a win-win situation.

Sometimes it felt as though Iran was already at war. At the mosque and on the news they would hear that Zionists controlled the world; that Israel could invade Iran at any moment. Newspapers ran shrill headlines: ISRAEL ANNOUNCES DATE IT WILL ATTACK IRAN.

The Supreme Leader's response always gave the boys hope. At a speech in Mashhad he had said: 'If Israel makes a wrong move, we'll level Tel Aviv!'

The Basij gave Morteza purpose and focus. Supplication to God and country strengthened his resolve to fight his debased feelings towards his sex.

As the boys entered puberty, a long line of clerics attempted to dampen their lust with lectures on the dangers of desire. The lessons only succeeded in arousing the boys' anger. Anger that they could not fight the urge. Anger at those who indulged. Anger at women who posed a temptation.

Morteza's anger was mostly aimed at himself, for inadvertently enticing the Commander's libido. Morteza thought the Commander could tell that he had been built *wrong* and he felt responsible for the weekly abuse, with the Commander continuing to rub against him until he cried. This must be what happened to boys like him.

The Commander invited a black-turbaned ayatollah to give morality lessons – *dars-e akhlaagh* – to the boys. The black turban perched on his head was his ace of spades, marking him out as a descendant of the Prophet. Through tireless self-publicity, the cleric had elevated his status to that of a leading purveyor of modern ethics and standards, as well as his bank balance. He only ever travelled in his white Mercedes. A huge billboard of the Ayatollah's smiling face stood on Vali Asr, near the Islamic Republic of Iran Broadcasting network, with an offer of his services at reasonable rates. The Commander had haggled ferociously with him for a discount on a series of lessons for the boys.

The arrival of a celebrity cleric was one of the highlights of Morteza's year. Even Gholam the caretaker was beside himself that such an exalted and virtuous cleric would be gracing his mosque. He had seen the poster and he had heard the cleric's adverts on the radio; he spent three days scrubbing and demanded his wife buy a new chador. Gholam had asked if his daughters could stand behind the door and listen to the cleric's holy counsel. He was berated for even thinking this would be acceptable. His daughters might still look like little girls, but they were dangerously close to bleeding age, which was banishment age at the mosque whenever the *basijis* were near.

The Ayatollah's lectures crystallized Morteza's resolve to fight his urges by devoting himself to God through his work with the Basij. But he could hardly bear to listen as the Ayatollah lectured extensively on the scourge of homosexuality. He would lift passages from the Koran, quoting paragraphs about Lot, who was punished by God for sodomy. Mostly he free-styled, crackling with repulsion as he told the boys gay men were lower than dogs and pigs and were to blame for Aids. With each new session, Morteza realized the magnitude of his sinful thoughts. After the fourth session, Morteza swore to himself he would never see Ebbie again. That was not hard, for Ebbie had stopped turning up. Morteza guessed why, but the two boys had never spoken of what the Commander did to them in his office. Morteza had heard that Ebbie had started smoking *sheesheh* in the local park with a bunch of down-and-outs.

A year later, Ebbie disappeared.

'He'll turn up, he always bloody does,' his father said. But he never did. Morteza cried when he heard the rumours: that his body had been found near Shoosh, where the shrunken corpses of drug addicts surfaced from time to time.

The Commander retired the same year that Ebbie went missing. A new commander of the Basij unit was appointed. Commander Abbas Yazdi wore a black and white *kuffieyh* scarf round his shoulders as a mark of solidarity with his Palestinian brothers. The Basij sessions took a more political turn: Commander Yazdi fed the boys with revolutionary stories and gave them reading lists. Morteza found a new hero in Ali Shariati, a Sorbonne-educated academic who was imprisoned under the Shah and who died before the Islamic Revolution. Shariati had unleashed a revitalized appreciation of the Islamic faith on the masses before his death, cleverly fusing Western philosophy and sociology with the principles of Shia Islam to create a doctrine that had class war, revolution and Islamic puritanism as its cornerstones.

Morteza's *Hezbollahi* uncle had recognized Commander Yazdi's name: he was a renowned war veteran and an original revolutionary who had worked his way up the ranks of the IRGC, the Islamic Revolutionary Guard Corps, also known as Sepah. Among his peers, Commander Yazdi had a reputation as a fair and incorruptible man. He also detested clerics. In the early days of the Islamic Republic, in the 1980s, Commander Yazdi had been the chief bodyguard of a prominent cleric. The cleric was an ultra-conservative and a vocal champion of stoning; he believed in the literal interpretation of the Koran and rigorous adherence to Islamic law. He was also under threat of assassination by the MEK. When the cleric was admitted to hospital, an informant had reported that the MEK were going to strike. Commander Yazdi stationed his men around the building and nervously paced through the wards, hand on gun. The MEK came for the cleric on the third day. A nurse had questioned a man dressed as a doctor. She knew immediately from his faltering response that he was an impostor. She shouted for help and he darted towards a back staircase. Commander Yazdi reached the stairwell in time to catch a glimpse of him and fired a shot. Somehow the assassin managed to escape. As Commander Yazdi neared the cleric's room, he panicked. The soldier guarding it was nowhere to be seen and the door was ajar. He took his gun out of its holster, edged closer and peered in. The soldier was lying on top of the cleric, who had his arms wrapped around him, pulling him down. Finally the cleric eased his grip and the soldier shuffled towards the door. As he emerged, Commander Yazdi slammed him against the wall.

'What the fuck was going on there?'

The soldier's face flushed red with embarrassment. 'Sir, you got to help me. He does this the whole time. He says holding me like that is for my spiritual development, so he can transfer God's energy to me through his body. One thing it doesn't feel is Godly. I don't know what to do!'

Commander Yazdi was furious. He marched in and told the cleric exactly what he thought of his 'spirituality'. The cleric told him to relax, and that it was hard for a common man, so far removed from God, to understand the workings of religion. Commander Yazdi marched out, pulling all his men from the operation. At a disciplinary hearing, at which a dishonourable discharge looked imminent, he made the charges against the cleric.

'Yes, we know. He's also been caught touching little boys. Listen, we applaud you for standing up to him. It shows you're a man of morals. But what can we do? You know his links. It's one of those things we have to let go,' the investigating officer had said. Commander Yazdi's charges disappeared, replaced with a commendation for excellent behaviour. But he could not let the case go, passing the allegations to a brigadier-general. He was in luck. The general had never liked clerics. He also happened to be a trusted confidant of one of the country's most influential politicians; but despite being kicked out of parliament, soon enough the cleric returned to public life. Commander Yazdi stepped back from his rising career in disgust. He insisted on teaching young *basijis* in the hope of instilling proper values in the new generation.

By the time the protests of the contested elections of 2009 started, Morteza was spending most of his time with the twins, who he saw as exemplars of masculinity. Mehran had already left. He had resigned when some of the boys in the group started stopping cars in the neighbourhood, intimidating those who played music too loudly. 'I don't want to be the arsehole that hassles people,' he had said, looking at Morteza.

At the *hosseinieh* the boys watched videos of rampaging protesters. State television was tirelessly reporting on these criminals who were threatening the security of the state. The boys heard about a *basiji* called Saaneh Jaleh who had been martyred in the line of duty, shot by a demonstrator. State television had broadcast a photo of a bearded Jaleh with his *basiji* colleagues. In fact, unbeknown to Morteza and his class, Jaleh had most probably been killed by a government sniper; friends of Jaleh declared he was not even a member of the Basij and that a picture of his Basij membership card had been Photoshopped by Fars, a news agency linked to the Revolutionary Guards. Jaleh was, they said, an anti-regime Sunni Kurd and art student, and the authorities had hijacked his death for their own propaganda.

Yet the boys wanted retribution for the killing of one of their brothers, and they were itching for some action. But they were deemed too inexperienced to be sent out into the fray. Older *basijis* gleefully described their street battles, showing mobile-phone footage of beatings and mass arrests. Morteza and the boys went out during the second week of the protests, on motorbikes donated by the twins' father, Haji Ahmadi. They had not been allowed near the action by the security forces, but the petrified looks on people's faces as their bikes neared gave them a thrill. Morteza did not feel the same. He was overwhelmed with sadness, which in turn made him angry at his wretchedness. He had taken to berating himself out loud: *You stupid idiot, what's wrong with you?* Once Khadijeh had heard him, but she had said nothing. She was relieved that Morteza was fighting his weaknesses.

A week after the protests started, Morteza heard Mehran and his family shouting *Allah Akbar*, God is Great, in the dead of night from the rooftop of their home. It was the cry of dissent, the same chant protesters had used against the Shah. Morteza was scared for Mehran's family; he knew that his unit were trawling the streets, listening out for that cry so they could storm the homes of those who dared to chant from their roofs. What Morteza did not know was that another Basij unit did storm Mehran's house, but that the commander had sent his boys away and let Mehran's family walk free; he did not agree with the violence against the demonstrators. Morteza also did not know that across the city some *basijis* had refused to beat protesters and had deserted.

After the demonstrations ended, out on the streets the Basij were more hated than ever. Grand Ayatollah Montazeri, one of the world's highest-ranking Shia clerics and one of the founders of the Islamic Revolution, had publicly condemned the Basij's involvement in the violence. Montazeri had already been sidelined from power and put under house arrest after speaking out against the mass killings of political prisoners in the 1980s.

At a football match, a few hundred supporters chanted at a crowd of *basijis*: *kos-e-nanat*, 'your granny's cunt'.

The protests changed the boys' allegiance to the Basij. It was now much more than a hobby; it was a matter of life and death. High-ranking Basij commanders briefed the boys on crowd control, on using weapons against the public and on obeying orders to shoot.

The tops of the trees on Vali Asr had been swallowed up by the night. On either side of the street, hundreds of dusty tree trunks disappeared into a black sky that pressed down onto the road below. Morteza, Abdul, Majid and the Ahmadi twins were standing near the intersection of Vali Asr and Parkway, a few hundred yards from Pop Stereo, which sold top-of-the-range sound systems for thousands of US dollars. On the way, Morteza and the boys had walked past a phone box on Vali Asr on which someone had daubed: DEATH TO THE DICTATOR. They had stopped to scrub it off.

They spoke in short, fast bursts, their speech speeded up by the excitement of their first real mission as *basijis*. They had been given a Colt and a pair of handcuffs each. The group began to unload the pick-up truck a few yards behind a new government poster: MY DAUGHTER, I'M TALKING TO YOU: IN GOD'S EYES, BY PRESERVING YOUR *HEJAB* YOU ARE SAFEGUARDING THE BLOOD I SHED.

For no particular reason other than the thrill of it, the boys radioed to the team that had been stationed at the northern end of Vali Asr, just past Tajrish Square. Both teams were setting up checkpoints, and had been instructed to stop anyone they deemed to be involved in immoral or dubious behaviour.

That turned out to be mostly attractive females. The Ahmadi twins waved a car over. Two pretty girls were manically readjusting their headscarves.

'What time do you call this to be out alone, dressed like that? Where are you going?'

'Just home,' one of the girls squeaked. The terror in the girls' faces roused the boys' spirits and their nerve.

'Where have you been? Both of you get out.'

Abdul and Morteza began to search the car.

'Have you been drinking?'

'No. As God is my witness, I have not been drinking.'

'Let me smell your breath.'

The girls, only a few years older than their teenage interrogators, knew they were in trouble. It was midnight, they were wearing tight party *manteaus*, had painted nails, lashings of make-up and, apart from having taken MDMA, had been drinking shots all night. They were on their way to another party.

'If you don't let me smell your breath now, I'm arresting you.' Majid flashed a glint of handcuff. The girl closed her eyes so she would not have to look at the twins glowering at her as she opened her mouth. They stared at her parted lips in wonder. The Ahmadi twins had never stood so close to a woman who was not their mother.

'You're not breathing out.' They stepped towards her. The girl opened her mouth wider, trying to hold her breath in. 'I want to hear your breath as it comes out.' Finally the girl expelled a puff of air, warm and stinking of vodka. A moist cloud enveloped the twins. One of them had even opened his mouth a little, as though trying to taste it. The girl opened her eyes and braced herself. But all the twins had smelt was the acidic smell of sour breath.

'There were these in the car.' Abdul was holding a handful of CDs, Shakira, Lady Gaga and some Persian pop. 'Shall I take them to the station?' He began breaking the CDs with his hands. He had not yet managed to get very close to the girls and wanted a turn.

'Please don't take us to the police. My parents have no money, we couldn't afford a court case. Everyone's got music these days, you know that.'

'Let them go. They're wasting our time,' Morteza shouted from the side of the road. There was silence. Morteza was acutely aware that he could not muster even a fraction of the rage that bubbled up from the others, frothing out of their mouths as torrents of abuse. When he saw his victims' frightened faces he could not help but recoil, hurrying away to pretend to check his mobile phone.

One of the girls had started drunkenly crying.

'Just let them go.' Morteza realized that he sounded as though he was pleading. The twins scowled.

'Get back in the car, and if we ever see you behaving like this again, you really will be in trouble,' said Abdul as he used his boot to slam the door shut.

'Fucking sluts, they'd open their legs to their own brothers if they got money for it.' The twins turned to Morteza. 'What's wrong with you? You've been like this since the protests. And we heard that you saw Mehran smoking a joint and you did nothing. Whose side are you on?'

'You keep letting us down, bro.' Now it was Abdul's turn.

'I think we should tell him,' said one of the twins.

'Tell me what?'

'There are rumours about you...'

'What rumours?' Morteza's voice was shaking.

'We're risking our reputations being seen with you.'

'I've told them the rumours aren't true. It's impossible,' said Majid.

'I don't know what you're talking about. Please just tell me.'

'That you're not a real man...'

'That you're a faggot.' They were all staring at him. Morteza was suddenly cold, and fighting the urge to let his teeth chatter.

'Who said that? I can't believe you're saying this to me,' his voice as faint as a croak. The four boys were motionless. They just looked at him.

'You believe me, don't you? I love God and my country, and it would be impossible for someone like me to be like *that*.' He tried to make his face grimace in revulsion, but his muscles were paralysed. 'I want to know who's spreading these rumours because they need to be taught a lesson.' Morteza was starting to sound more confident. This was a matter of survival. 'You're discussing immoral rumours like your gossiping aunts when we're supposed to be working.' Morteza put his arms square on his hips, as he had seen the twins do. 'Gossiping is more important than our work, I suppose?' He nodded towards a car that had slowed down as it approached their checkpoint. Morteza flagged it over.

'Get out.' It was a man in his twenties with long, curly blond hair in a ponytail. He was wearing a tight T-shirt and black skinny jeans. Both his ears were pierced.

'Driving licence.' The man fumbled about nervously; when he finally flashed his licence, Abdul noticed he was wearing black nail varnish.

'That bitch is wearing nail varnish.'

'Hey man, I like playing the electric guitar…it's not anything more than that…I don't drink, I don't party, I never break the law…'

'See, and because of your gossiping, you nearly let him go.' Morteza was ignoring the bumbling victim. He turned to Abdul, 'Hold him.'

The man had started to beg. The twins locked his arms behind his back and Abdul pushed his head down. Morteza got out the flick knife he kept tucked in his belt and started to hack at the man's hair. The man wriggled and yelled, chunks of his hair scattered near his feet. When he was done, Morteza punched him hard in the back, then started kicking him in his stomach and slamming his elbow in his face.

'Fucking queer bastard, you're lucky we're not going to kill you, you little fucking faggot.' Morteza looked at his black eyes, burst lip and blood-splattered T-shirt and decided to let him go. He turned to the boys. 'Don't you ever come to me with your filthy tales again.'

*

Morteza was at the mosque watching the Supreme Leader on television. He was warning his citizens not to discuss the biggest embezzlement scandal in the country's history. Bankers had used forged documents to steal over two billion US dollars from several state- and private-owned banks. For weeks nobody had discussed anything else.

The unit kept up to date with every Friday prayer and every word the Supreme Leader uttered, vigilant for any commands that required action and any opportunities to dispense justice.

As it got dark, the boys mounted their bikes and drove straight to Farmanich, a posh, rich neighbourhood where they had formed an alliance with some local *basijis* they had met at a summer training camp. Majid had a pair of nunchucks stuffed into his trousers that he had bought from Gomrok. When he had tried to demonstrate a Kung Fu-inspired move, one of the handles had smacked him in the jaw and the boys had bent double with laughter.

It was a Thursday night, party night. Within half an hour they got what they were looking for. Throbbing music and a stream of revellers dressed like *Westerners*. Morteza's unit had been told they should leave house raids to the police, but parties were raided less and less nowadays and the police rarely took up their leads. The boys lamented the power that was being sucked out of their eager hands.

They drove to the station. They were in luck; the officer in charge was bored, and he enjoyed showing these *basijis* who was in control. He told the boys they could accompany his men on the raid. The officer gathered a small team, including two soldiers on national service.

At a plain, stone-clad apartment block, the cop buzzed every single ringer and stared into the entryphone camera.

'If you don't open the door, I'll have my men break it down.'

A panicked voice crackled through. 'I'm coming down right now, officer.'

'He thinks he can buy himself some time. I don't think so.' Morteza and the boys smirked. They were in for a good night.

The moment the front door opened the officer pushed it wide open and streamed inside, his men and the boys following behind. 'Check the neighbours aren't hiding any of these idiots,' the officer shouted out. 'Whose apartment is this?'

'Mine, sir.' A man in his twenties was panting behind them, smiling. 'Can we sort this out, officer? In any way you like.' He moved towards the officer and tapped his wallet with his hand.

'Think you can bribe a man of the law?'

'Yes sir I do!' He slurred his words. His friends around him started giggling.

'Shut up!' the officer screamed. The giggles were becoming louder.

'I order you to stop laughing now!' At that, the group burst out into a collective roar of laughter. Morteza and the boys were confused.

'You need to teach these arseholes a lesson,' the Ahmadi twins were shouting. The officer slapped the boy across the face. He laughed harder than before.

'They're on drugs.' The officer shrugged. He was right; they had raided mid-acid trip. The officer in charge told the boys to search the flat. Abdul found condoms in the bedroom, to be used as evidence. Morteza walked to the back of the house and began checking the rooms. He opened a bathroom door and saw one of the young soldiers standing over the loo, emptying bottles of booze into it. When the soldier saw Morteza he froze. For a few seconds, they stared at each other in silence. Then the soldier whispered, 'They're kids. They're not evil, just having a good time. They're not even that rich, they'll be screwed with all this booze.' Morteza closed the door.

'Nothing back here,' he shouted out. He felt no guilt at having shown mercy. He had experienced a strange connection to the young soldier carrying out this random act of compassion.

The team led the kids outside; they were unsteady on their feet and unable to co-ordinate their movements while hand-cuffed to each other, which led to more laughter. Even one of the policemen had laughed.

'Hey guys, we should party sometime,' said a tall, lanky tripper to the cop.

'You should whack him!' said Abdul.

'Hey, you need to get laid, that would seriously chill you the fuck out.' The revellers burst out laughing and just as the Ahmadi twins were about to lunge towards the lanky tripper, Abdul calmly took a can of pepper spray out of his pocket and aimed it directly into his eyes. The lanky tripper dropped to the floor, rolling into a ball, crying in pain. His friend who was chained to him was dragged down with him. The younger cops rolled their eyes at each other. They hated these *basiji* boys. Another officer was trying to placate Morteza's group. As much as he enjoyed intimidating rich kids, he did not have the stomach for violence, and anyway he enjoyed an occasional tipple and toke of opium himself.

At the station the duty officer approached the partygoers, who had been deposited in a waiting room.

'Guys, they're going to give you a drugs and alcohol test. You're fucked. I want to help you – here, eat this, it absorbs the drugs and the booze, they won't be able to find a thing.' The officer handed them carbon paper. One of the kids high-fived him as he gobbled up the paper, wincing at its bitterness. Five minutes later the head of the police station walked in, a big man with a handlebar moustache.

'All the drunk, stoned motherfuckers with blue mouths get up.' This time the police officers were laughing as much as the kids.

The kids spent the next four days in an underground car park that had been transformed into prison cells. Their parents were not told of their whereabouts until the day they were released. All of them were ordered to appear before a court, and their parents were made to hand over the deeds to their houses as bail.

As Morteza and the group were leaving, a disabled man in a wheelchair entered the station, shouting with the full force of his lungs. He was leaning as far forward as he could go. Anger had engorged his face with blood. He spat as he yelled.

'Yes, my wife's a prostitute!' His left arm – his only working limb – was jabbing the air, his hand clenched so hard in rage that the white of his bones looked almost luminous under his stretched skin. 'She sells her body for money because that's the only way she can pay for my medicine. This is how the Islamic Republic treats its war veterans!' Beside him, his handcuffed wife was weeping silently, wiping her eyes with the corners of her headscarf. 'And as if you haven't emasculated me enough, now you want to arrest her. You think this is the way we want to fucking live?' Three policemen were trying to calm him down. 'Please keep your voice down, you're going to get into trouble.'

His wife had been caught having sex with a client in a car. Her husband was in his wheelchair at the top of the road. He always went with her when she worked, as it was safer that way.

'Fuck the Islamic Republic of Iran, fuck them all, this is what they've done to us! I can't make love to my wife, and now she has to fuck other men so we don't have to live like animals! Just kill me now!' The Ahmadi twins were shouting at the police officer to slap the cripple. You could hear his blasphemous screams from outside the station. He had drawn quite a crowd. The police chief had heard everything from his office. He emerged sighing and shaking his head from side to side. Whenever he thought he had heard it all, something would happen that would unsettle him.

'Just let them go.' The officers were perturbed enough to quickly acquiesce. They also knew better than to argue with the chief.

The Ahmadi twins stepped forward. 'She's a whore! She's defacing the name of Islam, and you want to let her walk free!' Majid and Abdul were also screeching their disapproval.

The police chief stepped towards them, bellowing so loudly that the whole station was shocked into silence. 'If you don't show some respect, I will have you dealt with – being a *basiji* does not make you immune to humility and humanity. Get out of my station and don't ever come back.'

As the boys left, Morteza turned round and saw that the war veteran's head could not have been held any higher as his wife wheeled him out of the police station. Morteza saw her stroke her husband's neck; in that tiny gesture he knew the police chief had been right.

Just over halfway down Vali Asr, tucked behind Tehran's City Theatre, is Daneshjoo Park, a small, landscaped slab of green, thick with trees and shrubs. At first glance it seems like any other park, where lovers come to take refuge from the city and its laws; the tell-tale signs of illicit behaviour are here: knees touching, fingers entwined, numbers being exchanged. But those who care to look a little harder will see something else is happening. Park-e Daneshjoo has been adopted by the city's misfits and deviants. Cruising gay men, prostitutes of all persuasions and punters of all ages do business among the benches and the fountains. A man with a shaved head, 500 Viagra pills, two vibrators and various other sex toys stuffed in his coat calls Park-e Daneshjoo Tehran's 'Little Pigalle', his reference to Paris's sex district – all the more impressive when you know he was born after the revolution and has never left Iran.

Morteza had heard the boys talk about Park-e Daneshjoo as a den of immorality that needed to be destroyed. Now he was on Vali Asr walking towards it. After years of repressing his desires, he could no longer resist.

A dirty beige smog pushed down on the city, trapped between the road and a dark blue sky. It was the day before a long weekend and Vali Asr was crammed with shoppers. Loudspeakers belted out the latest bargains and price reductions; Céline Dion and Europop blasted into the street from the clothes stores. Outside a shop selling yellow baseball caps stamped with SACRED HEART REGIONAL CANCER CENTER a green budgerigar chirped at passers-by from its cage. The traffic was at a standstill; Vali Asr had been transformed into an endless car park. On the side of the road a man in a ripped leather jacket was selling bottles of knocked-off eau de cologne from a tatty holdall. Morteza weaved through the cars, gulping mouthfuls of poisonous air.

Morteza was astonished by the theatre's beauty; a giant cylinder, a perfect mix of modern sixties and classic Persian architecture; concrete columns and geometric arches, intricate inlaid tiles dotted turquoise and green, big studded wood-and-metal doors. Morteza's reaction surprised him; he must have passed by the theatre hundreds of times on the bus but this was the first time he was *really* looking at it. Men and women were sitting on hexagonal cement benches talking, listening to music on iPods and reading newspapers and books. Morteza wound his way through the crowds to the back, down some steps into the small park, which was on a series of levels. He sat on the edge of a bench, scanning the scene around him. A girl with a visor over her black chador and Nike Air trainers was whispering in the ear of her married middle-class businessman lover. On a patch of green grass in front of him, a street sweeper was stretched out in a pool of sun, still in the lurid orange uniform that earned him the nickname of *haveech*, carrot, among Tehranis. He had taken off one shoe, on which he rested his head.

At first, Morteza wondered whether the boys had got their information wrong. Nothing was happening. Then he began to notice: the looks, the slight nod of the head, the almost imperceptible narrowing of the eyes. After nearly thirty minutes of summoning his courage, he dared to hold a man's gaze, and it was done. He followed the man to some public toilets where a line of young boys were cottaging. In a dirty, small cubicle he cried with pain as he was fucked. The man did not look in his eyes when it was done, he just disappeared out into the world.

The next week, Morteza went back to Park-e Daneshjoo. In the toilets he tried to kiss the stranger who had met his eyes. The man punched him in the face and walked out. The next time he picked up a man, he asked his permission to kiss on the mouth. This time the man called him a pervert before slapping him.

The woman at the door was wearing a chic beige trench coat that was cinched at the waist, a fake Hermès headscarf and no make-up.

'Salaam, my name is Nassim Soltani and I would like to speak to Morteza Kazemi.' Her husband and little boy stood beside her; it always worked better that way, people were less intimidated and more trustful of a woman with a family by her side. Nassim and her husband respectfully bowed their heads, greeting their growing audience; Khadijeh's sister and niece had grabbed their chadors and run to the door, where they stood gawping at the visitors.

'We think your son, Morteza Kazemi, may be able to help someone who is in trouble; we have heard Morteza is an honest young man who has served his country and God with a pure heart. You must be very proud of him.' Nassim had been dealing with women like Khadijeh for over ten years. She knew how to handle them. Khadijeh nodded in approval while her relatives whispered to each other. Khadijeh shouted Morteza's name without averting her gaze. Morteza had been listening to the conversation from the hallway. When he emerged, he made sure to step outside and close the door behind him. His family would be straining to listen. He nodded to Nassim and began to walk down the road; she quickly followed. The only chance she stood of persuading men like Morteza to talk was by extricating them from their families. After five minutes Morteza stopped on the edge of a park.

'I need your help. You're not in any trouble at all; but this is a sensitive matter.' She gave Morteza her business card and told her husband to go and buy some ice cream. 'I represent people who are victims of our justice system. I usually represent people no one else will touch. Are you happy to talk here?' Morteza looked around; nobody in sight. He nodded.

'Did you know that the old Commander of your Basij unit was stabbed to death recently?' Morteza bristled. Thought of the

Commander still made him shudder; he had tried to obliterate all memory of him from his mind.

Morteza had heard the news in the mosque a month ago. The Commander had been murdered by a madman. Not everyone believed the story. The mullah of the mosque had said the killing was the work of an undercover Iraqi spy who was seeking retribution for all the enemies the Commander had valiantly slain during the war. The Commander's close friends had said a drug lord had ordered the assassination for an enormous opium debt. The mosque had held a lavish funeral for the Commander. Hundreds had paid their respects. Food was handed out to the poor. Morteza had felt intense relief.

'I don't know how I can help. I was simply a student of the Commander. I hadn't seen him for years,' he said, staring at a patch of dried grass.

'But I believe you know his killer. Ebbie Haghighi.'

Morteza looked up in shock. 'But Ebbie went missing years ago, people said he was found dead.'

'He's very much alive. He suffered greatly under the Commander. He turned to drugs. Do you know what the Commander was doing to him?'

'No.' Morteza lied, instinctively and quickly.

'The Commander was raping him. Every week. Ebbie has admitted to the murder. He says he feels no remorse. He's very happy he killed the Commander. But he's about to be executed for it. Ebbie wasn't the only victim. If I can prove this happened to others, I have a good chance of saving him.'

Ebbie had never forgiven the Commander. He had left Tehran, wanting to be as far away from him as possible, and had worked on building sites across the country, until the need for vengeance grew so strong he could think of nothing else. He had returned to the city and headed straight for Gomrok, where he bought a serrated hunting knife. The Commander was still living in the neighbourhood. When he answered his front door, Ebbie plunged the knife into his chest and his stomach. The Commander fell backwards, but he carried on stabbing him, even when the Commander's wife ran to him screaming. When he was done, he wiped the blade on his jeans, calmly tucked it back into his jacket and walked to the nearest police station, where he handed himself in. The cops thought he was a lunatic, but he was simply a man at peace, resigned to the fact that he would soon be hanging from a crane – a small sacrifice for the satisfaction of revenge. When asked about his motives, he had kept silent. It was only after his case was assigned to Nassim that the truth came out. Nassim's instinct and experience taught her there was more to this than a straightforward killing. She had also dealt with enough cases of abuse to know there would be more than one victim.

'You're not the first person from the unit that I've spoken to. Obviously I can't give you any names, but three others have so far agreed to testify. The Commander abused a lot of young boys. The more testimony I get, the stronger our case is. Maybe the Commander didn't touch you, but if he did, I can guarantee that your family will not hear about it. Nobody will, apart from me and a judge. None of his other victims will present evidence on the same day; no one else will see you.' Morteza agreed to meet in Nassim's office on Vali Asr the following afternoon.

Morteza had never heard a woman speak with such candid honesty and unflinching openness. Nassim talked about genitals and sexual proclivities as if she were discussing the weather. The only other person who had been this direct was Ebbie. Morteza was immediately comfortable in her presence. He told her all that had happened with the Commander and agreed to testify.

The case was held behind closed doors, as Nassim had promised. Ebbie was found guilty of murder, but his death sentence was revoked. He would remain in Evin prison until he was an old man.

The week of Ebbie's appeal, newspapers had received an order from the Ministry that the word 'rape' was banned from use in all media. A few newspapers reported the crime of a stabbing of a Basij commander, but they were not allowed to name him. They stated that the assailant had been spared execution, as there was evidence that the Commander had *mistreated* him and other boys.

It was not until his epiphany at the secret Ashura, back in the room filled with blood and sweat, that Morteza realized that everything he had believed in was a lie; that he could no longer be a *basiji*, that he did not believe in what it stood for; more than that, that he did not like the people he called his friends. Until that moment, Morteza had expected to devote his life to the Basij.

He had been spending all his spare time at the *hosseinieh*, staying later and later. When everyone went home he would research his condition on the shared laptop, making sure always to wipe his browsing history. To his surprise he read that the state advocated medical intervention for people like him, and there was even a fatwa condoning it.

He had stopped having sex with strangers, but his thoughts were still transgressive. He had been grateful to the Basij for keeping him in line, acting as an extra incentive to fight his unnatural urges. He had believed it would be his salvation. But now he saw things clearly for the first time. Staying in the Basij would in fact be his ruin. He had to get out and turn his life upside down.

When he walked out of the secret Ashura, after managing to shake off the twins and Abdul, he wandered through the streets for a while and called Nassim. She was gentle and reassuring and promised she would help him. He returned home, announcing to Khadijeh that he had left the Basij. He wanted to tell her more, to tell her that he had felt duped all these years, but her reaction was bad enough so he thought it should wait.

The dawn light had only just started to smudge the night sky when Morteza heard the banging on the door. At first Kazem and Khadijeh thought they were being burgled. Then they heard the shouts.

'Fucking fag!' It was the Ahmadi twins. Kazem began beating Morteza about the head.

'Shame, shame, shame. You have brought nothing but shame on our family! Go out and face justice!'

Khadijeh began beating her own head and wailing.

'We know why you left Ashura! We have evidence you're a queer, we saw the filth you were reading on the computer!' More banging. Morteza cowered in the corner of the room. Khadijeh peeked through the curtains; she could see some neighbours looking out of windows.

'Why are they saying these things?' Khadijeh turned to Morteza. 'You need to leave and not come back. Your father will either kill you or have a heart attack. And I will never be able to face the neighbours again. Please go.' She hugged him as she led him to the back door.

*

Shireen leaves her job as a secretary on Fatemi Street early; she has a final appointment with the doctor who operated on her nose. It was worth paying the extra money as the surgeon is one of Tehran's best. When she leaves the consulting room she rushes home, buying pistachios on the way; tonight she has a special guest.

She lives in a tiny flat and struggles to make ends meet, yet Shireen is the happiest she has been in her life.

She cooks her guest's favourite dish: jewelled rice with saffron, almonds, pistachios and barberries. On top she scatters rose petals. She spends hours getting ready and puts on her best outfit, an elegant cream suit with nude-coloured peep-toe sandals. Her flatmate gives her copper-coloured hair a Farrah Fawcett-style blow-dry.

When Nassim arrives with two boxes of pastries, the women hug and Shireen introduces Nassim to her flatmate, who has heard all about this straight-talking lawyer.

Shireen has set the table beautifully, with a candle burning in the middle. The women eat and talk for hours. Before she leaves, Nassim tells Shireen how proud she is of her.

'I want to give you something,' says Shireen. From a box in the corner of her room she takes out a laminated card and hands it to Nassim. 'I won't be needing this any more.' Nassim laughs and kisses her. It is a Basij membership card. Printed on it is a small photo and next to it Shireen's birth name: MORTEZA KAZEMI.

SEVEN

ASGHAR

Nasser Khosrow Street and Shoosh Street, south Tehran

'I toast all you motherfuckers!' Asghar raised his glass, waving it across the room, 'and all the motherfuckers we've lost along the way!' He gulped the triple shot of *aragh sagee*, home-brewed vodka, and smacked the glass down on the small wooden table, sucking his teeth as the liquid burned the back of his throat.

'Ya Hossein!'

The regulars shouted back, over the sound of slamming, 'Ya Hossein!'

Tonight was a tradition that Asghar had lived by for over forty years: to mark the start of the holy month of Ramadan they would drink for four nights straight. It was the final hurrah, a celebratory blow-out drink before thirty days of fasting and abstinence, thirty days of a city full of hungry, bad-tempered people with bad breath. He looked around the room at all the new faces. How he wished the old boys were still here. Nobody understood the old ways any more.

After the toasts, the regulars all went back to playing, mainly poker and blackjack. It was nearly a full house tonight. Asghar was pleased. Until he heard her coming. Above the clamour, his doormen's voices pleading with her, trying to hold her back. He knew nothing could stop her. Pari threw open the doors and stormed in.

'You promised me! You promised me!' The men started laughing. They were used to Pari's dramatic entrances and public admonishments of Asghar. None of them understood how she ever made it past security; they joked that security probably pissed themselves in fear whenever they saw her black chador angrily billowing behind her as she strode up the stairs. Asghar ran over to her, his face red.

'Darling, it's not what you think, we're just having a drink!' He had his arm round her and was manoeuvring her towards the door.

'Don't you dare touch me! I can see the cards, I can see the money. You're a liar. You've always been a liar.' Pari started sobbing.

'Pari Khanoum, we just like to play snap, that's not un-Islamic!'

'Pari Khanoum, I swear, the only bet I've made is with Asghar – a million tomans that you would find out about tonight!'

The regulars began trotting out the usual jokes. None of them could understand why Asghar would get so upset by his crazy wife, or why he was so soft on her.

'Quick, someone get a doctor, Asghar's balls have just been chopped off!' The men were raucous with laughter. Pari stormed out. Asghar wanted to run after her and apologize, promise that he would close the place down in a few months' time when they had made enough money to pay off their debts. But he went nowhere. He was too embarrassed to chase his wife, afraid of subjugating himself in front of the men. It was his reputation, after all, that attracted so many of the young crowd who came here, to see Asghar the Brave, the man who once ruled the streets of south Tehran – a real-life, living, breathing old gangster, a relic of the city's history. His friends regularly berated him for not keeping his wife under control. They saw her as an interfering termagant who needed to be put in her place. They did not know that she had endured decades of broken promises. Asghar was angry with her for making him look stupid and he resented that she always made him feel pathetic. But he could never stay angry at Pari for long; she was his everything, his one true love. And he had failed her yet again. Asghar got back to pouring the drinks. He would talk to her in the morning.

After forty years, Asghar could still surprise himself with the force of his love for Pari. She was now nearly seventy years old, but when he looked at her he still saw the wide-eyed, carefree beauty he had fallen in love with. None of his friends could understand it. They all found their wives unattractive and boring. Asghar was the only one who had remained faithful to his woman. He had strayed early on in the relationship, before they were married, and Pari had found out. She had sent a messenger boy to tell him he was a liar and she never wanted to see him again. It took nearly six months to get her back, the worst six months of his life. He spent a week sleeping on the doorstep outside her house begging for a second chance. He was never going to risk that again.

Pari and Asghar had met in a cabaret club called the Moulin Rouge in Manuchehri Street. She was a showgirl and his crew were providing security. Mustangs, Chevrolets and Cadillacs were parked outside. Unlike the cabarets of Gomrok, where most of the performers were from France and Germany, at the Moulin Rouge the dancers and singers were all Iranian. Pari's wardrobe was a dazzling collection of fringed bikinis, beaded leotards and fishnet tights; she would high-kick while a live jazz band played and Asghar knocked back vodkas. Asghar had fooled around with most of the dancing girls, as they all had, but Pari was different.

She had an honesty about her that he had never seen before. He told the other guys she was out of bounds, and they respected that. Even in those early days it was obvious Asghar was on his way to the top – that he would *be* somebody. Asghar knew very well what dancing girls did, but that was not a problem. One of his brothers had married a dancing girl; he had simply taken her for *tobeh*, Shia baptism, to be cleansed of her sins by a mullah. Which is what happened to Pari when Asghar proposed. Asghar took her to a holy shrine where she repented her whoring and swore her loyalty to God and the imams as the cleric uttered prayers under his breath and splashed the backs of her ears with water. She was pure again. Asghar never held her past against her. Everybody makes mistakes and everybody deserves a second chance.

Pari was thirteen years old when her parents sold her to a man in his sixties. They haggled over her skinny, undeveloped body for ten minutes before they settled on her worth. The buyer got himself a bargain thanks to his excellent timing. He had arrived at the precise moment that withdrawal symptoms were taking hold of Pari's parents; their bodies shivered with need, they spoke in broken sentences. Pari's mother put her daughter's belongings in a blue plastic bag – a chador, a pair of trousers, two tops and some underwear. Pari was crying, but she knew better than to beg; it was bad enough that she was being sold, but to be beaten over the head at this moment would be even more humiliating. Especially in front of the man. Her new husband, Agha Mammad. As her mother handed her over to Agha Mammad, she kissed Pari's head, only the third time in her life that her mother had kissed her. There were no tears.

'Don't cry Pari *joon*, we're doing what's best for you, every girl needs a husband.' The lies came out in the same familiar slur, as they always did. Pari's parents had both been born in Nazi Abad, a deprived neighbourhood a little farther south than where Asghar grew up. Education, health care and regular employment simply evaded their families for generations. The men were mostly labourers who slaved whenever they had the chance to work, and died young. Most of them succumbed to addiction somewhere along the way. First it was opium and then, when a cheaper opiate came to town, they snapped it up. Pari's parents were quick to turn to heroin, as were so many of their neighbours.

As Tehran's early construction boom stretched south, Nazi Abad slowly transformed from a magnet for the poor and dispossessed to a suburb full of thriving shops and working-class hope. Pari's parents were soon priced out by rising rents and shamed by the creeping respectability of the neighbourhood. They headed one and a quarter miles north, settling in a new hovel – in the backstreets of Shoosh.

Pari was born beautiful. As a little girl her sharp cheekbones and naturally arched eyebrows made her look womanly before her time. Her looks tricked people into seeing maturity and allure when they were not there; it was hard not to be startled by her green eyes. When she turned twelve the marriage offers flooded in despite her parents being known heroin addicts. Her suitors were nearly always much older men. Pari would shake with fear whenever they came round, but her parents had promised they would not marry her off until she was at least sixteen.

Pari's husband robbed her of her virginity with as much care as a blacksmith hammering a nail. It was not a shock to Pari, nor did she put up a fight. She had been in the room when men visited her mother, and had seen her father mount her at night.

Her new home was nearly identical to all the others she had lived in: one bare room with cracked, dirt-streaked walls, rolled-up blankets in the corner and a gas stove. This room had a few extra luxuries: a small red television set on a wooden crate, a cheap Persian carpet on the floor and a round brown plastic clock propped up against the wall.

The next day a mullah came round to legalize their union and sanctify it in the eyes of God. The mullah was a good man; he was not dazzled by Pari's beauty but concerned for the frightened young girl that stood before him. He took Pari outside the room, making sure Agha Mammad did not follow. The mullah wanted to know if her parents knew about this union and if Agha Mammad had already defiled her. *Are you happy my girl?* Pari lied. Out of fear and out of habit. Even now she wanted to protect her parents, knowing they had done wrong. She did not realize the mullah would have helped her, for he had helped other young girls in the neighbourhood, without judgement. And so Pari was married to Agha Mammad on the spot.

Agha Mammad was a bricklayer but he rarely had work. He spent most of his time smoking opium. Sometimes the opium would make his erections last for hours and Pari got used to lying there while he did his business. He would give Pari opium too, and he was surprised by how much she could take without getting sick. Her parents had given her opium since she was a baby, first for her teething pains, rubbing it in tincture form onto her gums, then to shut her up when she cried.

Agha Mammad looked after Pari in a way her parents never had. When Pari had cried all the way to her new home, he had promised her they would visit her parents soon. He did not break his promise. When he took her back to see them three months later, they were gone.

When Pari was seventeen, Agha Mammad sold her to a local madam. He did not want to let her go, but he had high debts to pay. The madam persuaded Pari not to resist the work and told her sex was her ticket to freedom. Pari never got used to it, but had learnt from Agha Mammad how to endure it. Her beauty made her popular and soon enough she was spotted by a client who thought she should be aiming higher. He paid off her madam and drove her to his friend's high-class cabaret. They took her on immediately, housing her with the other girls, who taught her the way. She had been there for two years when she met Asghar.

Asghar was a *jahel*, from the Arabic word for 'ignorant'. *Jahels* are hoodlums-cum-gangsters, bred from pure working-class south Tehrani stock. They tried to project an image of honourable, lovable, well-mannered rogues and scoundrels – like a gentlemanly Mafia, with less violence and more compassion and courtesy. They had a strict code of ethics with chivalry and magnanimity at its core, not characteristics usually associated with gangland bosses. With a knife tucked in their trousers and God in their hearts, they were ready to defend the honour of their women, demonstrate their loyalty to their friends and defend the weak and the oppressed. The best *jahels* were Robin Hood figures who stole from the rich and distributed their booty among the poor. In the 1970s, after *jahel* culture was immortalized in dozens of Iranian films, they became heroic figures and the notorious *jahels* of south Tehran, like Asghar, were lionized.

Jahels had their own way of dressing: a black fedora hat tipped to the side, crisp white shirt, black jacket and trousers and black shoes that they had transformed into slip-ons by standing on the backs. Sometimes they wrapped a red scarf round the palm of one hand, or they would drape it over one shoulder. *Jahels* even had their own way of dancing, holding up a white handkerchief and spinning around. Asghar and his brothers had perfected the *jahel* gait, a wide-legged, languid walk, although their father said they all looked like they had shat their pants. They had their own language, slang that was delivered in a low, sing-song staccato, Tehrani Cockney rhyming slang. The more humble and deferential the talk, the better.

'I'm the dirt on your shoe!'

'I'm your slave!'

'I'm your donkey!'

They all had nicknames – the only name you ever needed to know. There was Mustafa the Nutter, Mehdi the Butcher, Javad the Upstart. And Asghar the Brave. The nicknames made him smile now, but back then, those names could strike fear through a man. Reputation was everything, and your name was your reputation. *Jahels* loved cheap prostitutes and alcohol almost as much as their religion, which they took seriously. Asghar had Imam Hossein's face tattooed on his back. On his shoulder was another tattoo, the Zoroastrian maxim: GOOD WORDS, GOOD THOUGHTS, GOOD DEEDS.

During religious festivals they would feed hundreds of poor, clubbing together to pay for food, generously fulfilling their *zakat*, giving-of-alms duties. If anyone landed up in prison, which they often did, the *jahels* would support the family until he got out.

But even if many *jahels* tried to fit the romantic mould of thug-with-a-heart, the truth, of course, was less alluring. They ran protection rackets, gambling and prostitution rings and regularly fought over turf and women.

Nobody in Asghar's neighbourhood was surprised when he reached the top of his game. His ascent had been astonishingly quick. Asghar was a born leader, charismatic, generous and a convincing liar. Despite having left school at thirteen, he was the brightest kid in the hood and the most fearless. Even as a precocious eight-year-old, Asghar was cunning and street-smart, outwitting the local coppers and the big boys, running in and out of the tea houses and the bazaar. He had the ability to tread the fine line between being a common thug – *laat-o-loot*, as they were called – and being a gentleman who aspired to notions of *javanmardi*, which meant showing restraint, grace and honour at all times. It was a difficult balance to achieve, a fist and a hand-shake not always going hand in hand, but Asghar had managed it. It was the secret to being a successful *jahel*. Everyone knew he was destined for fame.

Asghar was born in a small house in a dirt alley in the back-streets of Nasser Khosrow, just north of the bazaar, the son of a shoe mender and the middle child of thirteen siblings. Despite his father's cripplingly low income and the copious number of mouths to feed, there was always food on the table and their clothes were clean. Asghar said it was different in those days; nobody went hungry, you looked after each other. He liked to say that back then you worked a day to feed twelve; nowadays you had to work twelve to feed one, each man for himself.

From when the boys had first learnt to walk, it was almost as though the streets around Nasser Khosrow were run by Asghar and his brothers. They were big and loyal. Most importantly, they weren't afraid to use their fists or their knives. Honour was every-thing. They had all started out by running errands for mobsters, and learnt the trade at close quarters. They understood that to be a true force with a fighting chance of making money, they would have to stick together; strength in numbers. It worked. No bond was stronger than blood and, with nine brothers, the old guard were quickly pushed out.

They set up a fresh-juice stand on Nasser Khosrow. It was an instant success and they were selling juice by the gallon. With the money, they rented a shop where they sold juice downstairs and ran a gambling den upstairs. They always made sure punters were given a free *chelo kabab* at lunch. More money poured in. Asghar spread it around, buying loyalty and fans throughout the hood. And there were dozens of people to keep quiet. In the fifteen years they ran the gambling den, it was never closed down. The police left them alone; Asghar was paying every single cop in the area. It helped that some were distant relatives and others were neighbours. They widened their operations and began providing security at clubs, taking protection money to keep other mobsters out. Business was sweet. News of their outfit had spread far. For years the chief of police would attempt raid after raid, but word always got out. He gave up in the end; Asghar and his brothers were protected by everyone and he did not want a riot on his hands.

Fighting was part of the life. A true *jahel* was not meant to be a *chaghoo kesh*, a knife-wielding hooligan, he was meant to abide by the rules of *javanmardi* at all times; but the lines were blurred. Fist fights, group fights, knife fights, fights with billiard cues – Asghar had been in so many fights he had lost count. They were usually tame affairs, someone would get knocked up and end up in bed for a week with a few missing teeth and broken ribs. Or else there would be a knife wound to be dressed. The fights were not meant to kill. Occasionally they did; a knife would be thrust just a little too deep. They were the only times the police got involved.

As Asghar's fame spread so did his social circle. Celebrity directors, actors, artists and members of the bohemian set would invite him to their parties and mansions. But he would not leave south Tehran for anyone, so they would make the pilgrimage down south, marvelling at the rawness of the south of the city. They drank and whored and gambled and sang and danced.

'He's a friend of everybody except the Shah!' is what people said of Asghar. They were halcyon days when the toughest and the fairest men got the most respect. He had sixty guys working under him, and he was one of the most revered and respected *jahels* in Tehran. With Pari by his side, he was invincible.

Then the revolution happened.

Asghar and the other *jahels* were faithful to their religion and thought it would be wrong to stand against an ayatollah who spoke of social justice. They took to the streets, demonstrating against the Shah. None of them could have imagined there would be no place for them in the new Islamic order. The *jahels'* liberal interpretation of their religion was not what the Islamists had in mind for their citizens. In fact, the *jahels'* version of Islam could get them imprisoned or worse.

They came looking for him once, in the early days. He was saved by one of his brothers, who persuaded the young Islamist with a G3 rifle slung round his shoulder that Asghar the Brave was a film hero, not a real-life person. The young revolutionary at the door ended up believing these convincing miscreants and left, never to return. Pari and Asghar had heard them from their room upstairs. Pari had squeezed his hands and kissed him; she had not seen him cry since she had left him all those years ago.

A handful of *jahels* were executed for immoral behaviour and criminal activity. The new regime confiscated their property and money. A few of the dancing girls were executed, including Pari's best friend. A few escaped. One, who had become a famous singer, had been so scared of the new regime she had approached Khomeini himself for forgiveness of her sins. He personally baptized her.

Asghar's income disappeared overnight. Five of his brothers were sent to the front lines and three of them did not return. He sold his properties that had not been seized and used the money to pay the bills and look after his martyred brothers' families. He was relieved he had no children of his own to support. After a few years of marriage, it became clear that either he or Pari was infertile. They made a pact never to find out who was to blame. Asghar told Pari that she was all he needed in his life, and that was enough for her.

He was no longer King of the Streets, but he felt the same as before, the big boss who lived by the same rules. Only everything around him had changed. A few years after the revolution, Asghar took his first hit of heroin.

He had enjoyed opium, as they all did – it was no more harmful than a tipple. From time to time Pari would smoke it with him. But the opium and the vodka were no longer enough to ease the anxiety that had taken hold of him.

He had always resisted heroin. Too many times he had seen it kill off friends, big, famous *jahels* diminished to walking bones. He had heard that since Hossein-e Zahra, a *jahel* of repute, had turned to the drug, he now lived in a tiny hovel. He saw him once in the street, buying some bread, and he had almost cried at his shrunken face and shrivelled body – this man who used to be so big. Hossein-e Zahra died of an overdose a few weeks later. After the revolution some of the old boys had even started dealing in heroin, but it was risky. A few years ago Shapour the Bull-Slayer and Morteza Four Dicks were caught with more than a kilo of heroin and opium, and were charged with smuggling and banditry. They were both executed.

Asghar knew from his own neighbourhood that addiction was everywhere. An official had said there are ten million drug addicts in the country, two million of which are *chronic* addicts; all the statistics showed that Iran has one of the highest rates of drug addiction in the world.

For years Asghar did not venture outside. The few times he did, people treated him as though he was just another old man. He might have been able to cope if he still had money, but he had nothing.

Pari and Asghar were forced to move to Shoosh, the neighbour-hood Pari had escaped. The day Asghar told her they no longer had enough money to stay on Shariati Street, she cried silently for hours. He knew what Shoosh meant to Pari, but there was no other option for them; they were drowning in debt. A friend had a room there that they could have for free.

A long, forlorn road lined with car mechanics, tyre shops and ragged children, Shoosh has not changed much in over 100 years. Pari remembered the elderly men sitting on the street corner talking about some of Shoosh's former legendary residents as if they were still alive: the stories of Zeynab the Blind – whose eyes were so small everyone said she must be blind – who was one of the cheapest prostitutes around. Zeynab the Blind was very particular: she would only have sex with old men with thick moustaches. She wore a *sheleeteh*, traditional long red skirt, and when business was lagging, she would lift it up, flaunting her goods and advertising her wares. 'Roll up, roll up, I'm not a cheap *bazaari* who'll rip you off by insisting on having sex in the dark!' Zeynab was best friends with Long-Haired Mouness, a prostitute who was renowned as a class fighter; she could beat ten young men with just a stick.

Shoosh is still full of prostitutes, but most of them now are heroin addicts. It has become even more impoverished and deprived than when Pari was a little girl. Its twisting back alleys are filled with beggars and detritus. Its poorer residents huddle together in slums of crumbling brick and courtyards full of needles and human shit. It is a road of outcasts: Afghan families squatting in abandoned homes, one-dollar prostitutes working the streets surviving on bread and drugs. Charities periodically descend on Shoosh with condoms and needles in hand and psychotherapists in tow. But Shoosh is as stubborn as it is ugly and remained unprettified in spite of the efforts of the visiting good Samaritans. Civil society is not welcome in the Islamic Republic, and so some of the charities that came to Shoosh were kept on their toes with raids and threats of prison and closure. Soon after an addiction clinic in a dirty road that jutted off Shoosh made inroads with the queues of heroin addicts waiting patiently for their plastic cups of methadone, the two doctors who ran the place were arrested and imprisoned on charges including 'communicating with an enemy government' after they returned from a conference in the USA.

Shoosh is also the birthplace of Vali Asr; it is striking how such a majestic road has such humble beginnings. Tehran's main railway station, Rah Ahan, opens out onto a square, from which Shoosh crosses and from where Vali Asr shoots northwards, careering away from this pit of poverty and ruin for as far as the eye can see. Shoosh, so near to Tehran's beating heart, and yet on the edge of society itself. It may have been at the other end of Vali Asr, but for most Tehranis Shoosh docs not even exist.

Asghar and Pari moved into a neighbourhood where the roads were pockmarked with decaying houses shedding brick and dust into gaping holes; rotten cavities waiting to be filled up with the mounds of rubble and rubbish that were piled high on street corners. The area was made up of a network of alleys that spread out like rivulets, some barely wider than two shoulders, where dirt-encrusted children with matted hair played in the streets next to smacked-out prostitutes slumped on the cracked asphalt.

There were no billboards or posters. The walls were instead daubed with messages and warnings – names of the dead and stencils of their faces. On the side wall of Asghar's and Pari's building someone had written in blue paint: MAY YOUR MOTHER AND FATHER BE DAMNED IF YOU EVEN THINK OF LITTERING HERE.

Below the message a stinking mound of putrid litter grew bigger by the day. On a neighbour's wall was a warning to anyone thinking of parking a motorbike: BURST TYRE.

The air around the neighbourhood stank of drugs. Nearly all the residents smoked opium. Half were addicted to heroin, crystal meth and crack. Next door to Asghar and Pari, in a half-built wreck, a family of fifteen *kolee* gypsies were squatting, living by gaslight. The barefoot children sold daffodils in the streets in spring and *faal-e Hafez* all year round, slips of paper on which were written excerpts of prophetic poetry by the great poet Hafez. Pari had once bought one, out of kindness. The gypsies had no identity papers and few rights in the Islamic Republic; none of the children had ever stepped inside a school. They shared a washing-line-strewn courtyard with three Afghan families who were all illegal immigrants. The government had deported one of the families back to their village in Afghanistan, even though their teenage children were born in Iran and had never been to Afghanistan. It took them two months to make it back to Iran, walking through the desert mountain passes. Their little girl died on the way.

Pari took a job as a cleaner without telling Asghar; she knew he would not be able to bear the shame. Every day she wound her way through the alleys, past courtyards covered in needles, past the scores of car workshops and scrapyards that were squeezed together, black-greased men picking through the thousands of gearboxes, brakes, car doors, wires, engines, tyres, hubcaps and metal panels that lined the road. From the bottom of Rah Ahan Pari would get a bus to the northern top of Vali Asr and, looking out of the window, she would remember the past. There was not one bit of Vali Asr she did not know; as a dancing girl it was here, on the city's chicest road, that she would spend her money. Some of the old restaurants and cafés were still there: Nayeb, Pardis, Shatter Abbas; the *haleem* and *aash* shop; Yekta with the best café glacé in town.

When Pari was working, Asghar would smoke heroin, sometimes with the Afghan builder next door. They would sit in silence, the children playing around them. The only words the Afghan ever said to him were: 'A drowning man is not troubled by rain.'

Asghar had employed his nephew to sell fruit juice in the bazaar, but business was bad. The economy was in ruins and the price of food had shot up. Pari would try to find Asghar's stash, but after she threw a batch down the toilet, he decided to keep it hidden in his underpants at all times. To appease her, he promised to go to a Narcotics Anonymous meeting; NA centres had sprung up all around the city. He never kept his promise. It was only when he discovered that Pari was working as a common *kolfat*, cleaner, that he begged for her forgiveness, and promised her their lives would change; *this time*, he said, *I mean it*.

The only way he could secure their future was if he returned to doing what he did best: he would set up a gambling den. The stakes were different now, with the punishment for gambling up to six months' imprisonment and up to seventy-four lashes; being caught running a racket would incur a tougher sentence.

Iranians love to gamble. Families play cards for money all over the city; in backstreets of poorer neighbourhoods, groups of men gamble over dice games and cockfights. Not all gambling is illegal in the Islamic Republic. A few ayatollahs have declared that betting on horses and shooting are not against Sharia law. There is a racetrack at Nowroozabad, west of Tehran, where racegoers officially place 'predictions', and even an electronic screen where the message flashes up: *Make a prediction, win a prize.* 'Predictions' can also be made on the federation's website.

But real aficionados head to Tehran's illegal gambling dens. In the north of the city, the joints are accordingly classier and more sophisticated: private casinos set up in high-rise apartments where customers turn up in sharp suits and ties, where the croupiers are glamorous, the security personnel burly and where fortunes are lost.

Asghar found an abandoned building just off Nasser Khosrow that would be perfect for his new operation. Nasser Khosrow was not too different from when he was younger. There were more illegal pharmaceuticals being peddled than before, but the road still throbbed with the loud hum of hundreds of motorbikes weaving their way up and down the street, ignoring traffic lights, stop signals and one-way signs; like an endless stream of worker ants they zigzagged past pedestrians and barrow boys and shopkeepers and old men playing backgammon outside shop fronts.

He strode down the street in his army Puffa jacket, with his diamond ring (which he had sworn he would be buried with) on his little finger, a gold chain with a pendant that spelt out his name hung round his neck. He was in good shape for a man his age; the heroin had not ruined his looks yet. He was missing a few teeth, knocked out in fights, but he still had a full head of hair, thick and grey. The street was buzzing. Asghar felt at home right there, in the middle of it all, even if he no longer ruled it. A good-looking barrow boy lifted a toothless man in the air and joked to some pretty girls: 'Take a look at my stock ladies, I got the best stock in town.' Between the electric shops and the pharmacies, there were still remnants of the Tehran that Asghar had been born into, flashes of elegance in decaying buildings. An old man in a woolly hat was sitting on a concrete bollard, scores of scissors of all different sizes and shapes spread out in front of him on a makeshift table propped up by cans of industrial adhesive; he was in exactly the same spot as when he had first arrived in Tehran, when he had left his hometown of Hamedan nearly fifty years ago to make his fortune.

'Alright boss!' he shouted out to Asghar, just like the old days. Asghar threw him a 2,000-toman note. A man selling screwdrivers was eating his lunch; beside him a middle-aged woman was yelling, 'Cunts are made of gold!' Asghar smiled to himself. Nobody ever paid her any attention, but she had been shouting the same thing for as long as anyone could remember.

Asghar walked past the Shams-ol Emareh Palace, where it was said that 100 years ago slaves were brought over from Ethiopia and Zanzibar; the men were castrated and forced to guard the harem and the women were trained as informers and spies. He walked past the passageways that led to bazaars that snaked behind the streets and sloped underground; he walked past the open doorways where bowls of hot broth appeared; past the sweet stands and the rubber boots and knife displays. A man wearing a black and white chequered turban carrying boxes on his back stopped outside a shop that was advertising lottery tickets to win an all-expenses-paid trip to Mecca. As he turned into an alley, a young man shouted out to a passing woman, 'Hey gorgeous, let me suck some sweet milk from those tits of yours.' For the first time in years, Asghar felt alive.

With money borrowed from the owner of an electrical store on Nasser Khosrow, who remembered him from back in the day, Asghar set up shop. He hung his black and white photos of wrestlers on the wall, dead heroes who used to treat him like a god. He bought old tables and chairs. He served tea and *aragh*. After only a few months he had attracted a raft of regulars. Slowly, Asghar started making money.

Pari was furious when she discovered what he was doing. She had put up with it all, even the heroin, but gambling was *haram*, a sin. The baptism had changed Pari. She had taken it seriously; she prayed every day and read the Koran. Asghar was moved by her devotion and was proud of her. A few weeks after the revolution happened, she started wearing a chador and never took it off again. Asghar paid for her to go on a tour to Karbala. It was there that she had a dream so vivid that for a few days afterwards she thought it had really happened; she had been standing by Imam Hossein's tomb when God spoke to her. He told her that he accepted she had atoned for her sins, but unless Asghar stopped his immoral ways, they would never be reunited in paradise. She returned from Karbala on a mission to save Asghar from hell.

She pleaded and begged him to close the gambling den. Asghar was religious, but he had always thought God would appreciate the importance of his survival. When Pari found out where he had set up shop (by pressurizing one of his friends) she started storming into the club on a weekly basis, shouting at him in front of the customers; they got used to it. When he would try to reason with her, she would tell him she did not want to be without him in the afterlife; he was all she had in this world and all she wanted for the next.

*

After Pari ran out of the club the boys cracked even more jokes about Asghar the Henpecked, or Asghar the Brave – unless his wife was near, in which case he became Asghar the Coward. Asghar smiled and went along with it, but he could not help feeling guilty for having let Pari down yet again. In between shots and toasts, he tried to call her on the home line, but she was not answering. He would talk to her in the morning; he would promise her that within four months they would have enough money to shut down the gambling den and move out of Shoosh. And this time he meant it.

As it was their pre-Ramadan celebration, Asghar drank more than usual. He was so drunk by the time he stumbled home he could hardly walk. Trying to be as quiet as he could, he climbed under the covers, relieved that Pari was fast asleep. He kissed her goodnight. But he was too drunk to notice that her body was stiff and cold. Pari had died of a heart attack as she had got into bed.

In the morning, as Asghar rubbed his eyes and felt the hangover throb in his head, he turned round to cuddle Pari, as he always did. That is when he realized. He did not leave the bed for a long time, crying into her neck.

Asghar organized a grand funeral for Pari, spending nearly all of the money he had saved; with Pari gone, he no longer needed extra cash.

After her death, his life changed in a way it never had before. He made it his mission to fulfil all the promises he had made to Pari that had remained broken. It was less to soothe his guilt than to make sure they would be together in the afterlife. Asghar never gambled again. He shut down the business and cut off ties with that part of his life. He stopped drinking. He even started to pray. More than ever, he wanted to show Pari that he could be a good person, an honest person; that he could be the man she had always wanted him to be. His only real vice was the daily hit of heroin that oozed into his veins, warming his soul. And that was the beauty of Pari; even when he did wrong, he knew that she would understand.

EIGHT

FARIDEH

Fereshteh Street, north Tehran

No matter how hard she tried, she could not get it right – gyrating her hips while undulating her stomach. Farideh looked like she was frantically trying to keep an invisible hula hoop aloft. All the women were laughing at their own clumsiness.

Belly dancing at the health club had proved even more popular than the Bikram yoga classes. The dance studio had magnificent views of the mountains, but thick lace curtains had been drawn to shield the dancing ladies from view. The owner took every precaution to abide by the law.

It was then, mid hip-swivel, that four chador-clad women from the morality police entered the gym. They walked into reception and calmly told the duty manager to shut the whole place down. They then went upstairs into the dance class and one of them turned the Arabic pop music off. None of them shouted. They just issued a list of commands: *stop dancing; everybody get dressed; everybody get outside.* The teacher, a blonde dancer in bra top and hot pants, was terrified.

'I don't understand what we've done wrong?' She was pleading with one of the *chadoris*, who was shoving all her music CDs into a bag.

'These dancing classes are lewd, provocative, immoral and

contrary to Islam,' the *chadori* replied in a clipped monotone. Most of the women had already grabbed their *manteaus* and headscarves and raced outside, scared of being arrested.

Farideh was enraged; her weekly moment of joy had been invaded by *them*. She refused to be hurried.

'How dare you! You should be ashamed! When did dancing become illegal in your filthy minds? Even if there were men here, they would hardly be interested in us when there are so many young girls on the loose that *your* lot can't control.'

'But look, no men! *Mard neest!*' A beautiful French business consultant was trying to reason with the *chadoris* in her faltering Persian. The *chadoris* paid no attention to the foreigner. They had recognized the supercilious tone of Farideh's voice; it irked them that the Islamic Revolution had not managed to curb the superiority complexes of these rich old women. Farideh recognized it too, and she was always struck by her condescending manner towards *regimeys*. She could not help but look down on them, her anger at what the country had become manifesting itself as class hate.

'You—' Another *chadori* was pointing at Farideh now. 'Watch your tongue or I'll have you arrested. Unfortunately, old women like you still have libidos, and we know what happens when *your sort* can't get attention. This type of dancing clearly promotes lesbianism. It's disgusting the way you all behave,' she said.

Farideh must have looked shocked, for when she walked outside the other women grouped around her.

'We heard you shouting at them! What did they say?'

'They're afraid we'll turn into lesbians.' Some of the women began to laugh at the absurdity of it; Farideh just stood in silence. She was angry at herself for letting something so trivial upset her; it was not as though she would never dance again, but the dance classes were one of the few things she actually looked forward to leaving her house for.

Farideh dreaded her brushes with the city. Despite all the years, it was impossible not to feel stabs of longing when she drove through the streets for the Tehran she had loved, full of miniskirts, discos and pool halls; juice bars and vodka bars, donkey carts and new cars; the triumph of colours and music on the streets; the thrill and buzz of a new epoch; milkshakes and cigarettes and wine and song. She remembered one of her boyfriends coming back from a trip to London and announcing how the English were so *uptight*. How London was so *backward*. He told her British border police had never seen a watermelon, and insisted on slicing it open in case he was smuggling something inside it. He told her the food was terrible, you could not even buy garlic! And he had been threatened with arrest for indecent exposure because he had taken his top off on a scorching day. How they had laughed at swinging London.

There were plenty of her friends who were now happy to live in the bubble of north Tehran, acting as though the rest of the city did not exist. Farideh did not have that luxury. Ever since her husband Kaveh had died she had taken over his fight to claw back some of the family land that had been confiscated after the revolution. Kaveh had come from old money – lots of it – but a large portion was tied up in property and land, and most of that had been seized by the state.

For nearly twenty years Farideh had endured endless days in government offices, ministries and courts, forced to beg and flatter and fawn to various officials and judges who spoke to her as though she barely existed. Sometimes the first question they would ask was: 'And where's your husband?' Even when she explained that he had died, that she was now in charge, they did not take her seriously. She saw how differently they would treat the men. The process was torturously slow; the machinery of the Islamic Republic was encumbered by bribery, corruption, poorly educated officials, internal politics and crippling ineptitude. It took her five years to prove that the deeds to a building her father had owned had been forged by a civil servant who had claimed it as his own. And then, after spending over 50,000 US dollars on bribes, it took another two years to fight the (rich) civil servant's appeals, which were effectively greased by his even larger bribes to the judges. She spent six years trying to reclaim a plot of land north of the city where Kaveh's family once had a holiday home. After the revolution, it had been declared the property of the state. She had received five separate verdicts from five different courts, all in her favour. Yet still the verdicts continued to be contested, which meant another court case; another appeal; another few years.

Farideh often wondered if she should have left after the revolution. Her life had only just started to come together when it happened. She had finished her degree in art history and had been accepted for a job as curator of a small gallery. Kaveh had got his first promotion in the Oil Ministry and they were attending decadent parties at weekends. She had watched as so many of her friends fled, draining their prodigious bank accounts and siphoning the money into Switzerland; politicians and cohorts of the Shah plundered the treasury and the Ministries for every last shekel, frantically bankrupting the country in a whirl of greed, fear and violence, sucking the bone of its marrow. Whole packs of aristocrats and monarchists escaped in private planes and first-class seats, bound for their villas in the south of France, their pieds-à-terre in Paris, London and New York. And of course they flocked to the blue-skied glitz of Los Angeles, where Italian mottled marble, crystal chandeliers and gilded furniture would be soothing reminders of home. In time they monopolized block after block of Brentwood and Westwood, until Los Angeles became their *Tehrangeles*.

There were those who refused to be cowed, who refused to leave their glorious land, even in the face of death. Most of them were executed. Like General Rahimi, who was killed by firing squad on the rooftop of a school a few minutes before midnight on 14 February 1979. The General was the military commander and police chief of Tehran; he had also been a family friend of Farideh. She had watched his interrogation by the Islamists on television. They had beaten and tortured him, yet he refused to denounce the Shah. His last words, reportedly, were '*Javid Shah*', long live the Shah. But the Shah had already scarpered; the only battle he was now fighting was against the cancer that would soon kill him. Farideh still ached when she thought of those times and the friends she had lost.

She had chosen to stay. Kaveh had tried to persuade her to flee, but she could not bear the thought of leaving her parents behind, who were too set in their ways to start over. That was only one of the reasons. They had not been as canny as their friends; there were no secret offshore accounts. No homes abroad. No foreign passports. Farideh was afraid that if they left, their house would be taken. When the new state began to auction off thousands of people's homes, she thought she had made the right decision. They still had enough to afford a handsome life, better than anything abroad. Then there was the war. A new round of friends leaving, of parents packing their sons off to international boarding schools instead of the front line. The ones who stayed behind, like Farideh, retreated to the countryside when the bombings in Tehran started.

During the darkest days, they had partied the hardest despite the dangers, drinking and dancing and loving like they never had before. These moments, in between the terrors, were a perversely magical time.

Farideh had also stayed partly through loyalty and devotion to this cursed, wretched, beautiful land. These were her people, fanatical or not. She was a patriotic woman and talk of Cyrus the Great could still reduce her to tears; as for so many Iranians, it was not just the romanticism of him as a great, beneficent king, it was the fact that at the time of his rule Persia had been the envy of the world. She would suffer with her fellow countrymen. Although so many of them appeared happier now the Shah was gone. The extent of discontent had taken them all by surprise. She felt guilty for not having noticed. It was easy enough to call these others a bunch of *dahati*, illiterate peasants, but deep down it upset her that there was such a giant gulf between her and so many of her people, and she sensed they would edge no nearer to each other in her lifetime.

Some days she was sure she had made the right decision. She remembered her friends who had suffered far more, like Mr Karimi, an eminent chemical engineer reduced to being a London cab driver, and Mr and Mrs Ahmadian – he had been a high-ranking member of government under the Shah and spent his final years in a small two-up, two-down terraced house in Willesden, robbed of all his wealth, all his land taken. They were the honest ones. The ones who did not loot the country, but left with nothing, taking their naive, law-abiding ways with them, to stand in queues and beg for acceptance that would be issued on pieces of paper; to become refugees and immigrants; exiles.

*

The night after the gym was raided, Farideh was meant to be going to a wedding, but she was no longer in the mood. Besides, these big, showy weddings bored her.

The son of the head of a multinational company with a government contract was marrying an English model and the party was happening a few roads away from where Farideh lived. The father of the groom had pulled all the right strings and sweetened all the right mouths. The local police had been paid off. The party was going to be spectacular. They had hired top DJs, a band and a film crew to cover the event. The cost was rumoured to be a million US dollars. Hundreds of guests in expensive clothes were screened by security and were ordered to hand in their mobile phones before entering the gigantic luxury home. The north Tehranis were out in force, the spoilt layabouts, party lovers and hangers-on. The groom's mother was a *chadori*, and some of the partying would be carefully hidden from her. This was new Tehran, where tradition and class are blended together and trumped by money. Some of the upper-crust families kept away from these events, wanting to distance themselves from distasteful displays of wealth.

It was a huge operation. But by nine o'clock it was all over. The party had barely started when it was raided by the security forces. Terrified revellers scattered like rabbits, hiding anywhere they could. *Basijis* on motorbikes circled, looking for victims. A few truckloads were carted off and the father of the groom was led away in handcuffs. Everyone had their theory: somebody important had a grudge; his competition wanted his contract and this was the way to get it; he was a pawn in a political game.

When Farideh heard about the wedding raid, she did not leave the house for twelve days straight. She painted, tended to the garden and had friends round. But being at home was as lonely as being on the streets. And she was aware that she had to face her fears, get out there and carry on. She broke her enforced incarceration by agreeing to join her friend Lilly at an art class. Lilly had discovered a remarkable young artist, Golnar, who gave life-drawing lessons.

Farideh and the other women were drinking tea and smoking when Golnar arrived. She was alone, without her life model. It was obvious something was wrong.

'They raided a friend's lesson, I don't know how they found out. Dena was modelling.' Golnar started crying. 'They arrested everyone. They accused them of making porn, and when they didn't find any footage, they said it must have been an orgy. I didn't want to say what had happened on the phone.' Golnar explained that they had been on the thirteenth floor of an apartment block, a solitary building away from prying eyes, with wondrous light streaming in from huge windows. They had not seen a faraway neighbour spying with binoculars. It did not matter that everyone, apart from the model, had been fully clothed. The drawings, of course, made matters worse. They were propagating porn – an executionable offence.

'Where's Dena now?' Lilly asked.

'She's at her mother's, but they're trying to get her out.'

'How much will it cost?'

'About 10,000 US dollars across the Turkish border. Her parents have given her 4,000, all they've got.'

'Tell her it's OK, I'll pay the rest,' said Lilly.

Farideh stepped in. 'I'll help you Lilly, I'll give you half.'

Farideh had helped a few journalists and activists in the past, paying for their lawyers. It made her feel less useless. There were plenty of privileged women who could not care less, as long as they were safe and free and nothing threatened their splendid lives; and there were those who were too frightened to get involved.

She had tried everything to fight the increasing isolation. Yoga had helped, the breathing exercises calmed her and made her feel a little more whole, even if it was only for a matter of minutes. She had tried the Vipassana meditation retreat outside Tehran, where she took a vow of silence. It was full of lapsed drug addicts who had nowhere else to turn. She had emerged after ten days more accepting of herself and the world, exhilarated with new concepts like *mindfulness*, able to will the bad thoughts away. That did not last. A stay in an ashram in Goa had left her more empty than before, depressed that a country such as India had progressed so much while her own slipped backwards. Depressed that she had resorted to searching the globe for what she should be finding at home. By the time she decided to sign up for the Landmark Forum courses in personal development, another underground hit in Tehran, it had closed down.

She had even dared to try Christianity, more out of curiosity than a need to find God. A friend, a recent Christian convert, had convinced her to give Jesus a go. They went to a weekly night service, walking round the block three times, checking over their shoulders before entering an alley. They used a password to get in: *omeed*, hope. They walked through a large garden to a soundproofed room at the back of a house. The music was deafening: frantic, joyous singing; manic clapping and whooping to the clatter of a tuneless piano and rattle of tambourines. There were crosses hanging from the walls and teenagers jumping around like kangaroos. Nearly everyone here was a convert, risking death to pray to the same God, but a new prophet. Farideh was grief-stricken; she could not articulate exactly why she was so sad watching the fearless happiness and love around her; she had not seen people look this happy for a long time. She had later found out that the underground church was funded by a Christian union affiliated to a North American university, its money spent on proselytizing in Muslim nations. She was furious, suddenly so protective of the faith that she felt imprisoned by.

And yet Farideh had never felt so far from her religion. She believed in God. She loved the drama and humanity of Shia sacrifice, of battling for your beliefs. She did not hate all mullahs; in fact there were some she adored, with their wise words and modest behaviour. She had continued to seek spiritual guidance through her *estekhareh* sessions with a mullah who lived nearby. He had a good heart and he always got everything right, which was more than a coincidence. She was surprised by the strength of her superstition.

Over lunch with a Zoroastrian community leader, a charismatic charmer and intellectual with a ribald sense of humour who delighted women wherever he went, Farideh confided in him of her evangelical foray. He told her every month he turned away dozens of young kids wanting to convert to Zoroastrianism. The kids would plead with him, saying it was their true faith, part of Iran's glory years before the Arabs invaded and burned their books and gave them Allah.

'But why do you turn them away?' Farideh looked almost bereft.

'Apart from the fact I don't want to get anyone killed, it's all the bloody same isn't it? And they've got this romantic notion about Zoroastrianism. They think it'll fix all their problems, but it won't.' The Zoroastrian was murdered in an apartment in Paris a year later, his throat slashed by his ex-wife's lover. Some said the killer was an Iranian undercover agent. The authorities had been monitoring him for years. He had even been kidnapped in London, on his way to give a lecture at the School of Oriental and African Studies. Iranian intelligence agents from *ettela'at* had driven him around for three hours and threatened him, he had said. They should have known he was not the type of man to be intimidated. He had returned to Tehran with the same vitality as before, even more determined to help his Zoroastrian community.

A month after the arrests of the life drawing class, again Farideh felt unable to leave the house. Some of her friends thought her weak for letting *them* get the better of her, that it was just bad luck she had been caught in a freak wave of crackdowns that happened from time to time. Lilly persuaded her to go to a friend's dinner party.

Farideh flitted between a few different social groups. The handful of upper-crust, old-money families mostly stuck together. They were descendants of the Qajars, a Turkic dynasty who ruled Persia from the late 1700s to the 1920s. Being a Qajar was to be bandied about and made known, for it was a thing of stature and prestige; never mind that the Qajar rulers were oppressive, whoring gamblers who clung onto power and gobbled up the country's wealth while their subjects were devastated by famine. Blue blood was blue blood. A step down from them were the landowners, to which Farideh belonged. They had enjoyed being on the winning side of feudalism until land redistribution in the early 1960s, but even that did not seem to dent their wealth. There were the families of established merchants who had been trading across the Caucasus and along the silk routes for generations, selling to the royals and upper classes and spending money on education until they were, at last, assimilated into them. There were the academics and intellectuals, but they were rare, Iran being the victim of one of the world's most spectacular brain drains. Money was not strictly an indicator of class; there were enough struggling aristos to attest to that. In Farideh's generation, the new wave of industrialists was seen as uncouth, no matter how much money they made. Too *nouveau*. Artists, film-makers, actors, foreign visitors and diplomats dipped in and out of these circles, along with avant-garde bohemians and (educated) free spirits. Their homes were mostly clustered together in a few choice north Tehran neighbourhoods that curled around the foothills of the mountains: Niavaran, Farmanieh, Fereshteh; the Chelseas, Knightsbridges and Mayfairs of Tehran. A few of the edgier, younger generation had moved downtown, to be nearer to the soul of the city, among the hoi polloi where Tehran still had heart and vigour.

Farideh lived in Fereshteh, the first right turn off Vali Asr above Parkway, the final northern stretch of the big road. A quarter of the way down Fereshteh Street, opposite Bosni Herzogovin Street, is the luxury Sam Center, stuffed with shops like Chopard and TAG Heuer.

Farideh's home was a grand mansion with inner and outer courtyards, one of the few old houses still stubbornly standing in the area, squashed in on all sides by hideous high-rises. The house was exquisite; Farideh had an eye for design and style, cleverly mixing the old and the new. There were gigantic turquoise urns and ancient clay bowls on stone floors, priceless Persian carpets and antique tiles. On the walls hung paintings by the latest up-and-coming artists and in the garden there was a swimming pool surrounded by walnut and fig trees. She had lived here since her marriage, for over thirty years. It was where Kaveh had died, in their bed, after cancer dealt him three cruel years of pain. She had married Kaveh for love and for his goodness. He had been her best friend, a true, loyal companion in life.

Tonight's party was at a theatre producer's house in Niavaran, north-east of where she lived. The parties and gatherings kept them all going. It was part of their defence; it was what lent verisimilitude to their carefully crafted lives, as well as being the only possible means they could socialize, laugh and dance like the rest. But the community was small, even if the houses were big.

They were served canapés and wine in the garden in the last glinting shafts of the day's sunlight, enjoying the dewy smell of the cool air and the sensation of a new season lurking nearby. A few nightingales tentatively tested their voices; Farideh could smell a joint being passed around.

It was a mixed lot tonight. There were a few single girls in their thirties; one was an architect, another a poet and the rest worked in publishing. An international painter was chatting to a respected movie director. An eligible doctor in his forties was encircled by another group of single women. A gastroenterologist by profession, he was a secret stitcher of hymens on the side, restoring dignity and marriage prospects with a needle and a few inches of thread. His few friends who knew his secret had nicknamed him Dr Sew-up. He gave back virginity to the daughters of rich *bazaaris* and industrialists; to girls from religious families and *sonati* families rich and poor, even ordinary working-class girls. Having your hymen sewn up could cost from 200,000 tomans (about sixty US dollars) to seven million tomans (about 2,300 dollars) depending on who and where in the city your doctor was, but Dr Sew-up charged lower fees to his poorer clients as he had a strong sense of justice; it was not fair that these fearful women were being judged simply because they had been born into the wrong class. His own class had different rules. Western rules. He knew there were plenty of rich kids who wanted virgins, but they were never the true upper classes. He and his friends wanted the opposite: experienced women who would not simply lie back and give out in the hope of getting a ring on their finger. Dr Sew-up was regaling the women with stories of virginity kits that he had seen in the bazaar, consisting of a capsule filled with red liquid that was to be inserted into the vagina and would burst under pressure. Dr Sew-up was lying; he had not seen them in the bazaar, but had heard about them from one of his clients who had decided the fake blood was an unconvincingly bright hue.

At the dinner table, talk shifted from scandal to art, to politics and to work, the familiar rhythm of the subjects ticking along with the regularity of a metronome. A European businessman had left his wife and four children for a woman they all knew, a forty-something desperate high-class wannabe with a series of failed relationships scattered behind her. Copious injections of Botox had failed to dissolve her haughty look, a mouth permanently turned in disgust that she had learnt from her mother and practised since her teenage years in the hope it would elevate her status if her face suggested everything around her was beneath her. She taught French to rich kids and diplomats' children, and even spoke Persian with a faint, affected *Parisienne* accent. She had slept her way through a slew of married men, aiming for the ones with foreign passports, for that translated into *cachet*. She had finally struck gold.

There were a few new faces, part-time exiles dropping in from Milan and New York to buy art, socialize, speak their mother tongue and eat good food. There had been a flood of returnees in recent years, mostly the children of the Diaspora coming back with their sweet foreign accents and malapropisms that would endear them to the rest. They came to find themselves; to find husbands and wives, to party, to be sharks in a very small pool, which they were; for everyone was hungry to be touched by the

West with all its exotic chic and refined urbanity. Once these
visiting exiles had tasted the upper echelons of society, a tier they
did not inhabit in their host countries, many did not want to
return to the West. They simply cocooned themselves from the
real Islamic Republic. Just as Farideh and her friends had done.

'So what's the latest from New York?'

'Dull! New York is just about visual arts at the moment. So
boring. It *so* doesn't excite me. It's just not happening there,'
replied a striking woman who dabbled in interior design, as did
most of these females, spending their friends' money on exorbi-
tant furniture and overrated paintings. 'Everything's becoming
the same. I blame the bourgeois!' continued the dabbler. 'In fact
I *loathe* the bourgeois. Give me a working-class Englishman over
a middle-class anything, *any day*.'

'What about a working-class Iranian?' Farideh could not help
herself. 'Not a romantic gangster-with-a-heart type, but a real south
Tehrani, with a *chadori* wife and a picture of the Supreme Leader
on his wall?' Was it jealousy, she wondered, that provoked her
to cut them down, jealousy at the ones who liked to flash their
international credentials? Or just anger at the casual snobbery, the
objectification of the poor, seeing them as simply things of interest?

'Absolutely – give me him over the interminable middle class!'
Everyone laughed. Except Farideh.

'Maybe there is something exciting about *them* thinking of *us*
as immoral sluts.' The room laughed even louder, not noticing
Farideh's sarcasm. She forced a smile in time for her not to be
discovered. Recently at these gatherings she had had a habit of
sabotaging merriment. She could not understand why she was
being so defensive of a class she did not understand, of a class
she was capable of loathing, an entire stratum of society that she
could write off with disdain at their backwardness.

Farideh left early. She got stuck in the Thursday night traffic on Vali Asr, an endless line of cars crammed together, inching forward; the chug of engines, horns hooting, music thudding. A queue had formed outside the glass-fronted *aash* and *haleem* shop, where cooks in white overalls were scooping up ladles of thick bean and noodle soup and wheat porridge from massive steel vats. A woman in a chador and pointed silver spiked-heeled boots was eating her *aash* on a blue plastic chair on the pavement. Above them all, strings of fairy lights flashing different colours hung between the lamp-posts and the sycamore trees were lit by red, blue and green flower-shaped lights set in the pavement below.

At home, Farideh fixed herself a whisky. Her son Alidad was picking at leftovers in the kitchen. He had spent the afternoon playing polo and was now getting ready to party.

'Mum, did you hear about Delara?'

Delara was the young niece of one of her friends. For months, nobody had spoken of anything but Delara. She claimed to have been raped by three rich kids after they spiked her drink; Farideh had believed her story but many thought she had simply regretted a wild night out. Delara had a reputation. She liked to dance on tables in her bra drinking vodka and cherry juice; she liked one-night stands and she liked to hoover up lines of coke and pop pills into everyone's mouths.

'She killed herself.'

Farideh clasped her neck with her hand. Alidad ran over to her and hugged her, kissing her on the forehead. 'It happened tonight. She threw herself out of the apartment. And you know what, those bastards will be set free.'

After Delara had gone to hospital and then to the police station, all three boys had been arrested. But one of them had already escaped to Dubai. The remaining two had been sent to

Evin. Their fathers were rich and closely connected to the regime. Nobody thought for a minute that they would be found guilty.

Alidad offered to stay home and look after Farideh, but she insisted he go to his party. She began to cry as he closed the front door behind him.

Alidad had been out in the streets celebrating when Rouhani had been elected President; he had told her that everything would change, that everything would be different; it would just take time. She had heard this talk before – as far as she was concerned, change would not happen fast enough to make a difference to her life in Tehran.

She ran up to her room and started packing her bags. It was not too late for her to enjoy normality, to live out the rest of her years somewhere she would feel secure and free. She would go to London. Since the revolution her close friend Marjaneh had tried to persuade her to start afresh there. Now was her chance. Not that she could travel – she would have to get a visa first – but a packed suitcase, ready and waiting, would comfort her.

The rich kids were out in strength on Fereshteh Street; lines of glittering fast cars costing over 100 per cent extra with import tax – BMWs, Mercedes Benzes, Porsches, Ferraris, Lexuses and a Maserati – wound along the kerb outside the cafés and restaurants making the road look like a luxury car showroom. Alidad used to cruise here when he was younger. Once, near this spot, a *basiji* had searched his car and found a crate of Efes beer in the boot. Before Alidad had managed to stammer out 'I can explain…' the *basiji* had slammed the boot shut. 'Go on, get lost. And don't drive around with that shit in future,' was all he had said.

Alidad slowed past the gangs of gorgeous girls. A black Ferrari driven by a boy who could not be older than twenty sped past, zigzagging dangerously between the cars. A dervish was standing on the side of the road, bright green robe resting on his shoulders, long white hair flowing from a sapphire turban. In his right hand he was swinging a metal censer; white puffs of smoke from the burning of *esfand*, seeds of a weed, were rising out of it: spells to ward off the evil eye and expunge sorrow. The dervish's left hand was held out in supplication. Even the beggars on Fereshteh were upmarket.

By the time he got to Ana's house it was one o'clock in the morning; the party was pumping, Hot Chip was booming and everyone was dancing. Ana was single and in her late twenties, living on her own in a small apartment stuffed with retro shabby-chic furniture. She was one of the few Iranians who had kept the imperfect nose they had been born with, a handsome, strong, aquiline nose that had become her glory, a proud mark of her strength and individuality. Her nose would not be considered big in the West, but in Iran she had endured a lifetime of concerned relatives and family friends, even kindly strangers, cajoling her to have her nose carved into a more desirable shape, a more marriage-friendly shape – a narrow, pre-pubescent button nose, to be precise. She had refused. Ana was not one to conform. Growing up in the Islamic Republic had not impeded her dream of being a dancer. She trained in a studio in the city, where moves deemed too sexual by the Islamic Republic had to be scrapped. They could not even call what they did *dance*, but rather *movement*. Her troupe ended up touring Europe, working with celebrated choreographers in Madrid, Berlin and Paris. Now she designed jewellery.

Tonight Ana was dressed as a forties pin-up girl, hair in a quiff, shocking red lipstick on her pouty mouth. Beside her, a girl in a pair of brogues, pastel chequered trousers and a bow tie was smoking a skunk joint with a rock chick with a shaved undercut in a black jumpsuit. This was the trendy crowd, and they were the kind of girls who wore baggy, vintage-looking *manteaus*. They were surrounded by a gaggle of adoring gay boys. Ana was holding the party in honour of her friend Jamshid's 'coming out' to his parents. During the protests in 2009, Jamshid had been arrested out on the streets. He had been taken to Evin where he was held for three weeks and interrogated while blindfolded every day. His interrogators had forced him to give them his email and Facebook passwords; at that moment he had been petrified, thinking his life must be over. His inboxes were full of messages from ex-boyfriends and graphic photographs of himself that he had sent to lovers. But the interrogators never mentioned them. Finally, on the last day, one of them had whispered in his ear: 'We know all about you and we know exactly how you like it. But we don't give a shit about that. That's your fucking problem. We just wanted to know you hadn't been acting against the regime.'

In the bedroom, a group of boys were gossiping and drinking from a bottle of Mr Chavez Blended Special Whisky – Extra Special, an Iraqi brew. Jamshid's new eighteen-year-old boyfriend had just got an exemption from military service by claiming he was a transsexual, a condition the regime viewed as an illness.

'You know, he could have just told them he was gay, they think we're mentally sick too. What could they do? It's not illegal to *be* gay, only to have gay sex.'

'Well that's a good thing, cos then half the fucking city would be arrested.'

'All of south Tehran would, that's for sure.'

'Oh God, I got to try me some south Tehran man, I love those strapping rough-and-ready barrow boys.'

'You've seriously got to go south. If the middle classes are homosexuals, *all* the working-class boys are G-A-Y. Gay, gay, gay.'

'Listen, it's the same in any Muslim country, you can just clean up. It's cos these poor bastards can't get anywhere near pussy, that's why we're in business!'

The boys mostly met dates on the Internet. The Internet is the lifeblood of the gay scene in Tehran, specifically a gay social networking website called Manjam. Men all take risks – from webcam sex to picking up boys in Park-e Daneshjoo, cruising south Tehran and screwing in cars and alleys and public baths. The law on same-sex sodomy, which had just been amended, reflected the state's twisted attitude towards homosexuality: if the sex is consensual and the man playing the active role is not married and a Muslim, he will be flogged 100 times, whereas the man who plays the passive role will be put to death (unless he is a kafir having sex with a Muslim, in which case they will both be killed). It is better to bugger than to be buggered.

In the kitchen a guy in high-top trainers was rapping Rumi poetry to a group of women who liked to joke that they were members of the militant underground group Lezbollah. Among them was one of Tehran's most notorious lesbians, a hefty, butch woman who was startlingly successful at seducing straight marrieds. She had recently got married herself in San Francisco, to a blonde beauty who had left her husband – one of Tehran's most desired catches – for her. Another two women were kissing in the hallway, evidently also affiliated to Lezbollah. The punishment for lesbianism, *mosahegheh*, is 100 lashes, but if lesbian acts are repeated four times, the death penalty can be applied – although none of these women or any of their friends had ever been caught.

Alidad moved between the groups, downing tequila shots and

getting stoned. He had grown up with this quixotic, eclectic group of friends; they were privileged but good people, non-judgemental and accepting. Even the ones who could afford a life abroad chose to stay. But they all knew the dancing and the partying were vital to their well-being, so they made sure they did it well.

A European diplomat friend helped push Farideh's visa application through. A month later she was on a plane to London. The plan was to spend three months with Marjaneh while she looked for a small apartment to buy. She would then divide her time between Tehran and London, for as long as she was legally permitted to stay.

Alidad could not understand why Farideh thought she would be happier in the West. He had visited friends in London, LA, New York, Paris, Rome – all the usual places – and always looked forward to getting back home. He liked to dip his toe in, to party and pull exotic foreign girls, but his life was in Tehran. He embraced it all, the good and the bad.

Farideh's first week in London was heavenly; Marjaneh took her to galleries, museums and restaurants, showing her everything she had been missing. Farideh was overcome with guilt that she had made her husband and her child endure Tehran when they could have had *this*: real freedom and all that came with it. But as the weeks wore on, she began to feel strangely disconnected from this new society around her. Life was more disparate and impersonal here. The gatherings and dinner parties were cold affairs, lacking in intensity. The bonds between Marjaneh and her friends were looser too; people had their own families and jobs to care about. Everyone watched the pennies. Cabs were extortionate. People were aggressive; they shouted and swore at each other in the streets, even in Marjaneh's high-class area, something that rarely happened in north Tehran. When Farideh began to house-hunt, she realized how little her rials and tomans would buy her. Even if she sold everything and used up all her savings, she would only be able to buy a minuscule, dingy, one-bedroom apartment in Marjaneh's neighbourhood. Otherwise she would have to live in suburban hell, rows and rows of identical houses with crude gas boilers and tiny, sorry splodges of grass as gardens. And the weather never changed; one cold, grey, wet, drizzly day morphed into another.

After just two months, Farideh was surprised to discover that all she really wanted was to go back home. To Tehran.

'We had the first rain of the year last week. It was wonderful. Cleared up the pollution. You been away long?'

'A few months. What have I missed?'

'The same old – pardon my language madame – shit.'

Farideh laughed.

'Bet you wished you stayed away, eh?'

'Actually, I missed it here. Funny really.'

'I know, sometimes I think I want to take the whole family away from all of this, but I don't know if I'd be able to live anywhere else.' The taxi driver looked at her in the rear-view mirror. 'At least we're all in it together.'

Farideh smiled at him. 'Yes, you and I. Who would have thought.'

Now it was his turn to laugh.

The cab turned into Vali Asr. Two men were stripping a sheep's carcass in front of the Mercedes Benz showroom. Farideh wound the window right down and leant her head out. She never thought she would be so relieved to be back; wrapped in Tehran's mountains, protected under her startling blue sky and warmed by her sun, enveloped by her trees, licked by her breeze, bursts of umber, russet and ochre now bleeding out of the leaves. They drove past the fruit stalls filled with the autumnal yellows and oranges of lemons, quinces and persimmons, the jumble and the chaos and the clamour, the smoky smell of lamb on hot coals which rubbed against her cheeks, the mulberry trees and the jasmine, the layers of dust, the splutter of vans, the man selling puppies at the side of the road, the swarms of motorbikes criss-crossing between beautiful girls in defiant clothes, the juice stands, the gold shops, the ancient bazaars and tunnelled walk-ways, the chipped blue tiles on magnificent, crumbling manor houses and the hidden gardens.

Farideh closed her eyes to savour the moment.

EPILOGUE

Vali Asr

The first snow of winter falls on a queue outside the *barbari* bread bakery on the north of Vali Asr – the price of a few pieces of bread is now the same as a hit of meth. The road is splashed with bursts of ruby red from the season's pomegranates and beetroots. Two teenage boys with quiffs and ripped jeans dart between the cars, selling rap CDs and gum. On the pavement, an elegantly dressed woman with glasses sells cashmere headscarves; next to her an old man sits cross-legged, a pair of cracked scales in front of him. An eight-year-old girl on a piece of cardboard leans against a metal telephone exchange box, carefully writing in an exercise book as she takes a break from selling packets of tissues to do her homework.

Near Rah Ahan railway station, where Vali Asr begins its northbound ascent towards the mountains, thousands of mourners dressed in black stand in the cold outside a mosque. The crowd keeps swelling; part of Vali Asr has been closed off to traffic. An ambulance expels clouds of gritty black fumes as it waits beside the mourners. The mosque has opened its *hosseinieh* to cope with the numbers. Trays of dates, *halva* and herbed rice with lamb shanks are laid out on a table. After recitals from the Koran and the eulogy, the crowd outside parts as the body, covered in a sheet, is carried out on a stretcher and put in the back of the ambulance, which will make its way to Beheshteh Zahra cemetery where the body will be washed, wrapped in the white *kafan* shroud and placed in the earth.

'That's the end of the city as we know it. He won't survive without her,' says an old man in fingerless gloves as the doors of the van slam shut. He has taken a break from selling polyester socks on the corner of Vali Asr and Rah Ahan so he can pay his respects to the wife of Asghar the Brave, the toughest and most chivalrous *jahel* to have walked the streets of Tehran.

Two elderly women in chadors leave the crowd; one of them used to be a dancing girl with Pari. She limps from a bad hip. The women come across the stump of a sycamore tree. 'It was in the news. They said they're sick and they had to cut them down,' says her companion. The old dancer shakes her head.

The government did not immediately respond to the contro-versial felling of Vali Asr's sycamore trees. Now it says that the trees are diseased, that they are a danger to pedestrians. The women staring at the stump do not believe this. They have heard that the trees are obscuring police cameras, and that they are in the way of development plans.

But it is true. The sycamore trees are sick. They are slowly dying – mainly of thirst. A plan to pour concrete into the *joobs* went wrong; it prevented the water that ran down them from seeping through to the trees' roots. Some say pollution is making matters worse, that like Tehran's own residents the trees farther south of the city are choking. But everyone agrees on one thing: the trees were chopped down in the dead of night because the authorities knew there would be an outcry.

The women continue up Vali Asr, the gush of the water rushing down the *joobs* rising above the sound of car engines and horns. They walk under the dying trees, now grey, shimmering skeletons cloaked in a thin sheet of ice, stripped of their leaves by winter's cold hand. Soon they will be clogged in snow, the water in the *joobs* hard as crystal before it will thaw with the first warm breeze that will breathe life into the green shoots and roots, encouraging them to sprout again. Buildings will be built and torn down, people will demonstrate and celebrate, cars will crash, citizens will be executed, lovers abandoned, police corrupted, political dissidents imprisoned and freed, presidents will come and go; but Vali Asr will remain, a constant, unchanged by wars, dictators and revolutions. With or without its sycamore trees.

AUTHOR'S NOTE

It was Black Friday 1978 when my mother, brother and I landed in Mehrabad airport in Tehran to join my father for a new life. Martial law had been announced and the military had opened fire on an anti-Shah protest, killing and injuring dozens of demonstrators. It was the first time the authorities had reacted to a protest with such force. It was the start of the revolution; it was the beginning of the end of Iran as we knew it. It was an inauspicious day to be returning to the country of my birth.

My memories of this time are vivid: the dancing and the street parties when the Shah finally left; the jubilant mood that filled the city; men and even children carrying guns stolen from the national armoury, now adorned with flowers poking from the barrels. Yet the streets felt safe, and the majority of Tehranis were united in a way they never had been before. It was a time of hope.

I was only a child, but I soon sensed a change in the atmosphere: the streets became quiet, adults started whispering. Standing on our balcony, we would watch the night sky streaked red by tracer rounds. I remember evenings when we sat in silence and darkness in our flat as armed groups roamed outside our front door, firing their guns.

Nine months later we were on a plane back to London. My father stayed behind for another four months, awaiting the acceptance of his resignation from the navy. He had not wanted to flee his country and sever ties with the land he loved.

My mother and father had met ten years earlier at a party in Earls Court. He was being trained by the British Navy at the time. The minute he saw her, he fell in love. Like me, my mother was born in Tehran but grew up in London. Her father moved his family there in 1960 in self-imposed exile. My grandfather was a military man and during Mossadegh's term as Prime Minister, one of his jobs was to be head of army radio. He had been ordered by the Ministry of War to broadcast propaganda about Mohammad Reza Shah, who was in exile in Italy. My grandfather refused; he believed that the army was there to serve the people and should not interfere in politics. Mohammad Reza Shah soon returned when Mossadegh was ousted in a CIA- and British-backed coup. Word reached the Shah of my grandfather's defiance and he was repeatedly passed over for promotion. A brilliant polymath renowned for his honesty, he worked his way up the ranks through his abilities rather than bribery, connections and loyalty to the regime, as was so often the way. When he was finally made a general, it was too late for him. He was tired of the sycophants and the corruption – it was said that no one dared to lie to the former king, Reza Shah, and no one dared to tell the truth to his son and successor, Mohammad Reza Shah. He was also keen to give his children a British education. He left Iran and vowed never to return.

My grandfather's cousin, Hassan Ali Mansour, tried many times to persuade him to come back, but he would not be swayed. Mansour was appointed Prime Minister in 1964 and during the White Revolution he implemented the controversial and much-loathed 'capitulation' law. The law gave US citizens accused of crimes immunity from prosecution in Iran. Mansour told my grandfather that he himself had been forced to capitulate to the US's demands; he had accepted the US's terms in return for a loan of 200 million US dollars, money which the country desperately needed. But in the eyes of most Iranians, he had sold his country and the interests of his people to interfering imperialist powers. The capitulation law turned out to be a seminal moment in the country's modern history. It was condemned by a little-known cleric called Ayatollah Khomeini, who also denounced the Shah and the United States. Khomeini was promptly sent into exile where he used the capitulation law as one of the rallying cries against the Shah. And so the rumblings of a revolution began. Just over two months after Khomeini was exiled, Mansour was assassinated. His killer was a seventeen-year-old who worked with two accomplices, members of the fundamentalist Fadayeen-e Islam group. All three were executed.

Twenty-six years after leaving Tehran, I went back to live there. Although I knew little of my family history, I had an overwhelming need to reconnect with my roots. It also seemed to be the perfect place to launch my career as a journalist.

It was the summer of 2004, when I was the Tehran correspondent for *The Times*, that the idea of this book first came about. My press card had been revoked by Ershad, the Ministry of Culture and Islamic Guidance. This would occasionally happen to journalists living in Tehran. You would never be told what you had done to piss *them* off, but this time a particularly friendly official told me straight. 'Miss Navai, you covered a notorious human rights case and you wrote about people laughing at mullahs. You know they don't like attention on human rights. And as for jokes about mullahs…' At this point the official started to laugh. He told me to sit tight and give it a few months, while *they* 'taught me a lesson'. At least I would have some respite from the periodic secret interrogation sessions with intelligence officers that I had come to dread, and which the Ministry claimed were not carried out by their people.

I knew immediately what I would do. I had written a feature about a school run by a charity for street kids in Shoosh, south Tehran. I was so moved by the children's stories I wanted to help in some way.

I was asked to teach English in a school in the back alleys of Nasser Khosrow Street in the heart of downtown Tehran. The pupils here were paperless Afghans, gypsies and the illegitimate children of prostitutes; none of them had the right to an education. I loved my group of Afghan children, the most hard-working kids I have ever met. They fitted school and homework around paid work, toiling on building sites, in factories and shops. One of their favourite sessions was when I took my friend Angus to school; I had asked them to prepare a list of questions to ask the *Ingilisi*. Predictably, they were all about his romantic life. Angus happily answered. He was a hit.

Around the same time, I met a prostitute at a methadone clinic off Shoosh Street. Her once beautiful face had been pockmarked and clawed at by drugs and disease, but her intense green eyes still served to pull in the punters. We started meeting once a week for a tea. As I was an outsider yet still a Tehrani she could talk freely to me without feeling judged; our conversations were never guarded or censored. She took me around her stomping ground, among the pimps and the dealers, the madams and the working girls, through the crumbling alleys and needle-strewn parks where she hung out. Sometimes she would be too high to speak much; she had a serious heroin addiction and had just found out she was HIV-positive.

I was inhabiting two very different worlds. I would return

home to north Tehran, telling my friends – born and bred Tehranis – of life in the south of the city, only a few miles away. They listened in wonder, as though I was talking about a different country. And yet we were all connected by one single long road – Vali Asr.

The more time I spent with people like the characters in these pages, the more I realized we were connected by so much more than that one street. We faced the same frustrations and limitations of life in the Islamic Republic: irrespective of class, wealth or profession, we were all required to hide aspects of our true selves.

When Ahmadinejad was elected in 2005, he appointed a new minister to Ershad. His name was Mohammad-Hossein Saffar Harandi – his uncle was one of the boys who had killed my grandfather's cousin, Hassan Ali Mansour.

I never stopped going to south Tehran, even when my press card was reinstated. Over the years, more people shared their secrets with me and I discovered more dark corners of Tehran. The stories I heard painted a very different picture from the one I saw reflected in the news, with all its twisted political intrigues. I hope they make for a more honest, intimate and true portrait of the city that I love. This city of lies.

KEY DATES IN IRAN'S RECENT HISTORY

1921   The building of Vali Asr begins
Reza Pahlavi leads a military coup
Ahmad Shah, the last Qajar monarch, flees the country

1925   Reza Pahlavi crowns himself Reza Shah, replacing the Qajar dynasty with the Pahlavis

1935   Persia is renamed Iran

1941   Anglo-Soviet invasion forces Reza Shah to abdicate. This is after he refuses to get rid of his German advisers even though he has proclaimed Iran's neutrality during the Second World War
Reza Shah's son, Mohammad Reza Shah, takes over

1946   British and US troops are withdrawn from Iran. The United States assists Mohammad Reza Shah in removing Soviet troops

1951   Mohammad Mossadegh elected Prime Minister
Parliament votes to nationalize the oil industry, which was largely controlled by the Anglo-Iranian Oil Company
Britain bans Iranian oil in a bid to hurt the economy

1953   Mohammad Reza Shah flees
A coup orchestrated by the CIA and British intelligence
ousts Mossadegh
Mohammad Reza Shah returns

1963   The Shah launches the White Revolution, a campaign to
modernize the country, which includes land reform

1964   Khomeini sent into exile after speaking out against the
Shah and the United States when the 'capitulation' law is
passed by the Prime Minister, Hassan Ali Mansour

1965   Prime Minister Hassan Ali Mansour is assassinated

1978   Anti-Shah protests lead to martial law
Dozens of protesters are killed and injured when troops
open fire on a demonstration in Jaleh Square; the day
comes to be known as Black Friday

1979   JAN   Islamic Revolution
Shah and his family forced into exile

      FEB   Khomeini returns to Iran after fourteen years in exile
Hundreds of supporters of the Shah are executed

      NOV   Islamic militants take fifty-two Americans hostage
in the US embassy in Tehran, demanding the Shah
is returned to Iran to face trial

1980   War with Iraq begins when Iraq invades Iran
Shah dies of cancer in exile in Egypt

1981   Mojahedin uprising
American hostages are released after being held for 444
days
Ali Khamenei elected President

1988 End of Iran–Iraq war
Mass executions of political prisoners

1989 Ayatollah Khomeini dies
Former President Ali Khamenei appointed Supreme
Leader
Akbar Hashemi Rafsanjani elected President

1997 Mohammad Khatami elected President

2001 Mohammad Khatami re-elected President

2005 Mahmoud Ahmadinejad elected President

2009 Mahmoud Ahmadinejad re-elected president
Mass protests contesting election results

2013 Hassan Rouhani elected President

GLOSSARY

aragh sagee Home-brewed vodka, usually made of raisins. The name is a pun – *aragh* means vodka as well as sweat, *sag* is dog, so it is 'dog's sweat vodka'

Ashura Anniversary of the martyrdom of Imam Hossein

ayatollah Means 'the sign of god' and is the highest rank given to Shia clerics. To become an ayatollah, a cleric usually has to have gained a following and be considered an expert in religious, ethical, philosophical and legal matters by his peers. Ayatollahs do not exist in Sunni Islam. The next rank down is 'hojjatoleslam'

azan Call to prayer

bah-bah Yum-yum

Basij Paramilitary volunteer group

basiji A member of the Basij

chador Literally means 'tent'. An open black cloak that covers the head and the entire body. Historians believe the chador was introduced not long before the eighteenth century. Reza Shah Pahlavi banned the chador and all *hejab* in 1936, in an effort to modernize Iran. The police would forcibly remove veils worn in the streets. This policy outraged clerics and many ordinary Iranians who felt that being in public without the chador or *hejab* was tantamount to being naked. The ban lasted for four years until Reza Shah's son, Mohammad Reza Shah, came to power and women were once again allowed to cover up. Shortly after the revolution in 1979, the *hejab* was made compulsory

chadori A woman who wears a chador. Also used as a value judgement, to suggest someone religious and/or working-class

chaharshanbeh souri A fire festival celebrated on the last Tuesday night of the year; the name translates as the eve of red Wednesday. Bonfires are lit in the hope that fire and light will bring health and happiness

chapi Leftist

dampaee Slippers, which are usually plastic 'slides'

erfan **classes** Mysticism classes

esfand Seeds of a weed that are burned to ward off the evil eye

estekhareh Islamic divination

ettela'at Intelligence, refers to the feared Ministry of Intelligence

fatwa A religious edict issued by clerics

Haji The name given to someone who has completed the Haj. Can also be used as a term of respect

hejab A headscarf, or any garment used to cover the head and body in order to preserve modesty

Hezbollah Party of God, a movement that was formed during the revolution to help Khomeini and his forces. The term *Hezbollahi* refers to those seen as zealous or fundamentalist; a *Hezbollahi* is an ardent defender of the regime and can be willing to resort to violence to defend the Islamic state

hosseinieh A congregation hall used for gatherings and religious ceremonies

IRIB Islamic Republic of Iran Broadcasting

javanmardi A code of conduct that has chivalry, magnanimity and altruism at its core

jendeh Whore

joon/jan Dear, also used as a polite formality at the end of a person's first name

manteau An overcoat that must be worn over clothes to hide the curves and shape of a woman's body

MEK Mojahedin-e Khalq Organization (some other aliases: the MKO and the People's Mojahedin of Iran). The largest Iranian opposition group, committed to overthrowing the Islamic Republic. It was formed in 1963 by leftist students and has Marxist/Islamist roots. The MEK played an integral role in the Islamic Revolution, but was brutally repressed by Ayatollah Khomeini. Its headquarters are in Paris, under the banner of the National Council of Resistance in Iran

Muharram Month of mourning for Imam Hossein and the first month of the Islamic calendar

nazr A Shia tradition, a *nazr* prayer is a wish to God in return for helping the poor and needy. Prayers are usually made to God through one of the imams

Qajar The ruling dynasty of Iran from 1796 to 1925

regimey A supporter or member of the Islamic regime

roo-farshee Translates as 'on the carpet', meaning house shoes

sazman Organization. Also refers to the MEK

SOURCES

Whenever possible, I have used the characters' own words and language; many conversations and episodes that have been recounted to me have been written verbatim. Where inner thoughts have been conveyed, these have been written as they were explained to me by the interviewees. Descriptions of characters are, obviously, my own viewpoint.

All quotations from the Koran are taken from *The Holy Qur-an, English translation of the meanings and commentary* (King Fahd Holy Qur-an Printing Complex).

PREFACE

Tehran's population is from the University of Tehran website: www.ut.ac.ir/en/contents/About-tehran/About.Tehran.html

PROLOGUE

The history of Vali Asr: Dariush Shabaazi, *Bargh-hayee az Tareekh-e Tehran* (Notes on the History of Tehran) (Saless, 2011), pp. 353–4. The destruction of trees on Vali Asr: World Cultural Heritage Voices, 'Suspicious Removal of Trees on a Major Road of Tehran', 24 July 2013.

CHAPTER ONE: DARIUSH

Dariush's story is mostly based on my interviews with an ex-MEK member, who has spoken publicly of his MEK mission to Tehran to kill a former Tehran police chief. I have also used details provided by two other former MEK members living in Tehran and merged them with this man's story. Interviews with these former members also provided the details of the arrival in the country, family background, the MEK handler and the gun-runner. I have changed a few details of Dariush's assassination attempt. Descriptions of MEK meetings in the US are from current MEK supporters based outside Iran.

Current MEK members and some activists accuse the man on whose story this is based of being a regime spy, even though he left Iran after the protests of 2009 and has been granted asylum in another country.

Members of the MEK claim that since 2001 the group no longer sends its members for missions to Iran; instead they are chosen from an existing network already in the country. Between 2008 and 2013, five Iranians, said to be nuclear scientists, were executed on the streets of Tehran by assassins on motorbikes. The Iranian government says it is the work of the MEK with support from Israel.

Camp Ashraf was stormed by Iraqi troops in 2011, killing at least thirty-six people. It has since been closed down and about 3,000 MEK members were relocated to Camp Liberty in north-eastern Baghdad. They have come under rocket attack several times; a leader of the Shia militia Mukhtar Army has admitted responsibility.

The MEK was on the US list of terrorist organizations until September 2012, when it was delisted. There is talk within the

MEK of re-establishing its military wing with a powerful army, recruiting from around the world.

For the MEK see Ervand Abrahamian, *The Iranian Mojahedin* (Yale University Press, 1989), p. 1; on MEK weddings at Camp Ashraf, Masoud Banisadr, *Masoud: Memoirs of an Iranian Rebel* (Saqi, 2004), p. 311. The MEK bomb in Haft-e Tir is from Moojan Momen, *An Introduction to Shi'i Islam: The History and Doctrines of Twelver Shi'ism* (Yale University Press, 1987), p. 295.

CHAPTER TWO: SOMAYEH

Somayeh's story is based on that of a woman who wishes to remain anonymous; her relationship, from marriage to divorce, is as she explained it to me, including descriptions of her physical appearance and her dress. Conversations between Somayeh and her friends are conversations heard between girls of the same age group and from the same conservative families as Somayeh, or they are conversations recounted by Somayeh. Political conversations between the men were conversations I listened to in her area as well as conversations in a *mahzar* notary office shortly after Rouhani's election victory. I also interviewed several women in their fifties from conservative families for a full picture of Somayeh's mother, Fatemeh, and Fatemeh's friends.

Somayeh is currently living with her parents and her daughter. She told me she does feel lust from time to time, but she fights it hard, the only way she knows how, with fasting and prayers. Suitors come for her, but her neighbours and family were all right about one thing: none of them have been prepared to accept Somayeh with her little girl. Somayeh has said another *nazr* prayer, asking for a good husband who will love her daughter. She believes God and Imam Zaman will come good, as they have always done. She believes she is in store for another miracle.

Number of satellite television receivers in Iran: Asr Iran news website, quoting Javad Arianmanesh, 24 November 2008. Mullah condemns 3G mobile Internet service: ISNA (Iranian Students' News Agency), 10 February 2013. For social history after the revolution, see Ervand Abrahamian, *A History of Modern Iran* (Cambridge University Press, 2012), p. 180. The cleric discussing virgins in paradise on television was quoted on the IRIB (Islamic Republic of Iran Broadcasting) 3, *Samteh Khodah* (Towards God) programme. The Supreme Leader's response to the question about masturbation is from his website, question number 786: farsi.khamenei.ir/. Dubbing actors arrested: ISNA, 18 December 2012. Number of marriages ending in divorce: *Etemaad* newspaper, 29 April 2013, p. 13.

CHAPTER THREE: AMIR

Amir's story is based on that of a man who wishes to remain anonymous. The real Amir is not a blogger; I changed his profession at his request. I interviewed bloggers and student activists for all the details in this chapter. For information on the judge in Amir's story, I interviewed a former judge who was a judge in the Revolutionary Courts at the same time as the judge who approached Amir. All information on bribes, corruption and the incident of the stoning in Evin prison is as he described.

For details of Amir's parents' lives as dissidents, I interviewed several people of his parents' generation who were active at that same time. All details of parties and dissident meetings come from them, or from Amir's memory of his parents' gatherings. The account of the man on military service crying as he witnessed executions is from a man who had witnessed them in Evin prison following the 2009 protests; he told me that all the guards watching had cried.

The judge's son has also contacted Amir, asking him to forgive the old judge. The judge's son told Amir that his father has tracked down nearly all the children of those he condemned to execution, begging for forgiveness. Amir is the only one not to have forgiven him, and is the only one who has never accepted his gifts and his money. Amir is also the only child both of whose parents were executed.

When in prison, the blogger Sattar Beheshti publicly complained of being tortured and details of his treatment were published on the opposition website kaleme.com. An article in the *New York Times*, 'Jailed Blogger Not Tortured Before Death, Iran Says' by Thomas Erdbrink, 12 November 2012, quotes 'influential Iranian lawmaker' Alaeddin Borujerdi denying that Beheshti was tortured to death.

For the imprisonment and execution of political opponents after the revolution see Ervand Abrahamian, *A History of Modern Iran* (Cambridge University Press, 2012), p. 181; estimates of numbers eliminated by the Shah between 1971 and 1977, see Ervand Abrahamian, *Iran Between Two Revolutions* (Princeton University Press, 1982), p. 480; Khomeini's slogans, Abrahamian, *A History of Modern Iran*, p. 148.

Ayatollah Hakim's fatwa against joining the Communist Party, Baqer Moin, *Khomeini, Life of the Ayatollah* (IB Tauris, 1999), p. 144; the Ayatollah's younger son releasing a pop video, *Bahar News*, 13 January 2013.

On the exclusion of Baha'is see ISNA, quoting politician Javad Larijani, 14 May 2011 and Human Rights Watch, 'Barring the Bahais' by Faraz Sanei, 11 May 2010.

The number of executions ordered by revolutionary courts between the revolution and June 1981 is from Abrahamian, *History of Modern Iran*, p. 181 (the exact number given of those executed is 497).

Khomeini's secret order to execute all prisoners who remained opposed to the Islamic regime: Kaveh Shahrooz, 'The Iran Tribunal' www.irantribunal.com/index.php/news/articles/30-twenty-years-of-silence-the-1988-massacre-and-quest-for-accountability. The account of the court proceedings: see Muhammad Sahimi, 'The Bloody Red Summer of 1988', 25 August 2009, PBS Frontline/Tehran Bureau www.pbs.org/wgbh/pages/frontline/tehranbureau/2009/08/the-bloody-red-summer-of-1988.html.

CHAPTER FOUR: BIJAN

Bijan's character and details of his family life are based on one man. Details of crimes and criminal operations are based on the testimonies of several men introduced to me by Bijan. For obvious reasons, all locations have been changed. Nearly all conversations in this chapter are as I heard them spoken between Bijan and his group of friends and local gangsters, apart from conversations with the police chief – to be clear, the police chief was never present. The figure of one million US dollars' ransom money is from a friend of a friend who was kidnapped – this amount was paid by his family for his release.

On Iranians in Japan see Roger Goodman, Ceri Peach, Ayumi Takenaka, Paul White, *Global Japan: The Experience of Japan's New Immigrant and Overseas Communities* (Routledge, 2009), pp. 12, 161.

On drugs: the UNODC (United Nations Office on Drugs and Crime) report, *Transnational Organised Crime in East Asia and the Pacific, A Threat Assessment*, April 2013, p. 68, states that in 2010 the Islamic Republic of Iran ranked fourth in the world for licit pseudoephedrine imports (www.unodc.org/documents/southeastasiaandpacific//Publications/2013/TOCTA_EAP_web.pdf); Iran as fifth-highest consumer of crystal meth in the world, Tabnak news website, quoting Saeed Safaeeyan, 1 October 2013; champion wrestler tested positive for D-methamphetamine, *Donya-e Eqtesad* newspaper, article naming Alireza Gharibi, 23 June 2006. The figures for crystal meth labs in Tehran are from Hamshahri Online, quoting Morteza Tamadon, Tehran governor, 1 August 2013 (referring to 2012 and the first three months of 2013); popularity of *sheesheh*, Fars news agency, 5 March 2013 and Khabar Online, 5 February 2012; government claim to arrest thirty drug dealers and addicts every hour, Mehr news agency, 1 April 2013 and *Bahar* newspaper, 13 January 2013.

'This is Tehran / A city that tempts you till it saps your soul / And makes you see you were always meant to be / Nothing more than dirt', translated into English from 'Ekhtelaf' from the album 'Jangale Asfalt' ('Asphalt Jungle') by Iranian rapper Hichkas.

Special treatment for Basij students: Mehr news agency, 18 May 2010 and Hamshahri Online, 9 July 2008, article by Mina Shahni, quoting Reza Sahrai, Director of Higher Education, Martyrs' Foundation.

CHAPTER FIVE: LEYLA

Leyla's character and details about her upbringing, family and work as a prostitute are based on one woman. Kayvan is a composite character based on several people.

The real Leyla is still, happily, alive. The story of Leyla's death, however, is based on the real case of a woman who was executed for making a pornographic film. In 2001 a woman was stoned in Evin prison, charged with moral corruption. According to newspaper reports, the police had tracked her down using the serial number on her electricity meter, which was visible in the background of her porn film. The BBC quotes *Entekhab* newspaper on the woman stoned to death in Evin prison in 2001: news.bbc.co.uk/1/hi/world/middle_east/1343058.stm. I changed Leyla's death to hanging as, officially, nobody has been stoned to death in Tehran since 2001: Tabnak news website, 12 November 2012.

The Iran Human Rights Documentation Center estimates there are currently around 200–300 women facing the death penalty in Iran. Lawyers working there say it is not known how many have been charged with crimes related to moral corruption.

On prostitution: average age, Shafaf news website, 23 December 2009, article by Leda Ayaaz; camps for 'reformation', Mehr news agency, 10 July 2012 quoting Morteza Tamadon, Governor-General of Tehran province; Akbar Hashemi Rafsanjani's sermon: Robert Tait, *Guardian*, 4 June 2007, www.guardian.co.uk/world/2007/jun/04/iran.roberttait.

Information on the cyberpolice is quoted from the cyber-police website, www.cyberpolice.ir; crackdown on the Internet and Facebook pages: ISNA, quoting Kamal Hadianfar, 3 October 2013.

Report on Tehran's police chief being caught in a brothel is from BBC news website, 'Iran anti-vice chief "in brothel"', 16 April 2008, news.bbc.co.uk/2/hi/7350165.stm. Proposal for licensed brothels, Jim Muir, BBC, 28 July 2002, news.bbc.co.uk/2/hi/middle_east/2156975.stm.

Immoral women blamed for deterioration of society, earthquakes and the state of the economy: ISNA, quoting Tehran's Friday Prayers leader, 17 April 2010. Parliament bill on porn: Sepah News Service, 3 September 2013.

CHAPTER SIX: MORTEZA

Morteza's story, of a member of the Basij having a sex-change operation, is based on the story of a colleague of a friend. However, as she was too scared to give much detail of her life, I have drawn on the experiences of three former members of the Basij and two transgender male-to-female Tehranis from conservative *basiji* families, all of whom I interviewed.

As she was from a religious family, the catalyst that really encouraged Morteza to embrace her transsexuality and act upon it was a fatwa given by Ayatollah Khomeini himself, condoning sex changes. In 1984, a hermaphrodite called Fereydoon sought counsel from Khomeini, describing his mental and emotional state and explaining he was a woman trapped in a man's body. Fereydoon asked Khomeini for permission to change his sexuality; Khomeini agreed. A number of *mojtaheds*, high-ranking clerics who are able to issue fatwas, also accepted transsexuality, including the Supreme Leader Ali Khamenei. Since then, thousands of gender-reassignment surgeries have taken place in Iran, but there have been many reports of botched operations. Dozens of male-to-female transsexuals have filed complaints of being left unable to have sex after surgery, their sexual organs having been butchered or built the wrong size (www2.ohchr.org/English/bodies/cescr/docs/ngos/JointHeartlandAlliance_IRQO_IHRC_Iran_CESCR50.pdf). Even though the Iranian health service claims to have allocated a budget of 350,000,000 tomans for gender-reassignment surgery throughout the country (ISNA,

21 November 2012), operations are still expensive, costing at least 3,000 US dollars – nearly double someone like Morteza's yearly family income. Several cases have been reported of gay men who have been forced into having sex-change operations by their families, as being transgender is more acceptable than being gay. Many people from the transgender community have spoken of daily abuse and persecution.

'Shireen' had her gender-reassignment surgery in Thailand. She is no longer in touch with her family as they have been unable to come to terms with who she is.

ISRAEL ANNOUNCES DATE IT WILL ATTACK IRAN: *Khabar Eghtesadi* newspaper, khabareghtesadi.com, 9 May 2012; Imam Jomeh, Jiroft, 24 July 2013; Supreme Leader's response: IRIB 1, Supreme Leader's speech in Mashhad, 21 March 2013.

The references to the Ayatollah's lectures are drawn from Rasa news website, based on the words of Ayatollah Abdollah Javadi-Amoli, 26 May 2012.

CHAPTER SEVEN: ASGHAR

Asghar's story is based on interviews with friends and family members of a couple of well-known *jahels*. All names of famous *jahels* are real, apart from Asghar's, to protect the family's identity. Pari's story is based on the story of somebody I know, and on a showgirl married to a *jahel*.

Shapour the Bull-Slayer and Morteza Four Dicks caught with more than a kilo of heroin and opium: Tabnak news website, 27 July 2008. Number of drug addicts: Mehr news agency quoting Rasoul Khezri, a member of parliament's health committee, 11 September 2013 and Fars news agency, quoting Mohammad Esmail Motlagh, Director-General of Health, Ministry of Health, 14 September 2013

Ayatollahs declared that betting on horses and shooting is not against Sharia law: *Hamshari* newspaper, 30 October 2012. Accounts of Zeynab the Blind and the African slaves working as spies and guards are from Jafar Shahri, *Tehran-e Ghadeem* (Old Tehran) (Moin, 2004), volume 1, pp. 28–9 and 97.

CHAPTER EIGHT: FARIDEH

Farideh is a composite character based on several women. Farideh's son, Alidad, is also based on several people. Social events here are either as witnessed by myself, or as described to me. All other incidents, including the rape and suicide of Delara (not her real name) and the arrests of the artists and life models, are as told to me by witnesses or friends and acquaintances of those involved.

Details of General Rahimi's execution are from Michael Axworthy, *Revolutionary Iran, A History of the Islamic Republic* (Allen Lane, 2013) p.14.

ACKNOWLEDGEMENTS

To every Tehrani who shared their life story and secrets with me, I hope I have done you justice. It was a privilege to be allowed into your world. This book is as much yours as it is mine.

To everyone who helped me in Tehran: you went above and beyond to connect me to people and to show me all the hidden corners of our city. You are the brave ones, risking your freedom in pursuit of the truth in Tehran. In particular, Mr Smiley and Ms Kickass, it was an honour. A heartfelt thank you to Ali, Amir, Amirali, Arash, Arash, Asghar, B, Behnam, Hadi, Hiva, Majid, Minou, Mohammad, Mona, Mr G, Mr H, Mr M, Mr S, Mr T, Nahid, Saadi, Saeed, Saeed, Sara, Shadi, Sina, Sohayl, Vahid and Zahra.

To Monsieur K, thank you for your help – even when you were ill and tired!

Outside Iran, thank you to all who gave their time, thoughts and information: Arash, Dr Ghassem Khatib-Chahidi, Jane Khatib-Chahidi, Gissou Nia and team from the Iran Human Rights Documentation Center, Farrokh Negahdar, Arsham Parsi from the Iranian Railroad for Queer Refugees and your contact N, Hossein Rassam, Maryam Sinaiee and Reza Zia-Ebrahimi. A huge thank you to Aliasghar Ramezanpoor for your invaluable help and input.

I had the very good fortune of having a few brilliant readers. Thank you Roxanna Shapour for your sharp eye, loyalty and endless help. Thank you to Negin Shiraghaei for your excellent suggestions. A special thank you to my soul brother, Amir Paivar, for always being there.

To my fantastic, fearless and dogged researcher, Nikoo: *damet garm jeegar talaa*.

To the Tehran crew, thank you for your support, stories and making me laugh. You are always magnificent: Amirali N, AmirM, Arash, Aresu, Behnam, Bobs, Dr M, Kaveh, Mana, N, Nassim, S, T.

To my wonderful friends and family for cheering me on from the sidelines, for listening to my stories and for your advice, thank you: Steve Allen, Babak, James Brabazon, Jamsheed, Kate Brooks, Elisabetta Cavanna, Aaron Chetwynd, Anna Chetwynd, Libby Dempster, Miranda Eeles, Zoe Eisenstein, Tom Griffiths, Michael Ireland, Kambiz Karimi, Peyvand Khorsandi, Kathi Kosmider, Hannah Lambert, Claire McFall, Angus McDowall, Deborah McTaggart, Ramin Navai, Rick O'Sullivan, Tom Parker, Sasha Pick, Graeme Robertson, Lavinia Range, Mehrdaad, Siobhan Sinnerton and Paola Victoria.

Thank you to my aunt Shahla Ireland and my uncles Hadi Samsami and Kazem Samsami for your memories and for recounting our family history.

Thank you to the brilliant illustrator who also happens to be my father-in-law, Robin Range, for the beautiful map of Tehran at the beginning of this book.

Thank you to those who I can no longer thank in person but who made my time in Iran that much easier: Richard Beeston, for being the most encouraging editor; Kasra Vafadari, for showing me so much.

Thank you to all at the Royal Society of Literature Jerwood Awards, in particular Paula Johnson. The award enabled me to do so much more than I ever envisioned.

An enormous thank you to my phenomenal editor, Bea Hemming – it has been an honour to work with you, as well as such a joy.

To the best agent an author could wish for, Sophie Lambert at Conville and Walsh. You could not have been more supportive, encouraging and generous with your time, advice and notes. Thank you so much.

To the kindest and most compassionate people I know, thank you to my mother Laya and my father Kourosh. My gorgeous mother, it is because of your sense of justice (and your sense of mischief) that I do what I do. To my father – the father of all fathers! – living in Tehran with you was one of the best times of my life.

Finally, to my man, Gabriel Range, whose suggestions and ideas helped shape this book. Being with you makes me feel like the luckiest woman around. No words are good enough, but, I love you.

RAMITA NAVAI is a British-Iranian journalist and reporter for Channel 4's foreign affairs series, *Unreported World*. She has reported from over thirty different countries, including Sudan, Afghanistan, Egypt, Nigeria, El Salvador, and Zimbabwe. She was awarded an EMMY for her undercover reporting from Syria. She has also worked as a journalist for the United Nations in Pakistan, northern Iraq, and Iran, and was the Tehran correspondent for *The Times* from 2003 to 2006.